Tanya Heaslip was raised on a cattle station in Central Australia during the 1960s and 70s and learnt about the outside world through the Correspondence School, School of the Air and story-books. She spent many hours dreaming of the overseas lands depicted in those studies and stories. Tanya went on to become a lawyer but never stopped dreaming. In between practising law, she travelled to many of those lands, and has since written about her travel experiences in *Alice to Prague*, published in 2019. Tanya lives in Alice Springs with her husband. She is the Regional Vice President of the NT Writers' Centre.

TANYA HEASLIP

An Alice Girl

ALLEN&UNWIN
SYDNEY·MELBOURNE·AUCKLAND·LONDON

Allen & Unwin
83 Alexander Street
Crows Nest NSW 2065
Australia
Phone: (61 2) 8425 0100
Email: info@allenandunwin.com
Web: www.allenandunwin.com

A catalogue record for this
book is available from the
National Library of Australia

ISBN 978 1 76052 977 2

Set in 12/17 pt Minion Pro by Midland Typesetters, Australia
Printed and bound in Australia by Griffin Press, part of Ovato

10 9 8 7 6 5 4 3 2 1

The paper in this book is FSC® certified.
FSC® promotes environmentally responsible,
socially beneficial and economically viable
management of the world's forests.

To Dad—for everything

Contents

Prologue

The Cattle Duffers

'Cooeeeee!'

The call ripped through the hot, still air. I swivelled in the saddle, hands tight on the reins, straining to catch the direction of the sound. My skewbald mare Sandy moved restlessly under me, her ears pricked, sensing my anxiety. To the west lay a rocky rise, shrouded by blue-grey mulga, but if the sound had come from behind the rise it was impossible to tell. Behind me a dry creek bed dropped away to the south, lined by river gums wilting in the afternoon heat. There was no sign of anyone there. Nor did it seem a likely hide-out.

I cupped my hands around my mouth and shouted in return, 'Cooeeeee!' The words hit the low hills and reverberated back, while above a hawk rose high into the vastness on the currents of a willy-willy. Like my shout, the hawk was soon a speck in the emptiness, swallowed by the big, blue bowl of sky above. Sweat ran down the back of my thin cotton shirt. The sun burned my arms. Time was running out.

'Cooeeeee!' I tried again desperately.

Then I heard it, in bursts, through the thicket in the direction of the southern fence. 'Tanya—over—here!'

I then realised it was M'Lis's voice, followed by the sound of stockwhips cracking and the thunder of hooves beating through the bush. Perhaps the cattle were breaking away to the rocky outcrop, which would give them cover until they reached that fence. I looked over to what lay between here and the fence. Long, low, flat mounds of red earth sweeping towards the glint of wire in the distance, potted throughout with rabbit holes, treacherous for horses. One misstep and they could break a leg. My sister was calling for help and that route was the best way to head off the mob. But I couldn't risk Sandy going down a rabbit hole. So, I took a deep breath and leaned low over Sandy's neck. We came up straight and fast along a cattle pad, a narrow, dusty track created by cattle meandering to waterholes over the years. It ran across the side of the hill, which was a slightly longer way. Soon my ears were filled with the sound of Sandy's hooves and my pounding heart. I kept swivelling.

'Here!' M'Lis's voice came to me through the scrub. Then I glimpsed her crouched over a grey horse, hat flattened on her head, flying in pursuit of the fleeing cattle. Behind her came her friend Jacquie, standing high in the stirrups of her horse, UFO, her blonde ponytail swinging wildly.

'Where are the others?' I called frantically.

They should be nearby. We were a team with a job to do. I just hoped they were covering the flank on the other side of the hill, stopping the cattle being driven down there. But I couldn't see anyone in this hilly, scrubby corner. Out there, unseen, was my little brother Benny on his grey pony, Lesley, and our friend Donald on his bay gelding.

In the distance I knew my brother Brett, and Jacquie's brother Matthew, would be heading our way. He'd have my friend Janie with him, as well as another great horse rider, Joanne.

But now everyone seemed lost in the blur and brushlands.

'They've got them!' M'Lis's voice came out in frantic bursts through the thick trees. 'They're getting away! You take the fence side . . . we'll cut them off before they reach the creek.'

Our one, desperate job today was to stop the cattle duffers.

Sandy and I cut towards the south, then plunged down towards the length of Kangaroo Flat, focused only on turning the mob. They had a lead on us and I knew we were struggling to make up the gap. If we could stop them reaching the creek, we'd be in with a chance. *Where* were Benny and Donald?

We knew that the cattle duffers had stolen Dad's cleanskins— young cattle that had not yet been branded—and were now driving them hard towards their own bush hide-out. And the duffers knew the best secret gorges or wild scrublands to push the cattle into. We knew what they'd do if we didn't stop them. They'd build makeshift yards to trap the stolen cattle. Next they'd brand the cleanskins with their own illegal brand and sell them on. And for all we knew, they had some of Dad's best branded steers, and were intending to cross-brand them too. While the steers wouldn't be as easy to sell, cattle duffers were cunning and clever and usually found a way to persuade the right kind of people to buy.

We couldn't let that happen. We were here to protect Dad's cattle—all of them—at any cost. There was no time to waste.

Then, as one, M'Lis, Jacquie and I were both out onto the open flat—past the rabbit holes, racing across the gibber stones, nothing in our minds now but the safety of the mob, and the protection of the herd. It was now or never to get the cattle out of the clutches of the duffers and herd them back to safety. Our destination still seemed far away. A long, low washout stretching north to south on the eastern end of the paddock, across the dry creek, and then a scramble up the flinty hill that squatted in the middle of the paddock. It was a wondrous hill, we thought, and many years ago M'Lis, Brett and I had named it House Hill.

House Hill boasted a 360-degree view of our world, including the homestead that sprawled away in the distance to the north. On the very top of the hill sat a solitary prickly orange tree. It had defied the droughts and the desert winds year after year, its bark rough and sturdy and its incongruously green leaves pointing defiantly to the high blue sky. We were so proud of the orange tree. So proud that, many years before, we'd crowned it Home Base. That meant freedom and safety for the cattle and us.

'Hey, Tanya!' A shout came from behind me and I glimpsed Benny and Donald pointing towards the top of House Hill, then heard the crack of more stockwhips.

Through the air came the cackle of evil; the sound of wild, whooping laughter. It was the cattle duffers above us, galloping side-by-side along the crest, thrusting their arms in the air in victory, pushing the cattle ahead of them.

'Noooooooooo!' I shrieked but my voice was lost in the wind, my tongue now raw with dust and salt from sweat.

Brett, Janie, Joanne and Matthew were the cattle duffers today and they were getting away with the precious herd. Dad's livelihood depended on us getting the cattle back.

Suddenly ahead of us, there it was—the slim gap between the gum trees that disguised the entrance to the washout and the creek. I flew through it, just as Brett and Janie came around the other side, with Joanne and Matthew riding pincer action. Then, just in time, M'Lis was also there, and Donald and Benny, and it was a race to the top of House Hill.

It was a whirl of horses galloping, nostrils flaring, hooves hitting the flint of the rocks, and our hearts banging in our chests. The air was filled with the sound of cracking stockwhips and shouts of *'Har hut there! Hut hut! Walk up bullocks, walk up! Get 'em out of there!'* With fierce determination, M'Lis, Benny, Donald and I swung around in a loop to cut off our enemies before they reached the orange tree.

'Home free!' Benny's voice came out in gasps as he reached out his fingers to touch the rough bark. He was only five and this had been a huge ride for him, clinging to his pony as he'd followed Donald. But he'd begged to come out with us to take on the cattle duffers this afternoon, and Mum had said yes, if he was good and if he was careful, and if we looked after him. Luckily, he'd stayed on his horse, because once we were all in full flight, it was every rider for themselves. And now he was the first to reach home base, winning the game for our side. I reached across from my mare to hug him, and saw his eyes big and shining as he gazed up at me delightedly from under his over-big hat.

'You did it, Benny!' Eldest child to youngest, I was as proud as punch.

The remaining mob raced to a dead heat, yelling at the tops of their voices.

'We won!'

'No, *we* won!'

'You cheated!'

'No way, we got here fair and square, and we got those cattle back!'

'Not a chance! We're ready to truck them off to the border!'

And so it went on as we slapped each other's backs and circled our horses around to cool them down, breathing heavily, the sweet smell of horse sweat rising up from under the tangled manes and saddle blankets.

Brett and Janie, Joanne and Matthew each had Mum's black-and-red headscarves tied on their hats to denote they were the cattle duffers. They pulled them off, waving them in the air like pirates. But the rest of us weren't having it. There were more fists in the air and shrieks. Eventually, when we all managed to stagger off our horses, we agreed it was a dead heat, and the cattle could be returned safely to their owner.

Of course, in reality, there were no cattle.

All the cattle on our station were precious and Dad would have personally hung us upside down in a tree if we'd used them in our games.

But we didn't need real cattle. They were as vivid and alive to us as if we'd had a full mob at our disposal. Our imaginations easily filled in the gaps. Besides, when we weren't playing our favourite game of cattle duffers, we were mustering or working with cattle in the yards, so we had no difficulty visualising those beautiful beasts as we flew to protect them, up and down the Horse Paddock, as we had today. Each time we played we alternated roles, but I secretly thought Brett and Janie, Joanne and Matthew had played the baddies rather brilliantly this afternoon.

It was so wonderful having friends with us.

For the rest of the year, it was just us four kids: me, M'Lis, Brett and Benny.

But these school holidays, Jacquie and Matthew had come in from Mount Doreen Station, nearly five hundred kilometres away towards the Western Australia border.

Janie, Donald and Joanne had arrived at the start of the holidays, too. They'd ridden their horses out from Alice Springs along the winding, narrow creek beds to get to us. It was a long, full-day trip. We'd met them halfway in a hidden tea-tree gorge, a perfect horse hide-out. There were no adults involved in our daytrip, no communication with any parents—just bush savvy and the total sense of adventure we kids instinctively carried as we rode through the hills to meet one another.

The nine of us had then headed to Dad's stock camp. Now, two weeks later, we had successfully mustered and branded all the cattle, they had been trucked off to market, and we had been given this one free day—the last day of the holidays—as a reward.

The Horse Paddock was our own special space. All the other station paddocks housed cattle, and were used for grown-up purposes, but this one was next to the homestead, reserved for horses, and we'd unofficially claimed and named it as our own.

We were never too old for playing cattle duffers, our favourite game, even though it wasn't easy. First, we had to fetch the horses, which meant walking out several kilometres through the bush and rocky hills to find them, and once we had done that, we needed to throw a bridle over those we caught, and ride them bareback to the yards. Then we'd saddle them up, after which we would return to the paddock for action. The preparation could take hours and we'd usually be gone from late morning until dark. Fortunately, the horses didn't seem to mind; ears pricked, eager, obedient. I often thought they loved the chase as much as we did. And Mum was just pleased we were out of her hair, active and occupied.

As I dismounted Sandy, I looked up to the mountain ranges rising high behind the creek line, and my heart twisted painfully. Next year I would be gone from this beautiful place that was my home, a place where I felt strong and where I belonged. Where the games we played made sense, and the person I was fitted in, and was normal.

After the next school holidays, I was off to boarding school. It was a girls-only school, sixteen hundred kilometres to the south in a city called Adelaide. Mum had already bought the maroon tunic uniform, belt, white shirt, tie, stockings and lace-up shoes. They were hanging in my cupboard. I'd tried them on, but the collar felt tight, the tunic was itchy, the stockings scratched and the shoes pinched. I'd never worn such strange clothes before and I couldn't imagine wearing them all day every day. So, I took them off quickly and just hoped they would feel better when I was actually there.

Part of me was excited. I'd read all the *Malory Towers* and *Twins at St Clare's* books, as well as Nana Heaslip's 1920s *Girl's Own Annuals*. In these books, boarding school seemed a very jolly place. There would be midnight feasts, grave and wise mistresses to help me along my way, caring prefects to inspire me, and adventures with other girls in tunics. It was also the chance to immerse myself in books and study, which were already my favourite things in the world to do.

But I was also fearful. Boarding school was a life as far removed from mine as imaginable. I had only ever worn checked shirts, jeans and riding boots to school. And my schoolroom was a little stone building next to the homestead, where I did Correspondence School lessons with M'Lis and Brett, and spent half an hour a day on the two-way radio with School of the Air. Next year, Benny would take my place in that schoolroom. I couldn't imagine not being in my small sanctuary, where I studied happily with my sister and brother. I had never sat in a real classroom with other kids. I didn't even really know any city kids, just bush kids, who all rode horses and lived my kind of life.

What if things went wrong? What if I was sad or scared? What if, just by some unhappy chance, the mistresses and prefects weren't as kind and wise as they were in all the books?

Mum would be so far away. She wouldn't be able to make things better with just a kiss and a smile. I would only be able to tell her about my new life through weekly handwritten letters (or telegrams in emergencies). I had never lived away from Mum or my family or my home. I didn't know how I would survive without them. They were my whole world.

I roughly pushed the vision away and wiped my eyes with the back of my grubby hand. I refocused on the Horse Paddock, this place of freedom.

'C'mon!' said Brett. 'Time for some water. We've earned it!'

Water was our most precious commodity, and Dad never let us drink too much. If you ran out of water, you could perish. He constantly told us that we should learn to do without, so that we would become tough, rather than vulnerable. Dad's lessons were hard, because he wanted us to learn to be hard too, to make sure we survived in this arid landscape.

So, we always saved sips from the hessian water bags that hung off our saddles for when we really needed them. That was usually intermittently during the day and when we were close to finishing work—or in our case today, at the end of our game.

But today we weren't far from the homestead, and Dad wasn't here, so we allowed ourselves long, luxurious gulps to wet the dust and dryness in our throats. Then we poured a small pool into our hats and held them under our horses' noses, so they could lap up the remaining drops. We—horses and kids—would have a long and proper drink once back in the house yards. Luckily, unlike on a long muster, they weren't far.

Eventually the sun slipped towards the ranges and the glow of gold and pink and purple highlighted their ridges. We mounted our horses regretfully—it was always hard to leave our personal world, where we revelled in the freedom and fun we created. Then we meandered back along the old cattle pad towards the house creek as the shadows lengthened, telling jokes and talking about cattle-duffers again. They were the stuff of legends and bush poems and songs. We could talk about cattle duffers forever. As we could about the old saying: '*Got an eye for a neighbour's calf . . .*'

That was because it wasn't just professional cattle duffers who stole cattle. It was easy to ride across a far-flung boundary fence, pick up any young unbranded heifers and micky bulls (uncastrated young male cattle) you could find, and ride them back across the fence to safety. In these vast spaces, no one would ever know they were gone.

Well, not on our watch! Dad's cattle were safe with us.

I wondered if anyone down south would understand cattle duffing.

We crossed the house creek and all turned in our saddles to take in our last glimpse of House Hill, the scene of our last good works where the goodies beat the baddies.

The orange tree stood proud and silhouetted against the darkening sky. All around it, the ancient landscape folded onto itself into dusk. It was so beautiful, it took my breath away.

The thought of losing my home stabbed my heart. And yet I knew that leaving here next year was just the start of a long journey. The land would go to the boys when they grew up—that's just how it was in the bush—and I would have to find somewhere else to live, something else to do. So would M'Lis.

My hands trembled on the reins as I contemplated my unknown future.

'Righto—let's race along the creek.' M'Lis's command cut through my thoughts. With more than a year to go before she faced boarding school, she was still happily living in the present. 'Last one to the yards has to make up all the feeds for the horses tonight.'

And so it was on. Under the dusky skies we raced through the dry creek bed, waving our hats, shouting and laughing, doing everything we could to draw out the last precious moments of the day.

As the house yards came into view, I thought of Dad constantly instructing us, teaching us, to become better at everything we did, and a terrifying thought crept into my mind.

Who will I be, if I'm not here, on this land, under these skies?

How would I find the answer to this question? I had no idea.

Then another thought replaced it. A strong, powerful thought.

I will go away and live in the other places I've read about in my beloved books. I will do exciting things. Then, one day, I will write about this life and this land, so it's always with me, forever.

We galloped into the yards in a dead heat.

1

Where It All Began

My life as a cattle duffer chaser came about because, once upon a time, a beautiful woman named Janice married a handsome man named Grant. They left the safety and security of South Australia to take up a small cattle lease in remote Central Australia.

Mum and Dad were just twenty-six years old, I was three, M'Lis was two and Brett was one. It was the middle of a ten-year drought that had destroyed the country, and everyone thought they were crazy.

But we loved it. As far as our little eyes could see were miles upon miles of emptiness, huge blue skies and bare earth. We heard pink cockatoos squawk in the gum trees, and crickets click and clack at night. But it was also a place of silence. There was not a person or town to be seen. We could shout into the hills and hear our voices echo back to us. We could lie on our backs at night and imagine the sky of stars swallowing us whole. We knew we could die out here under the savage summer sun and our bones would turn white and dissolve in the dry winds, just like the bones of the kangaroos and dingoes. Nobody would ever know we'd been there. We thought that was kind of exciting.

Our property was called Bond Springs Station. It was first settled in the 1870s by two men who walked all the way from Adelaide to get there. It took them a whole year. I often thought how tired they must have been by the time they arrived, but how happy to discover this beautiful land.

Each sunrise and sunset, the high mountains filled with the colours of the sky. Colours so soft and beautiful after the harshness of the day that it always made my heart sing. Shades of red would turn to apricot, then soft pink, layers of purple, and finally black as the hills dissolved into the night. Every morning, the skies and hills would light up again, changing colour in reverse. It was like magic, and I would try to draw it with coloured pencils but could never capture its true beauty. Nature had its own special paint set.

Colour came in other surprising ways, too. Even in drought years, mulga trees gave us flowers that shone gold in the sunshine, and thick spinifex that looked like straw, making the plains dance with light.

It was a land rich with stories of the past. There was the Aboriginal Dreamtime and the sea that had once covered everything here. The powerful forces that had pushed the earth up into the sky, creating huge rocky ranges that ran from east to west, known to locals as the MacDonnell Ranges but to the local Arrernte people as Caterpillar Dreaming.

Bond Springs was a small block, just north of Alice Springs, nestled inside the MacDonnell Ranges that fell away to the east, with scrubby, red lands to the west.

I loved the eastern side best. It was magical country, filled with hills of all shapes and sizes, gullies and sandy creeks, and ridges shimmering on the horizon. Dad called it 'the sweet country', because that's where most of the rain landed. I also thought it perfect cattle duffer country. The western side was boring to me, but Dad would say, 'This is the soil left from the inland sea,' so I gathered it was also important and useful, and cattle somehow survived, despite it not being as sweet.

We came here because Mum and Dad were pioneers without even realising it.

They were born eleven days apart, in 1939, in the mid-north of South Australia, in the shadow of the magnificent Flinders Ranges. Mum grew up in the farming town of Orroroo, and Dad on a sheep property called Glenroy Estate.

'Tell us the stories about you and Dad again,' we would beg Mum. We were always longing to know about when they were young. In later years we also asked Dad, but Mum's stories were the best.

'Well,' she'd say, a big smile on her face, 'I came up to Alice in 1957 and became a governess on Hamilton Downs Station. I fell in love with this country. I wanted to fly away from my old life.'

'But why? What was wrong with your old life?'

Here Mum would pause, and then tell us different bits and pieces.

The outbreak of the Second World War followed the births of Mum and Dad, and it shaped the direction of the rest of their lives.

First, Mum's father, Papa Parnell, went off to fight for the Empire. When he finally came home again, Mum was five. She and Nana had to get to know him all over again. Papa had been a hero, one of the Rats of Tobruk, and after a final stint in Papua New Guinea he returned riddled with malaria and trauma. He became an alcoholic to drown his demons, and life was tough.

Things brightened when Mum's little brother, John, came along, and she helped Nana care for him. But her schooling ended at fifteen and she felt stifled. She worked at every job she could, and then, aged eighteen, scored herself a one-year office job with the stock and station agent Elder Smith Goldsbrough Mort in their Alice Springs branch. It was the perfect way out. She'd read *A Town like Alice*, and the tiny, dusty frontier town beckoned.

But it wasn't easy to leave Orroroo. Friends and family were dismayed. 'Terrible things could happen to you up there, Janice! The north is wild, savage, untamed.'

Only our darling Nana Parnell understood Mum's longing to spread her wings.

How brave our mum was, we thought, *to go against what everyone said, and head off like a pioneer!*

Mum told us that she flew up to Alice in a little old plane, a trip that took all day, with refuelling stops at Woomera, then Oodnadatta. It was a long, bumpy trip, but she was absorbed by the endless desert plains and wide empty sky.

When she landed in Alice and saw a landscape framed by enormous red ranges and blue skies, she knew she'd been right to come here. She said to us, 'This big land was just what I had expected, and almost immediately I felt that I wanted to belong to it.'

We looked at old photos of Mum from that time. We thought she looked just like Audrey Hepburn: huge brown eyes, an elfin face, cropped brown hair and a twenty-one-inch waist. She lived with another girl in an old Sidney Williams corrugated-iron hut at the back of the Elders' offices, and wore pretty dresses she made herself. There were card nights and dances, and a world of charming young stockmen who arrived out of the bush in their moleskins, RM Williams elastic-sided boots, press-stud shirts and huge hats. In Central Australia, Mum said, nobody cared who you were, where you'd come from, or what your parents did, and she revelled in her new-found freedom.

'Tell us more about Hamilton Downs,' we'd beg.

Mum's smile would grow. 'Well, Aunty Dawn and Uncle Bill needed someone to teach Gary, who was just starting school, and to look after little David and baby Wendy.'

Dawn and Bill Prior weren't really our aunt and uncle, but they'd been so much a part of our lives for as long as we could remember, we thought they were. They lived on a cattle station to the northwest of Alice Springs, nestled up against the ranges.

'Aunty Dawn advertised for a governess in the local paper. She had her hands full with cooking for so many stockmen; she didn't have time to be Gary's teacher, too. The Priors became my family. There was a big Aboriginal community living there, too. It was a different world to anything I'd ever experienced. Everyone welcomed me in.'

'What about the snake story? Tell us about that again.'

Mum said she hadn't been at Hamilton Downs very long when some of the young Aboriginal women told Aunty Dawn, 'There bin mulga snake in house here, Missus.'

Mum was standing nearby and nearly dropped the dishes she was wiping up. She already knew that the mulga snake, also known as the king brown, was enormous and deadly.

'Don't worry, Jan,' said Aunty Dawn comfortingly, 'they're part of life out here.'

But Mum wasn't comforted. The following night she was asleep in her cot bed on the enclosed veranda when she awoke to a sound. A slithering sound. In the moonlight she saw a huge snake moving up and down the wall, and the door, obviously trying to get out. She realised she was trapped in there with it. She screamed and screamed, until Aunty Dawn finally woke on the other side of the house.

'The snake!' Mum kept repeating frantically. 'It's in here!'

Uncle Bill was out in the stock camp, so Aunty Dawn ran to get the bore mechanic, who dragged himself out of his swag. He arrived in shorts and bare feet, cranky, and carrying a huge shovel. As he pushed open the door, he saw Mum standing on her bed. She was still screaming. He shouted, 'Shut up, Jan! Shut up!' and took on the enormous snake. When he'd finally killed it, there were bits of bloodied snake all over the veranda.

Mum was so traumatised, she had to go and sleep with Aunty Dawn for the rest of the night.

But before long she was able to recount the story as an old hand. 'You just have to deal with snakes,' she'd say, firmly. 'Can't have them in the house. Even have to be careful in the children's sandpit.' And ever since we could remember she kept a large shovel close to the kitchen door, just in case.

Every morning and every night she saw the raw colours of Central Australia rise and fall over the ancient ranges, and knew station life was for her.

She stayed there for two years, but finally she was drawn back south. She missed her family. And a young man named Grant.

'Tell us again about meeting Dad,' we'd say, mischievously.

Mum's eyes would again take on that faraway look. 'We actually met when we were thirteen. He caught the train to boarding school from Orroroo. I would wave goodbye to him.'

I could imagine Mum, standing in her little school dress, waving her handkerchief at a young boy with a freckly face, dark hair and a cheeky grin. We loved that image: Mum and Dad, young, with their lives ahead of them.

Dad's story was harder to piece together. He came from a sheep property, Glenroy, graced with a beautiful old homestead, wide creeks lined with gum trees and a long Heaslip heritage. His family were part Scottish and part Irish, and had been in Australia for five generations. He told us stories about his ancestors often, because he said it was important that we know what they had suffered, and how hard they had worked to give us the chances we now had in Australia.

'Glenroy was named after our family's home in Scotland. In 1692 our family, the McDonalds, took in the Campbells and showed them hospitality. In return, the Campbells massacred everyone.'

We weren't sure what we were meant to take from the story, especially because Mum was constantly taking people in and showing them hospitality, but we always nodded seriously.

'And our Irish side—well, they came from a farm in County Cavan. The Heaslip head was called Ben of the Rock. The family were starving in the Potato Famine. So, they made a decision: one son stayed and one son came to Australia, in 1853.'

Dad knew dates, names and history off the top of his head.

His family were a strong Methodist clan. They were devoted to the land of South Australia and to hard work, and they adhered to strict rules for living. They also saw developing land and stock as a way to get ahead after the Great Depression and war years. For a long time, they held coupons for fuel and lived *frugally* (Dad told me that word, which I thought sounded important). They skinned and sold wild rabbits and kangaroos to get by. The only time Dad stopped working was to play football or cricket on Saturday, and go to church on Sunday.

From an early age, it was drummed into Dad that his family were caretakers of the land. He could have gone on to be a great sportsman, but he set aside those distractions to focus on his duty and his passion for the land—and for one gorgeous Audrey Hepburn lookalike, who could join him in his quest.

'Dad persuaded me to come back from Alice,' said Mum. 'And then he asked me to marry him.'

'How beautiful!' M'Lis and I gazed up at Mum, feeling so happy.

'I said yes, if we could go back to the Territory once we got married.'

Dad liked the idea of forging a new life. Papa Heaslip controlled Glenroy, so moving north would give Dad independence and the chance to make his own mark.

But heading back to the Territory didn't happen immediately.

First, Mum and Dad nearly didn't get married.

'Tell us about the night of your wedding, Mum,' we'd chorus.

Mum would squirm a bit, then say uncertainly, 'Well, the night *before* our wedding, we had a big fight. I threw a bucket of water over Dad. It was winter and cold. He marched off. I cried all night.'

Silence. 'Then what happened?'

'Dad came back. And we got married. It was the happiest day of my life.'

We pored over the photos of their wedding, which Mum had pasted into a big white album. She arrived at the church looking like a princess, dressed divinely in a satin gown she'd designed herself. Dad looked so handsome, his black hair combed back like Elvis Presley's, a huge grin across his face. The love between them bounced off the pages of the album.

We looked at the proud face of Nana Parnell, her hair beautifully curled, and Papa's tired but happy eyes. We studied Nana and Papa Heaslip; Nana slim and elegant, Papa handsome with a silver moustache. Both our Nanas wore long gloves and hats.

Standing next to them were Dad's younger sister, Aunty June, and Mum's younger brother, Uncle John. They were both teenagers, seven years younger than Dad and Mum, and they were beaming. We loved them; they were fun.

'As a wedding present, Dad made me a kangaroo skin blanket,' said Mum. 'He used skins that he'd saved, and he sewed them together with a big needle. I've had that blanket on our bed ever since.'

Dad was nothing if not a practical man.

For their honeymoon, he drove Mum through drought-stricken outback Australia in a little Volkswagen. I didn't think that sounded very romantic, but they visited the Priors at Hamilton Downs, which must have made Mum happy, and gave Dad the chance to inspect the inland. The Priors promised to look out for properties for them. What Dad thought of that landscape, with its dust and scrawny cattle, I can't imagine, but he wasn't put off. If anything, he was inspired by the courage of those he met.

On his return, he wrote in his work diary, '*My main appreciation of the trip was to see the way that other people run their places, the way they handle difficult problems, the interest they have in their work, and their outlook on improving their stock and management.*'

At age twenty-two, Dad was a serious young man. What with the Scottish massacre, the Irish Potato Famine and the Methodist work ethic, he didn't have time for self-pity and never considered giving up. He admired those who pushed on, and cared for the land and their stock, no matter what obstacles were put in their way.

He would go on to spend the rest of his life trying to condition his wife and children in this way, too. 'For better or worse,' Mum would say, faintly.

'Then what happened?' we'd ask, going back to the wedding and Mum's happiest day. That was an easier story to listen to.

Once married, in 1961, Mum and Dad promptly had three children: me, M'Lis and Brett. Their first home was a tiny cottage at Glenroy.

'Dad worked for Papa and graded roads for the council. I cooked for the shearers. We were always trying to earn extra money.'

I spent my first few years in that little cottage, close to Nana and Papa Heaslip, whom I loved. When M'Lis was just a few months old, we moved to a sheep lease called Witchitie. It was also held by Dad's father, and was east of Glenroy and deep in the Flinders Ranges saltbush country. A long row of curving purple hills separated the two properties.

That was Mum and Dad's first dance with semi-independence. There they built a house and water tank, out of bricks and cement they mixed themselves. Mum continued to look to the north and longed for the life of freedom she'd once had there.

When we asked her, 'When did you want to go back?' she said without hesitation, 'The moment I left.'

Mum said that I often cried at night. Nothing she did could pacify me.

'It was terrible. I was following the old rules,' she told me. 'We were told we were only allowed to feed our babies at certain times. I had all this milk ready to give you but I was told I wasn't allowed to. You were so hungry and I was so distressed.'

I would hold my tummy at that point, looking at her anxiously.

By the time I was about sixteen months old, Mum couldn't bear it any longer. 'At about two o'clock one morning, I was desperate,' said Mum, her face flushed at the memory. 'I didn't know what else to do. So, I wheeled M'Lis in her cot into your room. She was two months old. I said to you, "Here we go, Tanya, here's M'Lis."'

I took one big, choking breath, and stopped crying.

And I didn't cry at night after that. Hunger aside, I was obviously waiting for my sister soulmate to arrive. We were inseparable from that moment on. We shared a room for the rest of our childhood.

We were like twins. Mum made our clothes, which were identical, and we didn't go anywhere unless we were together.

We did look very different, though: I had a blonde mop and M'Lis had dark curls. I was a serious-faced and serious-natured child, while M'Lis was merry, with bright sparkling eyes and a happy grin. She brought fun and companionship into my life. When Brett came along, with his earnest blue eyes, I looked after them both, taking on the protective role of eldest child. We three were like puppies, rolling and scrapping together, and over time I learned what they needed to be happy and safe.

———————

In the meantime, Mum and Dad's new life at Witchitie was busy. Dad spent most days mustering sheep on horseback. He would kill one animal each month for food and hang its carcass in the meat house, some distance from the house. Mum had a kerosene fridge and cooked over a wood stove. Every morning, her first job was to light the wood stove, which was a battle, then put the kettle on to boil. Inside the kettle were three bottles of powdered milk, bobbing away. We were like baby birds, lined up inside the nest with our mouths open and cheeping noisily, waiting for the next feed.

Every afternoon Dad chopped wood for our 'donkey' hot-water system (a forty-four-gallon drum and woodfire) that heated water for baths. Next to the house was a 'Freelite' windmill that gave us thirty-two-volt power in the mornings and evenings—if there was wind.

Mum and Dad planted trees and a lawn. We had picnic teas on the lawn and played games where Dad threw us up in the air. We were so little, and Mum said we laughed and laughed as Dad held us up, our baby faces filled with happiness, our eyes shining.

———➤◆◄———

Dad built a little office at the back of the Witchitie house where he kept his accounts and wrote in his work diary every evening. His father and uncles and grandfather before them had done the same. The diaries dated back generations, crammed with details about stock and prices and the weather; a living record down through the years so that each could compare seasons and rainfall and mutton and wool prices and sales. The Heaslip men never missed a day.

Dad was very proud of his diaries. Whenever we asked him about something important that happened, he'd say, 'It's all in the diaries,' and pat them confidentially. 'One day, you'll get to read them.'

———➤◆◄———

'Tell us how you got to Bond Springs, Mum!' We always wanted more.

'Well, in 1964, Bond Springs came onto the market. The drought was terrible and the Chisholms, who also owned Napperby Station to the north, were selling it.'

By now, Bond Springs held only 150 skinny cows, boasted no permanent waterholes or springs (despite Mr Bond's mistaken belief when he named the lease back in the 1800s), and had never been run as a standalone property. Elders GM and all the locals said that, despite being eighteen hundred and thirteen square kilometres in size, it was unviable on its own, and needed to be run alongside something much bigger.

'Dad did the figures and worked out we could run it with Witchitie. And—best of all—it was next door to Hamilton Downs!' said Mum, as though that had settled matters.

Dad told us he persuaded Elders GM to lend them most of the

money to buy it. Papa Heaslip, and Dad's Uncle George, agreed to loan Dad the rest.

'I had to pay them the going interest rate of the day, twenty per cent,' he said, with a wry grin. 'No free handouts for family.'

But Bond Springs nearly didn't happen at all.

The government also had to agree to the sale, because it was a leasehold block on Crown land, and the government were the ultimate owners.

'But the government was thinking of turning Bond Springs into a park because of the drought,' said Dad, frowning, when he told me this story many years later. 'We had to wait about six months, while they went backwards and forwards between departments. Finally, they decided to grant the lease. But it came with a kicker: we had three years to make all sorts of improvements and meet their strict rules, or at the end of those three years they'd take Bond Springs back. We'd be given nothing for our investment, either. We'd have to return to Witchitie, with our tails between our legs. It was a big risk for Mum and me.'

Especially at a twenty per cent interest rate.

Friends and family were worried at the time, too, just as they had been when Mum went up there in the first place. They said Dad had no experience with cattle—only sheep—and that was true. He'd never lived in Central Australia. True, too. Mum had worked there for several years, but as a governess, not running a property. It was a four-day drive to get to Bond Springs from Witchitie over rough, corrugated dirt roads. Communication was limited to telegrams and letters.

But Mum and Dad were 'young and bulletproof', as Dad would later say, believing hard work would solve all problems. Mum said, 'In those days, obstacles were just something to jump over,' and Dad added, 'We never considered we might fail.'

And Mum was happy. We'd ask her, 'What was it like to get back to the Territory at last?'

'Heaven,' said Mum, and a smile always lit up her eyes. 'I'd come home.'

2

Cattleman—*Har Hup*, There!

People said that Dad was not a big man, but he was a giant to us. He filled every space he entered; owned it, commanded it. Mostly he marched about, giving orders or asking questions. But when he relaxed, he grinned a lot. His eyes would sparkle and twinkle, right at us, and we couldn't help but grin back. It always made us feel everything was right with the world when Dad was happy. Before bed, he would recite a nonsensical ditty about farm animals called, 'Bed, Fred in the Shed,' and kiss our little cheeks with his stubbly one. When we grew up, we'd recite it back to each other, thinking it the most comforting, happy poem ever.

And years later, if we begged hard enough, Dad would tell us about the early days on Bond Springs.

Like bringing cattle in for the first time.

'That must have been exciting, Dad,' we said, looking up at him, eagerly.

'No, it was a necessity,' said Dad, reminding us right up front that his story was about *work*, not excitement. 'We had to introduce good breeders and quickly rebuild the herd because a hundred and fifty skinny cows weren't going to help us keep our lease.'

'Ah,' we sat back.

'There were no cattle to buy around Alice because of the drought. Elders agreed to extend the overdraft and we bought cattle from Adelaide and waited for the drought to break. It was a tense time.'

'Of course,' we nodded dutifully.

Mum added, 'Rod and Judy Hodder managed Bond Springs for us in the first year. They really helped us.' She turned to us. 'It meant Dad could go between Witchitie and the Bond, and I could mostly be at Witchitie. It was easier not to travel such distances with you little ones.'

Mum and Judy were old friends from school in Orroroo, so it was a good outcome for everyone. Best of all was when Rod sent news by telegram to Witchitie in late December 1965, telling Dad that summer rains had broken the ten-year drought in Central Australia.

'Huge relief,' Dad confirmed, and Mum smiled at him and the memory.

On 23 January 1966, a further telegram from Rod led to Dad scribbling in his diary: '*Some more rain, now feed. Rod says 400 cattle can go up now!*'

'That was a lot of cattle to get to Alice, so I took Papa Parnell with me to help,' explained Dad. 'We loaded the cattle on the Ghan at Maree. Left about ten-thirty at night. It was still thirty-eight degrees inside the goods compartment, stinking hot.' Dad shuddered. 'That's where Papa and I spent the trip, close to the cattle.'

Later that night, Dad crawled out onto the little steel lattice landing that ran along either side of the train to get some relief.

'I tied my left hand and left foot to the side of the landing posts so I could have a bit of a camp, and not fall off.' He told us those ties kept him safe. 'Miracle I survived that trip.'

After a long three-day journey they arrived in Alice Springs late at night, and it was 'still stinking hot'. Rod Hodder was waiting. He'd brought two horses through the back hills and creeks. The horses were poor but they were all Rod had available. He and Judy had also driven in the station's little old green Land Rover, packed with a tucker box, swags and feed for the horses.

'The plan was to camp the night at the yards, then next morning drive the cattle through the outskirts of Alice and into the hills, then on to the Bond Springs boundary,' said Dad. 'The creeks met there, just before some old wooden yards. We were going to spell the cattle there overnight, then push on to Bond Springs the next day. Papa would follow behind us in the Land Rover.'

Dad paused. 'I didn't know the route, hadn't seen any of this country, had to rely on maps from the Lands Board, and Rod, who didn't know the country either . . .' He was anxious from the start, and it seemed he had good reason to be.

To start with, the cattle and horses 'just wouldn't travel'. That wasn't surprising. The cattle were exhausted from the train journey and the heat, and unnerved by the new landscape and the sight of houses. Soon, Dad and Rod's big overland trek was behind schedule.

There was another problem; one that Dad could never have predicted. A storm was building. Central Australia had been in drought for so long that people were desperate for more rain. But today of all days?

'I can recall the exact moment I heard the first thunder crack,' he told us.

We could imagine the cattle, already fatigued and disorientated, snorting, the whites of their eyes showing panic. Dad said the light was fading and he was worried. The last thing he needed was for the mob to stampede.

'Push 'em on!' he shouted to Rod. 'Got to get 'em to the boundary, over the creek. Can't lose 'em now.'

As Dad told us what happened next, we could see and hear it all—a whir of sounds: stockwhips cracking, the men yelling hoarsely, cattle bellowing in fright, horses whinnying in fear, thunder banging all around them. Then, we could smell the first drops of rain. Sweet and heavy. It must have been terrifying as the water fell out of the sky, almost blinding them.

'By the time we got to the creek, it was already flooded.'

The cattle came to a forced halt, milling manically around the creek's edge. The water was rising fast, pounding and roaring in their ears.

Dad told us he forced himself to concentrate on Plan B.

'We'll have to hold 'em here, and keep 'em safe through the night.'

Temperatures plunged. Dad said he and Rod were starving and freezing. But Papa couldn't get through, so there was no food, no swags and no time to sleep, anyway. The rain was still hard and lightning sent jagged flashes through the sky. Dad and Rod moved around and around the mob, soothing the cattle, trying to hold them together in one group. They were shivering in their saddles, with soaking clothes and aching bellies; it was a long night.

As the light of dawn finally struggled through the drizzle, Dad could see that the creek was now well and truly flooded. But despite the horrors of the previous night, they still had the mob pretty much in one group.

'The relief was overwhelming,' Dad said. Now they just had to keep them all in the one place until the creek went down.

By mid-afternoon, the clouds had cleared. Steam rose off the wet land. The water in the creek had dropped. 'Righto,' Dad decided. 'We'll have to swim 'em across.'

With much cracking of stockwhips and shouting, they coaxed their unwilling and exhausted horses and the cattle down into the brown, murky water. It was still a risk. They didn't know what was underfoot, and both the horses and cattle could slip, become entangled in branches or knock into obstacles, and drown.

But Dad didn't dare stay any longer. There was a greater risk he would lose them all if he didn't get them to the other side, and soon.

'*Har hup, there! Walk up!*' Crack! Bellow. '*C'mon cattle, move it through!*'

Dad and Rod drove the mob through the muddy water, yelling, pushing, with fear in their throats.

'It seemed to take forever,' Dad told us, and he never exaggerated anything.

Dad said that just when he and Rod thought they couldn't go on any longer, the cattle and horses hit the bank. From there they struggled up the other side to high ground. Within half an hour, the men had them inside the wooden yards beyond. They collapsed off their horses.

'*Hell of a journey,*' Dad later wrote in his diary. '*Hard job. Horses had had it. Men had had it. But looked as though we got most of the cattle.*'

Dad was not only a man who never exaggerated, he downplayed everything, so his words showed what a hard time it must have been, especially as he considered what he might have lost. But when we asked him in person, he simply repeated, 'Hell of a journey,' and that was that.

It was hard to get any more detail out of Dad. He'd exhausted himself and his memory going back to that traumatic day. I did read in his diaries that it took another two days before he and Rod got the cattle to the homestead yards. Papa was waiting. Dad recorded in his diary: '*Amazing result—only nine short in a total count of 365.*'

Dad didn't write in his diary about the hunger, fear or exhaustion—or the fact the weather was quickly blazing hot again—but went on for the next two weeks to set out in detail how much rain had fallen from that wild downpour, the next round of mustering, numbers for drafting and branding, and notes of a quick trip to Hamilton Downs.

Then, three weeks to the day after he arrived, he and Papa caught a ride with an Elders GM representative back to Witchitie. Mum was waiting anxiously for him, as she'd received no news during that time. She remembered falling into his arms with relief.

They were so young, I thought. *Just over twenty-five, three little ones, and such pressure not to fail.*

There were more challenges ahead. Dad had to keep buying more stock to rebuild the herd now that it had rained. But he didn't want to go through the difficulty of bringing cattle up from south again, so he bought the next herd of cattle locally.

'Luckily there were some big rains out to the west in early 1965, and some months later the Braitlings from Mount Doreen ended up selling nearly a thousand Poll Herefords,' he told us, when next we begged for more stories. 'So, we put in an offer to buy part of the mob.'

Dad was happy about this purchase because the beautiful brown-and-white Poll Herefords were the breed he wanted to develop. He'd been told they were tough and resilient in outback conditions. And he'd already become friends with Wally Braitling, from Mount Doreen, to the far north-west of Alice.

Dad had met Wally, and his gorgeous wife Barb, when he first came to Alice. Mum was close to them, and the four immediately became great friends. That cattle purchase would also be the first of many business ventures between Dad and Wally.

But that cattle droving trip too nearly ended in disaster.

It was a five-hundred-kilometre trip. Midway, an unexpected storm hit, just as it had done during Dad's trip. The cattle stampeded and the stockmen feared they'd lose the lot. But as the cattle headed into the ranges, they hit a corrugated dirt road. Awash with rain in the evening light, it looked like a river. The cattle hadn't seen a river before—the drought had been so long and harsh—and they baulked, terrified.

That moment gave the stockmen the chance to cut off their escape route. But the cattle were stirry and unsettled from then on, and the stockmen 'didn't take their boots off' for the rest of the trip.

It took another week and a half for the mob to reach the boundary of Bond Springs. Dad (who'd come up from Witchitie), Rod Hodder and four young Aboriginal stockmen rode to meet the mob at Corkwood Bore.

'Rod hired the young blokes from the Mount Nancy camp in Alice,' Dad remembered. 'We knew we needed more men for such a big job.'

Dad hadn't ever worked with Aboriginal stockmen before, but he knew they were renowned as natural horsemen and cattlemen. He thought he might be able to engage the stockmen on a muster-by-muster basis if they wanted the work. They did.

It took all day for the six of them to ride from the Bond Springs homestead to the western yards. They arrived just before dusk, the air full of dust and the cattle bellowing. Dad said he felt overwhelming relief as, just on dark, the mob were herded into the yards and the gates shut tight.

He bought nearly eight hundred cattle, extending the Elders GM overdraft yet again to do so.

'It was another big gamble. We needed more rain so we could fatten the cattle and sell them. It was a big race to meet the lease conditions of three years, and pay back our loans to Elders and Papa and Uncle George. Every step of the way, we could have gone broke.'

But Dad's pluck paid off when almost one year to the day he sold the first lot of steers, bulls and heifers.

Dad recorded good prices in his diary, scribbling the details down in such a rush they were hard to read. Dad didn't mention how he felt—nor did he tell us—but, no doubt, he felt huge relief.

I trembled at the thought of what might have happened to us had things gone wrong. The ever-present fear of failure, and hunger for success, drove Dad forward, relentlessly, as he worked harder than he'd ever done.

Over time, the pressures would start to show, cracking the surface, taking their toll, shaping and moulding Dad into a man as hard and unyielding as the red, dusty land he was seeking to tame. But, in that first year, his diary recorded all that needed to be said.

Success.

And relief.

3

Our Very Own Palace

I loved Bond Springs from the moment we arrived.

To start with, M'Lis, Brett and I had endless amounts of space to play.

We had to watch out for big lizards—perenties—and if we ever saw one we could only shriek in awe and excitement at their magnificence and the speed at which they could run and climb. And there were, of course, snakes. Most feared was the king brown, especially after Mum told us about her first encounter with one at Hamilton Downs. We'd had snakes at Witchitie too, so we were trained to look out for them, especially when playing near bushes, shrubs and piles of rocks, all the places we knew they loved to live. From an early age, we were ever alert to danger.

M'Lis was adorably cute. She sucked her thumb and twiddled the ends of her hair when she was thinking hard, and she had a strong sense of her own self, even as a young girl. Brett's tiny face was freckly, framing intense blue eyes, and he was full of mischief from the start. We were inseparable.

Mum was our rock and anchor, ever present. She didn't stop running from one end of the place to the other, making the house our home, but she always had time for kisses, cuddles and stories. She told us constantly how much she loved us and we felt completely cocooned in that love.

To me, every part of Bond Springs was a palace. It boasted a rambling stone homestead with whitewashed walls and louvre windows. These were thickly covered in dust from the huge dust storms that rolled in from the southern and western deserts during the drought years. The floors were cement, although the large sitting room was pasted with cracking lino. At the front, French doors opened off a bar room (complete with a real bar) onto a flagstone patio.

In the heat of the day M'Lis, Brett and I would lie on the cool cement floors of the breezeway, which was right in the centre of the house. The original rooms—a sitting room and kitchen with fireplace—were built in about 1930, and the rest were added in a haphazard fashion over the years.

The homestead was surrounded by athel pines and pepper trees for coolness, and two beautiful lawns that were hand-watered to survive the drought. They offered the blessing of green against the baked, dry landscape.

Red-and-white painted posts cornered each side of the lawns. We thought they were wonderful, and Mum agreed, calling them 'a grand colonial gesture'.

Lining the patio were pots of brilliant green jade and faded green succulents called 'pigface'. But apart from the trees, lawns and those few tough plants, there was barely any other garden.

Water was not only limited but harsh with chloride and salt and undrinkable. It was bore water, drawn from one of the few bores that had been sunk over the last century, or a deep well situated down near the creek, which we were forbidden to go near.

All water was precious but none more so than our drinking water. It was taken from the white tank set against the laundry, and the greatest sin was to waste even a drop.

'Our drinking water comes from the rain, and if we run out, we will *perish*,' Dad would say with such finality that we were terrified at the very thought. I imagined us drooping around the house, slowly dying a hideous death of thirst, until we were nothing more than grey corpses. It was a constant fear, drummed into us so hard we made every drop count.

We shared a bath at night, squatting in an old tub with about two inches of the brownish bore water from the grey tank. (It was essential to know the difference between the two tanks. A mouthful of bore water would see us gagging and spitting.)

Just to the back of the kitchen, and partly hidden by athel pines, squatted a tin shed for the generator. It was tiny, yet it managed to rumble and reverberate through everything and everyone when Dad started it. Nearby, perhaps a little too close for comfort, were two incinerators and a large wood heap.

To the south of the house sat an original settler's hut whose walls were made of logs and filled with straw and daub, built in the late 1880s. I spent hours imagining the pioneers in the early days and what it must have been like for them to live in that hut, especially in the scorching summer, lying on a bed made from gum logs and covered in cattle hide.

To the east stood a two-room, tin Sidney Kidman cottage built in 1910. This cottage was grand in comparison to the hut, with its very own veranda on two sides. It was raised on stilts, no doubt to limit snake access. Next to the cottage were rooms that had been added sometime in the 1930s.

In total, the sprawling homestead comprised nearly twenty rooms.

Definitely a palace!

Further south again were a series of wooden horse yards and stables, built around the early 1900s. At the bottom of the yards was an old log saddle shed, filled with oiled saddles and bridles, and a blacksmith's forge—complete with a huge old anvil that had been used to make horseshoes, and other work tools—built almost entirely out of local golden-brown stone brought up from the nearby creek.

A number of other sheds and horse yards, a meat house and a chook shed made up the working buildings around the house. We spent a lot of time in the chook shed, which we loved, patting the new hens that Mum introduced, collecting eggs and watching for holes in the wire that might indicate the presence of snakes looking for a feed.

On the other side of the Bond Springs creek, on top of an adjacent hill, was a large, flat area with some empty tin houses with low verandas. Dad told us how Aboriginal people, originally from Napperby Station to the north (which was held by the Chisholms, the family from whom we bought Bond Springs), had lived in these houses during the 1950s and early 1960s but left during the long drought when the station ran out of feed, trees, stock and horses. Some of them, Dad said, moved to Mount Nancy, an Aboriginal camp in Alice Springs, where the four young stockmen had come from.

Further up the hill, out of sight but not out of hearing, were large wooden cattle yards. Built by Sidney Kidman, it was the place cattle were brought in for drafting, branding and trucking. When there were cattle in the yards, the constant bellowing reverberated through the homestead. I loved that sound from the first moment. It was the sound of our new world.

Down at the creek were the remnants of a big old wall, built in about 1915 to dam water when it rained. The wall was constructed out of the same beautiful old rocks as the blacksmith forge, and we found it so exciting to play around and on it despite its tumble-down state.

Summer kicked off about mid-September, grew in intensity from late November to late March, and didn't subside until mid-April.

We slept in swags on the lawn during summer because it was suffocating inside the house. Mosquitos would descend like blankets as night fell, leaving us tossing and turning under the canvas of our swags, sweaty and fitful, bitten and itchy. We'd wake at daylight to flies covering our faces, the heat of the desert already seeping through the dry air.

One night, Mum woke to see the shapes of three dingoes on the lawn, sniffing our swags. There were often dingoes about, howling eerily across the flat and up into the hills. But on our lawn, Mum said they were like silent, watchful hunters.

'Grant!' she called out, in fear.

Dad jumped out of his swag and growled, 'Get out of here!' They slunk off into the darkness, but we were all awake by then, and I was frightened. I imagined them hiding in the bushes, watching us, waiting for their chance to eat us.

Mum had read us *Little Red Riding Hood* and I believed that dingoes were just another kind of wolf (only with yellow coats, instead of grey). They gave me nightmares. They came back again and again, at night-time, because, Dad said, the drought was so bad. Luckily, we always woke before they could eat us, but that didn't stop the nightmares.

Winters were short but beautiful.

'The wind's straight off the Simpson Desert this morning,' Dad would say, rubbing his hands. The house pipes froze at night and frost covered the lawn in sub-zero temperatures. But by mid-morning we'd have taken off our jumpers, and by lunchtime we were often running around in shorts and T-shirts in the warm sunshine. By dusk, the temperatures would have plunged again, and Mum would light a fire in the sitting room hearth every night.

Spring and autumn skipped by, lasting about two weeks each, and just as we'd got used to them, they'd be gone again.

———⟶●⟵———

From the start, Dad made daily bore runs, driving all over the property, checking and fixing pumps and dams and fences. We all went with him, squashed into his little Land Rover. Eighteen hundred square kilometres of Bond Springs might have been small in Central Australian terms, but it meant a lot of driving.

Whenever we stopped for Dad to do something, we'd clamber out and play in the shade of a nearby corkwood or mulga tree. We'd create our own little world in the red dirt, using sticks and fingers to draw winding roads, yards of all shapes and sizes, tilting wind-mills and cattle. Our little minds were always busy, and for me it was a welcome distraction from the heat and dust of driving.

Being so young, I couldn't understand Dad's desire, and capacity, to drive and drive and drive. I didn't realise the import-ance of those early trips for Dad. He was not only checking waters, yards and animals, he was carving the property into his very being with every trip.

As he drove, he was learning more about Bond Springs. Every curve of the landscape went deep into his memory, each dip of the hill and sweep of the creek, every ridge and mile of scrub, soon seared tightly into his mind. He was determined to know his property at every turn, so that before long he would know it better than anyone else. He was the protector of his piece of earth and the herd he was building. And each season would bring different warnings and challenges, for which he would be ready.

Over time, we absorbed the importance of his learning. When we weren't playing, we would sit in the sand and dirt and watch him silently.

He'd dig the toe of his boot into the dust and draw part of a fence, and describe the section that needed to be fixed. Or he'd use a stick to point which way the gully had washed out and the cattle had headed. Or read the soil and the skies and the trees to understand the seasons and then teach others.

He was called Boss by the two local stockmen who lived with us on the station, Ross Coop and Colin Ansell. We kids just thought Dad was born that way and bowed to him without question. He might not have seemed old to himself, but as I gazed at his set jaw and listened to his unequivocal directions to others, he seemed as old and wise as time.

From the start, Dad got straight into meeting the government's requirements. With Ross and Colin, he replaced the old, rotting wood in fences and cattleyards with barbed wire and steel. He built new fence-lines and sank bores. Because Bond Springs had no permanent fresh water, he had to find other ways to get water for stock.

His idea was to turn the big paddocks into lots of smaller paddocks to make them more workable, and then put bores into as many of those paddocks as possible. Over the years, however, bore sinking proved expensive and unreliable. Most of the bores on Bond Springs turned out to be duds or unusable, because the water either couldn't be found, or was undrinkable even for stock. So, Dad built dams to supplement the bores—each named after us, or events that were happening around us—and to make the most of rain when it came.

———✦———

During the early years, Dad drove constantly between Witchitie and Bond Springs to keep both places going, and we usually went with him. I hated those drives—four days of heat and boredom along the red, deeply corrugated dirt roads south—and I always got carsick. Dad drove with furious concentration over the ridges and pot-holes, no time for conversation or cranky kids, and Mum tried to keep us occupied so Dad could focus.

But one trip, M'Lis and I were whinging so much that by the time we stopped for dinner camp we had worked ourselves into a frenzy. We sat on the ground and sobbed. Mum threw up her hands in despair. Eventually Dad strode over to us. He squatted down and put his arm around both of us.

'Tanya and M'Lis, if you don't stop crying, I'm going to give you both a big smack,' he said, his voice rough with exhaustion. 'And then you'll really have something to cry about.'

We both heaved and swallowed our sobs as best we could.

'There,' said Dad, getting up wearily. 'It wasn't so hard, was it?'

It didn't stop me hating the trips, though. They never got any easier.

And Dad didn't get any cheerier.

———✦———

Finally, after three years of constant driving and constant working, Mum and Dad met every rule imposed under the lease, and the government said they could keep Bond Springs.

'Jan, it's here!'

When the telegram from the government arrived, Dad's face split into a boyish grin. He waved the yellow paper around, looking like he'd just won Best and Fairest in every cricket and football match of the season.

'We can stay!'

He put his arm around Mum and twirled her around the kitchen. She sparkled then, too—young and beautiful and carefree—for one precious moment.

The government had set many rules around stocking and waters and fencing, which were tough, but Mum and Dad had got through those first years, and that was success enough. They still had to repay Elders GM and Papa and Uncle George, and that would take years, but they had a future now they could depend on.

And even though it meant Dad and Mum would be working harder than ever, we felt safe and protected. We could run free and wild in bare feet without a care. It was a happy life and we knew nothing else.

4

'I Belong That Country'

Plenty of naysayers predicted Dad would eventually fail: he hadn't grown up in the bush, didn't know cattle or the harsh seasons and had the wrong experience. But Dad had an innate sense of business. And one thing he did know: no stock sales, no money.

So mustering quickly became our life.

Station maintenance, such as checking and fixing bores, fences, tanks and yards, continued all year round, but the mustering season took place from April to September, before it got too hot.

Dad and his stockmen would ride from paddock to paddock, muster the cattle in each one, and drive them towards the nearest yards. Most of the paddocks were large and wild and miles from the house, so the men would ride out as a big expedition, then set up camp next to the yards of each paddock to be mustered.

Once the cattle were in the yards, drafting would then start; it was a long, hot and difficult process that could take days, even with a lot of men to help.

Dad would separate out cows, calves, micky bulls (uncastrated young male cattle), heifers, steers and bullocks into different yards, so he could look at the numbers and monitor how the breeding process was going. This was followed by searing the hide of any cleanskins (usually young cattle) with the BST brand, and castrating the young male cattle and any wild scrubber bulls that had got away last muster.

Then came the business side of it. Dad would arrange to sell the best of the herd (usually steers and bullocks, but sometimes also heifers and cows). Those cattle would then be trucked off to market.

The men could be gone for weeks, moving from paddock to paddock, coming back in to the homestead only to refresh horses and provisions. Food had to be organised carefully. The men needed enough items that wouldn't go off in the heat to last them while away. Luckily, Mum had some experience of this from her time at Hamilton Downs. The men used pack horses to carry large leather bags of flour, tea, sugar, water and salt beef, and they led the horses from camp to camp.

We loved watching the stock camp head out. Even as little ones, we sensed the theatre and drama of it all as the men prepared.

Finally, everything in place, swags rolled and the horses saddled, we would gather by the saddle shed for the farewell. Ross and Colin and any other men Dad had hired would sit easily on their horses flicking flies, their eyes shaded by their low-brimmed hats, and wait for the nod from the Boss. The pack horses would stand patiently, ready to be led by whoever drew the short straw.

If Dad had hired Aboriginal stockmen for the muster, which he started to do more often, they would sit quietly on their horses too, grinning shyly at us, while we looked up at them and grinned shyly back. We'd never seen Aboriginal stockmen before coming to Bond

Springs. They wore shiny press-stud shirts and big hats and Dad told us they were the best with horses and cattle.

We had seen pictures of traditional Aboriginal people in books, hunting with spears, their chests painted with white and red. We thought them bold and fierce and brave. We knew they were also called natives, because they were native Australians, and had lived here for thousands of years, well before the white people came. Mum told us they could track animals through the dirt and throw curved pieces of wood called boomerangs to bring down birds or kangaroos and could go without water much longer than even Dad.

Mum had learned these things on Hamilton Downs when she was a governess because of the big Aboriginal community that lived there. Her charges, Gary and David, played with the Aboriginal kids and spoke Arrernte as well as they spoke English. Mum saw firsthand how the traditional ways blended with those of the station. Often the camp disappeared on walkabout and no one knew where they'd gone or for how long. Traditional business took precedence over everything else and Aboriginal timing was an 'unknown' for the whitefellas.

We were fascinated by Mum's stories, and excited when the Aboriginal stockmen came to do musters for Dad. To bring in the stockmen, Dad had to fill in 'Aboriginal wage forms' and tell the government the men were working for us. At the time, the wages for Aboriginal stockmen were lower than for the white stockmen, which made me ashamed when I grew older and learned this, but it was the way things were done back then. Dad was new to working with Aboriginal men but he respected their skills and was glad to have them.

On the day, Dad would be the last to mount his horse. Once in the saddle, he'd turn and wave to us with a grin, before leading the team out through the wide homestead gate. Mum held our little hands as they cantered out and probably wondered when and if she would see Dad again.

———※———

With Dad away, our axis moved, tilted, and Mum took a huge load of responsibility. But she was happy to be back in Central Australia, and strong, which was lucky, given the amount of work that fell daily on her slim shoulders.

Dad's work was the station itself. Mum did everything else. She looked after us and the homestead, and cared for everyone. Her workload was enormous. The years of drought were marked by terrible dust storms, which would arrive from the south, blanketing the sky with red and black and leaving everything coated with thick, red dust. Mum spent hours scrubbing and sweeping out dust, which turned out to be a thankless task, because the dust storms only continued.

It seemed to me that Mum was constantly washing.

Every day she gathered up piles of Brett's dirty nappies (all towelling cloth), right through to filthy men's clothes, covered in bulldust, and headed to the laundry. Perched just outside the kitchen, the laundry was open-air and used by everyone on the station.

In the corner sat a crumbling, rusty copper into which small amounts of precious water was poured and then boiled to wash the clothes. A fire was lit underneath and during the summer it was unbearably hot within a good thirty-yard radius of the laundry. Mum's curls would cling to her forehead with sweat as she chopped wood, lugged it to the laundry, lit the fire, boiled the water and washed the never-ending filthy trousers and shirts of men. Just the boiling of the water alone could take hours and I stayed well away from the whole washing process.

Mum wasn't always so joyous on those days.

Apart from the endless cleaning of house, clothes and children, Mum made food for the many men who came and went on the station. There were not only those who lived there, including Ross and Colin, but an endless stream of dam builders, fence builders, stock agents, bank managers and neighbours from other cattle stations. Ten to twenty at any one sitting was not unusual.

The Hayes were a large, local family from several stations that bordered us: Undoolya and Deep Well to the south. Old Ted, as Mr Hayes was called, knew the country backwards. His sons, Jimmy, Mickie and Billy, were great riders and bush men. Sometimes they'd ride over (a day-long trip from the boundary fence through rough country) to say g'day and see how the 'new kids on the block' were faring.

The Goreys lived on Yambah Station to the north and the Turners on The Garden Station to the east, and each family welcomed us from the beginning. As did Aunty Dawn and Uncle Bill to the west. Mum was often saying, 'Aunty Dawn taught me this . . .'

Providing so much food for so many people was a big job for Mum. Dad shot a beast every month to provide meat for the station. It was called a 'killer' and we ate beef three times a day. Even in the summer when temperatures exceeded forty-five degrees, Mum worked over an ancient Aga stove, cutting up the huge slabs of meat that Dad hung in the meat house to 'rot' in the open air for tenderness.

She also found different ways to add variety to our diet. When the beef was fresh, she would bake, roast or grill it, then salt, crumb and curry it as it got older. At night, it was accompanied by potatoes and pumpkin. If it was a special occasion, we had tinned peas and carrots. But it was hard to do anything very creative with such limited options.

Every meal came with huge chunks of damper and jam from tins. The bread was invariably dotted with weevils that lived in the huge sacks of flour, but Mum always said cheerfully, 'Weevils don't eat much.'

When Dad kickstarted the little 32-volt generator at about 5 a.m. (or Mum did, when Dad was away), Mum would whip up steak, onions, gravy and toast for the men's breakfast by the poor light, and use the power for cleaning, washing, ironing and whatever else she needed to prepare for the day. Then the engine would go off about 9 a.m. and the still hush of the bush would descend upon the house for the day. Mum did the same tasks in reverse during the evening when the power came back on again before dark. Once night fell, however, it was difficult to read or write because the light was faint, so bedtime for everyone was early. Eight p.m. for the grown-ups was considered a late night.

The Aboriginal people, when hired for mustering, didn't usually eat with us. They preferred their own community and food, up in the old huts on the hill. Sometimes they brought their families. They caught kangaroo, goanna and snake and often went walkabout, too.

I remember Margaret, a tall, skinny and stately woman, who sometimes visited, and took us with the other women and Aboriginal kids for walks.

Those were wonderful times. We looked for wild honey and birds' eggs in the trees, and dug for grubs. M'Lis, Brett and I would be gone for hours at a time looking for bush tucker. The women walked in bare feet and carried big sticks. They spoke a smattering of pidgin English, enough to point to tracks in the dust and say, 'Big perentie', and, 'Long snake'. We trotted along behind them—down the creek, up the hills, over the flats—and they carried Brett on their hips when he got tired.

Mum was just happy we were in their capable hands because it freed her up.

From Margaret and other old ladies taking me into that country at such an early age, I acquired a deep love for wandering through the bush, taking in the sky and the trees and the landscape, and feeling utterly safe there. Those ladies helped me develop a feeling for this place; in my skin, bones and heart. They gave me a head start in learning to understand this wild, new country in which we had arrived.

Such a precious gift.

The land would soon shape the way I felt and thought and lived. It was like an anchor deep inside, holding me fast to the rocks and earth and hills around me.

'I belong that country,' I often heard Aboriginal people say, and my whole being would vibrate, *Yes, I know.*

5

Dick and Dora,
Nip and Fluff

In 1968, I was five, and it was time for me to start school.

'Time you stopped running all over the station barefoot, with wild hair and no education,' said Mum, but I was ready and hungry to learn.

I spent hours flicking through Dad's encyclopedias, even though I couldn't read a word. But I longed to. They were almost bigger than me, and when I lifted them unsteadily to my nose, they smelled exciting. Old, musty, full of mystery. I laid them flat and traced my fingers over the letters, hungering to know what they meant. They held an air of promise, and I was drawn to pages and the letters on them, more than to anything else.

Besides, they belonged to Dad, and therefore they must be important. That was another reason to learn to read. Without even realising it, I wanted to do things that Dad considered of value.

Fortunately, Mum knew exactly what was needed for this next step. A governess to teach me Correspondence School, and support me on School of the Air.

Mum now completely understood why Aunty Dawn had needed her. A bush woman's workload was all consuming. Mum still managed to dispense hugs and kisses whenever she could, patched up scratched knees and elbows, and found time to tell us bedtime stories—but the demands of her world took almost all her time. If she had any spare moments, she opened up her old-fashioned Singer sewing machine and made us clothes. She mended and darned everything, including Dad's socks, which always had holes in them.

Mum's only concessions to herself, as far as I could tell, were the Audrey Hepburn trousers and pretty blouses she made on the Singer. And she never came to dinner without lipstick on.

If Mum had any other spare time, she tried to fix up the garden. The decade of drought had destroyed it, but following the rains, Mum planted oleanders and jade and succulent pigface, determined to bring some colour and beauty to the homestead. The water was so harsh and heavy with calcium it was difficult for anything much to grow—certainly not vegetables or flowers—but she persisted with what she could. Gardening was her solace and escape.

Papa Parnell stayed with us often in those early days. He had what Mum called 'a green thumb', and he helped her in the garden, which was a lifesaver. Our isolated home also offered Papa space and quiet to deal with his illness and trauma. I recall him as a stooped, silent man, carrying his kit bag with his beer inside, and a face and eyes filled with the sadness of what he couldn't forget. He had his own quarters and lived mostly there. If visitors ever came to Bond Springs, he'd say to Mum, 'Don't introduce me, I don't want to see people,' and hide away.

Years later, M'Lis wrote a song about Papa Parnell's eyes and the grief he carried from his war memories. I think Mum and Dad were very glad to be able to offer him time at Bond Springs to recover a little.

And his presence gave Mum that extra bit of support.

In the meantime, a governess couldn't come soon enough, so Mum put an advertisement in the *Stock Journal*.

By now, I was desperate to learn, and M'Lis needed more of Mum than she was getting. She would trail around behind Mum all day long, sucking her thumb, gazing at her imploringly, waiting for Mum to finally stop running and working and rushing so that M'Lis could climb into her lap and be loved.

Luckily, Nana Parnell, whom we adored, came up every now and then to help Mum. When she did, Papa Parnell would return to Orroroo. We loved it when Nana visited because she gave us all her undivided attention.

M'Lis soaked up Nana's kindness, and spent every moment possible with her. Nana read *Brer Rabbit* to us, her glasses perched on the end of her nose, and we—M'Lis especially—basked in her attention and love. When Nana eventually had to leave, M'Lis would be inconsolable, and as she got older she started saying that she wanted to live with Nana. It was her way of saying, 'Mummy, I'm sad because I'm not getting enough of your time or attention.'

Brett was also becoming increasingly naughty, which was his way of trying to get Mum's attention, too.

Mum was nearly beside herself. She didn't have enough hours in the day for everything and everyone.

One day, when M'Lis was trailing behind Mum, pleading for

the two-hundredth time that she wanted to live with Nana, Mum realised she had to do something.

'Come with me, M'Lis darling,' she said, gently, and led her by the hand into the sitting room. She then turned the knob on the door of Dad's bar. M'Lis's eyes widened. No one was allowed in Dad's bar. That, and his office, were strictly off-limits to everyone but him. But Mum needed to go where they wouldn't be disturbed and it was the only properly private room in the house. Dad was out in the stock camp, so it was a safe bet he wouldn't discover them.

The bar was a beautiful old room off the sitting room. It had a built-in bar, which we thought terribly grown-up, and French doors that opened out onto a jade-fringed patio. It was there that Dad went after dinner, when he was home, to recover from the day and think about what he had to do the next day, and the next and the next . . .

Mum didn't have a room of her own, despite the sprawling many-roomed structure of the homestead. So, she opened the bar door and led M'Lis in. Mum sat on a chair, looking very serious, and pulled M'Lis into her lap. M'Lis gazed up at her.

'M'Lis,' she said, 'I know you love Nana. But we love you too and you are a part of this family. This is where you belong. This is the place for you. You can visit Nana, but this is your home, and this is where you must live. Because we love you.'

M'Lis continued to gaze back at her. Eventually, she smiled.

Mum hugged her and kissed her and said, 'Good! Now, let's go and find Tanya and Brett to play with, shall we?'

And after that, M'Lis was just fine.

And the lovely Lesley Clarke came to be our governess.

And everything got better.

'Miss Clarke', as we called her, moved in as though she had always been part of our family.

She came from the Flinders Ranges, very close to where Dad grew up, and he knew her family, who lived on a sheep station there. She was young and sensible, tall with a beautiful smile. We loved her immediately.

Miss Clarke was like a younger sister to Mum and Dad. Mum was happiest around people, and she'd always had lots of girl-friends. She never complained about missing them but it must have been such a relief when Miss Clarke came.

'Come along, Tanya, M'Lis and Brett, time for a bath,' Miss Clarke would instruct briskly, and we'd trot along after her, adoring and obedient.

I couldn't have had a more wonderful teacher to start my edu-cation. I wanted so much to learn and Miss Clarke was eager to teach.

At the start of 1968, we were at Witchitie for shearing, so that was where I started school. Mum and Miss Clarke cleaned out a little outside room next to the laundry and put fresh lino on the floor and bought two desks, one for me and one for Miss Clarke.

I remember the smell of lino—delicious, unlike anything I'd smelled before—and the thrill of being given my very own books for writing and reading. In my writing book, I learned to copy the letters—a, b, c—and from my reading book, I learned how to say, 'Dick and Dora, Nip and Fluff'. Bit by bit I worked out what the words meant.

Once I could pronounce them and put letters together and make other words, it was a breakthrough moment for me, a sense of knowing and excitement. I was later absorbed by the story of Helen Keller, whose governess traced words with Helen's finger under a water tap and the moment Helen realised the movements of her fingers meant letters and then words and then speech, followed by understanding and freedom.

But school brought one big downside for us.

M'Lis, Brett and I had never been apart, having only each other for company, except when we were with our grandparents.

On my first day of school, poor M'Lis was inconsolable again. She sat outside the school door, staring broken-heartedly at the meat house and creek, waiting for me to come out. She sat by the door for days and then weeks. My faithful, beloved sister. Mum couldn't move her. Eventually Brett managed to persuade her to come and play in the dirt with him. And Dad would sometimes pick her up in his arms and take her off with him in the Land Rover for a bore run. But once she was back, she would come running as soon as she heard the door open. I would re-enter her world, blinking and heady from the day, and everything would return to normal.

When it was time to head back to Bond Springs, Mum and Miss Clarke cleaned out a stone building near the old Sidney Kidman cottage.

They painted it and put in three desks: one for me, one for Miss Clarke and one for M'Lis, who was nearly ready to join me. The schoolroom, as we called it, was freezing in winter and boiling in summer, with just one tiny window. We would start at seven-thirty each morning, rush out at ten when Mum rang the huge smoko bell, return to school at ten-thirty and then finish at one for lunch.

M'Lis did not enjoy school anywhere near as much as I did, and once she started, it was poor little Brett's turn to be inconsolable. However, Dad had other ideas for his young son. He thought that Brett was ready to start learning about his responsibilities. From the time he could walk, Brett had to go everywhere with Dad, learning about tanks and bores and fencing and cattle and stock.

He would often be gone for hours on end and Mum would worry about him out in the heat and cold, but he always turned up, covered in dust, his blue eyes looking out for her, throwing himself into her arms when he arrived back.

In the meantime, I was absorbed by this glorious thing called school.

My lessons came once a fortnight from the Correspondence School in Adelaide, just as they had when Mum was a governess on Hamilton Downs. They covered the three R's (reading, writing and arithmetic) and every student had one teacher. Mine was Mrs Layton. I couldn't see her but she sent back my lessons with gold stars on them and ink-stamp imprints of little animals and wrote encouraging words. I thought she was wonderful.

At the end of my first year, the Correspondence School sent out its annual magazine. It was filled with stories and photographs of students in South Australia and the Northern Territory, all of whom were station kids, and occasionally some in mining camps or Aboriginal communities. Inside the magazine were photographs of all the teachers.

I quickly scanned down the little black-and-white photos until I reached the name Mrs Layton. Smiling back at me was a middle-aged lady, with glasses and hair set in waves. She looked like a very serious teacher, perhaps like a headmistress.

She was an important lady, I could tell.

A report card came with the magazine. Miss Clarke and Mum read it and then I was allowed to see it. I gazed at a two-page card brimming with sparkling gold stars and top marks.

'This is wonderful, darling,' said Mum, beaming. 'Dad and I are so proud of you.'

I felt a rush of something new. I felt proud of myself. Sometimes I'd feel those feelings when I looked after M'Lis and Brett well and

Mum was pleased with me. Or when I'd done a job for her that made her happy. But this was something more. This had come from my own work—my very own being—and I stood back and was amazed at what I'd achieved. So, I soaked up Mum's hugs and praise.

'Does Dad really think so?' I asked her, again and again. Dad was in the stock camp, so I wasn't sure when he would have had time to look at it.

'Oh yes, you can ask him when he comes back in,' Mum assured me, giving me a kiss.

When Dad came in from the stock camp at the end of the week, he was tired and dirty. He didn't have time to talk and went straight to his office. I waited for him to come out, but I had to go to bed before he did. And the next morning at breakfast he was too busy talking to the stockmen, so I missed my chance then as well. When I saw him at smoko, pouring a cup of tea, I leaped.

'Dad! Dad!' I rushed up to him, waving my report card. 'Have you seen this?'

Dad picked up the paper and looked at it. Then he looked down at me, with a smile crinkling his face.

'Good job, Tanya,' he said, handing me back the report. He gulped his tea. 'Keep up the good work.'

Then he was gone. Cup back down. Striding off to his next job.

I held the report card to my chest and breathed in and out like I'd just run from Bond Springs to Witchitie and back, feeling the glow of Dad's praise deep inside my heart.

I'd taken away the message that good grades earned Dad's praise. So, I would do anything and everything possible to achieve good grades in the future.

Dad might no longer be there for picnic teas or games or to throw us up in the air, but I longed to know I mattered in some way to him. To grasp a short-lived but wonderful moment in which I could bask in his approval. It brought unfettered and complete feelings of joy.

Even at age five, it was a primal need.

6

Four Good Men

Mum and Dad had not been at Bond Springs very long when a number of government rulings awarded long-overdue rights to Aboriginal people across Australia.

In 1967, after ten years of campaigning by Aboriginal and social justice groups, a referendum was held to change the Australian Constitution. For the first time, Aboriginal people were included in the population census, and the Commonwealth was given the right to make specific laws for Aboriginal people, instead of the states. There was great celebration across Australia as its traditional people claimed an important moral and symbolic victory.

In 1968, there was also a Conciliation and Arbitration Commission ruling on equal wages for the Northern Territory cattle industry. This was the result of a long-fought battle by the North Australian Workers' Union following the Wave Hill Station walk-off.

The background to this was long and complicated. Wave Hill

was a huge cattle station in the far north of the Territory owned by British pastoral company Vesteys. It was also the traditional land of the Gurindji people, who had lived and worked there for many years under Vestey's poor conditions and poor pay. They wanted change, equality.

In 1965, the North Australian Workers' Union brought a case on their behalf for 'equal wages for Aboriginal pastoral workers' across the Northern Territory. At the time the cattle industry, for example, was not legally required to pay Aboriginal drovers much more than three pounds per week while white drovers were paid five times this amount.

In 1966, two hundred Gurindji stockmen, domestics and their families courageously walked off Wave Hill and went on strike. Vesteys wouldn't negotiate initially, later coming back with concessions and offers, none of which were acceptable or accepted.

The Wave Hill walk-off went on to lead to important changes for Aboriginal people over the next decade. The Gurindji's claim became about far more than just wages and living conditions. They wanted their traditional lands back.

It took nine years of negotiations but in 1975 the Gurindji were handed back a portion of their land by the Commonwealth government in a historic ceremony. It was a wonderful moment for the Gurindji, their supporters and their courage. Their case then went on to be a catalyst for the passing of the *Aboriginal Land Rights (Northern Territory) Act 1976*. This was the first piece of legislation in Australia that allowed Aboriginal people to claim title over traditional lands.

At last, Australia was starting to make up for its wrongdoings towards Aboriginal people, but it had a huge, unexpected impact on the cattle industry. The cattle industry had told the Equal Wages court that they wouldn't be able to afford to pay those award rates as well as support the Aboriginal communities living on the stations. And unfortunately, that's what happened.

To put their concerns into context, in 1966 and 1967 (the years during which the case was being heard) Central Australia was coming off the back of the devastating ten-year drought. Cattle stations were still struggling to get back on their feet and rebuild their stock. By 1968, they hadn't yet had sales of cattle to put money in the bank. If they had endured the drought, they had been able to do so for a number of reasons, including an arrangement with the Aboriginal communities on their stations. A large Aboriginal stock camp helped keep the station going and was affordable for the station because of the low wages. In return, the Aboriginal stockmen had a home base for their community of women, children and elderly. They were given a regular supply of food and clothes, medical treatment and other provisions. Supporting Aboriginal communities in that way was a legal requirement for all station owners and it mostly worked for everyone. At that time, it was an accepted way of life, for better or worse.

Aboriginal men's ongoing cultural commitments also meant they often went away on traditional law business or walkabout. The cattlemen didn't know when they would go or how long they would be away. That meant if cattlemen had to pay equal wages for all stockmen, they would now be more likely to employ white stockman who were there full-time. Thus, the decision to raise wages for Aboriginal stockmen, while so important and overdue, had what I thought were sad consequences. Over time, fewer Aboriginal stockmen would be employed by, and fewer communities would live on, stations.

Throughout the Equal Wages case, Mum and Dad looked at what it would mean for Bond Springs. There were still only four or five Aboriginal stockmen working there off and on, along with some of the women and community members, also off and on. Although money was tight, Mum and Dad were determined to find a way to pay all their workers properly. Dad believed strongly in the importance of the native stockmen continuing to work with cattle and stock.

However, fate and Northern Territory laws intervened.

In 1964, the Northern Territory Government had lifted restrictions on the right of Aboriginal people to drink alcohol. While that was clearly a long-overdue social justice right as well, alcohol had unforeseen and devastating consequences for many Aboriginal people in Central Australia.

Due to our proximity to Alice Springs, by 1966 the Aboriginal people had already started walking into town so they could get 'grog', as it was called—full-strength beer or flagon wine. They left the stock camp and the house. They went alone, in groups, then in droves. They walked to the road and hitched a ride. Eventually they started to vanish before our eyes.

The women first disappeared when the men were away at the stock camp. On returning to find their women gone, the men would front Dad and demand, 'You take us to town, Boss.' Dad would drive them in to Alice Springs in his little old green Land Rover. Then they would scour the creek beds of the Todd River. The women were scattered around the various camps that had sprung up to accommodate the increasing number of Aboriginal people arriving in Alice Springs for the grog, and it was often a long and fruitless investigation well into the night. Often Dad just had to leave them there and go back the next day.

It was a difficult position that Dad found himself in. If he'd said no—he wouldn't take the men into town—he feared trouble. Or the men would simply have walked in and possibly not come back.

Before long Dad couldn't hold the stock camp together. In a last-ditch attempt, he would drive into Alice before dawn to look for his stockmen. He'd go to the camps, opening up swag after swag along the riverbed in the pre-dawn light. 'Tommy?' 'Billy?' Bleary-eyed men would stare back at him, most mumbling, 'No, Boss.' If he got a 'Yes, Boss,' he'd ask them if they wanted to come back to work. Some would come but others increasingly stayed in town.

Some of the Aboriginal men and women then started using taxis.

I remember waking up to the revving engine and horn of a taxi pulling up in front of the house about 4 a.m. Dad would have to go out and pay an angry taxi driver who was returning a group of loud and drunk people.

Before long the community drifted into town for good and we never saw them again. The call of the drink was overwhelming for people who had been denied legal rights for so long. The effect of alcohol was swift and devastating. Proud horsemen with cattle skills and a deep understanding of the bush way of life over the next few years became lost in a haze of alcoholism.

Within ten years, Dad's four top stockmen were dead. Alcohol poisoning and alcohol-fuelled car accidents were the cause.

'They were the best,' Dad said sadly, angrily.

7

'Delta Queeee-Bec Golf'

Dad made two important decisions early on. It meant spending more money, but by now he had become quite good at doing that, with the help of the Elders GM overdraft.

'Sometimes you have to spend money to make money,' he'd say, then add sternly, in case we got the wrong idea, 'but only if you know that you can pay it back.'

First of all, he bought a beautiful thoroughbred stallion and several good mares. The idea was to breed foals so he would have good horses in the future to manage his new cattle herd. We only had a few bony old stock horses left after the drought, and some skinny, poorly bred brumbies. None of them were much good for stock work. The stock horses had been too knocked about by the drought, and the brumbies were wild and difficult to train. In one diary entry, Dad wrote about one of those brumbies being broken in: '*Ross rode Toothpaste first time. Got thrown sky high first attempt.*'

Dad's big hope was that the new mares would deliver strong foals, and that the current old stock horses would survive long enough for the foals to grow up and take over. He wanted to avoid using brumbies wherever possible, especially Toothpaste.

Next, he thought we needed a better way to get around. We were wasting so much time on the road between South Australia and the Northern Territory (with this I agreed, heartily) and he wanted to get to places quicker and faster.

So, he bought a small plane, a Cessna 182.

Then he graded a dirt airstrip at both Witchitie and Bond Springs. He studied flying papers at night and practised with a pilot who had flown in the war. That pilot did loop-the-loops to thrill us all. 'He was a *hero* in the war,' Mum whispered to us. We thought he must have been too, as he dived all over the Witchitie plains like a bird catching the winds. We stood on the veranda, gazing up at the plane, awestruck.

Dad wasn't interested in the thrills. 'Flying is the quickest way of getting from A to B,' he told us, and proved his point by flying back and forth between Witchitie and Bond Springs as soon as he got his licence.

'Be careful, Grant,' Mum would say, looking anxious, every time he climbed into the little cockpit. But Dad showed no fear at all, only his usual resolve to succeed. We thought it was the most exciting thing imaginable.

So began a whole new way of life for us. The dreaded four-day trips by car were replaced by eight-hour trips by plane. We would all squash in, and fly across empty landscapes and deserts, higher even than the eagles and hawks.

The plane's call sign was 'DQG', short for 'Delta Quebec Golf'. Dad would call the air-traffic control tower over the plane radio and pronounce it 'Delta Queeee-bec Golf'. I thought he sounded *so* important!

I loved flying with Dad in DQG from the very first moment. I felt alive and happy up there in the clouds with him. I beamed with pride from inside that my Dad could be so clever, so strong, such a hero.

He flew through the air just like God.

It wasn't so much fun for the others. M'Lis and Brett got airsick. Mum and Miss Clarke had to nurse either M'Lis or Brett, who usually got sick in their arms. And Mum was terrified we were all going to crash, sooner or later.

There were some things I didn't like about flying. There was no toilet—only a tin—so we had to hold on, which we sometimes couldn't do, and the plane was constantly filled with the stink of wee. Not to mention the sickening smell of vomit, and mutton sandwiches (if coming from Witchitie) or beef sandwiches (if coming from Bond Springs).

Luckily, I could hide away in my imagination (and a story book when I got older) and forget about everything as we crossed the wide, empty spaces below. From that moment on I only ever wanted to fly.

We would always land at Oodnadatta *en route* (Dad taught me this expression and I liked it a lot, because he said it was *foreign*). We couldn't make the whole trip on one tank of avgas, so we had to stop halfway.

Oodnadatta was a place of shimmering silver and pink gibber plains. The heat rose in waves off the tarmac like it might melt before our eyes. As soon as Dad had landed and taxied up to the fuel tanks, we would tumble out and rush to the cracked, concrete toilet block on the edge of the airstrip. Mum followed us, usually carrying a tin full of wee to empty into one of the old toilets.

Then we would all stand outside and drink in deep breaths of hot, sandy desert air while Dad pumped fuel into the tank. Family friends the Greenwoods (such a beautiful and soothing name, I thought) would sometimes visit during our stopover, and letting them know that we were there was the best fun. Dad would zoom low over their house. The silver corrugated-iron roofs of the town under the plane seemed to blend into each other, so I was always amazed that Dad could pick out theirs from the air.

Dad's strict instructions were to be *quiet* on take-off and landing, and diving (we weren't allowed to distract him, otherwise Mum said he might crash) but we always forgot in our excitement.

M'Lis, Brett and I would squeal, 'Ahhh!' when Dad went into the dive and then as he pulled up out of the dive, we'd squeal, 'Ahhh!' again.

Dad would roar, '*Quiet!*' and we'd push back into our seats, shutting our eyes.

I secretly wondered whether Dad was even allowed to dive over a town, especially to dive-bomb a house, but he did it regardless, and we loved it.

Once Dad had landed, we'd forget the trouble we were in, jump out and wait for the haze of dust as the Greenwood ute bounced down the road to greet us. Sometimes it would take ages for them to get there, and we'd hop up and down, hoping Dad wouldn't say, 'Oh well, they're not there, climb aboard, we'll head off.'

But they always came, even if it took a while. They'd bring cold drinks, which we'd fall upon, and after hugs and rapid conversations we'd depart with promises to 'come and stay soon'.

If we had more time, we would stay overnight. Mum and Dad always had a happy time, then. We'd huddle around Mum's legs and gaze up at the Greenwood kids, Billy and Lindy, who were older than us. We were mostly too shy to get words out.

'Is this why Mrs Greenwood is called Mrs Greenwood?' I asked Mum on one visit, gazing at the glossy green leaves of the beautiful plants and ferns that were growing around their weatherboard house. They offered blessed, cool relief.

'No, darling,' Mum said with a smile. 'Mrs Greenwood and her green plants are just what is called a coincidence.'

I wasn't sure what she meant, but I loved the word.

There was another reason Dad liked stopping at Oodna (as the locals called it).

A man called Peck was in charge of the airstrip and fuel, and Dad liked talking to him. Mrs Peck ran the local store. They were refugees who spoke broken English and who'd turned up in Oodna after the war. Dad was fascinated by their stories.

While Peck refilled the plane, he and Dad would talk about things happening in the big, wide world, mostly the wars that had been, or were going on now. I didn't know a lot about them but I did learn very early on that there was the First World War, the Second World War and a Cold War. And other wars, further back in history. Dad had uncles and relatives who had been in both the First and Second World wars, and of course we knew that Papa Parnell had been a famous Rat of Tobruk. We feared not just the Germans and the Japanese, but now also the Russians. It was all very complicated.

After talking to Peck, Dad would often share stories and thoughts with Mum (and any other adults who were around). I would listen quietly, taking it all in. Dad said he truly believed that if people didn't understand world history, it would repeat itself, and the world would suffer from ongoing evil, wars, droughts and starvation. For Dad, it seemed the greatest evil during his time was Hitler, Stalin, Mao, and communism and socialism in their many forms.

We may have lived an isolated life, with no phone and only letters, telegrams and the two-way radio to communicate with the outside world, but Dad taught himself everything by reading and talking to other people. He hated ignorance. He asked us questions constantly to make us learn and understand things, too. He knew that knowledge was power. I guess that's why he had those twelve beautiful encyclopedias on his shelf.

Instinctively, I wanted to learn about things Dad was interested in. It made me feel a connection with a father with whom I otherwise had not much in common. I was a little girl and he was an exceptionally busy and driven man, focused on paying back a huge overdraft and meeting the Land Board NT's conditions.

After all, if anything went wrong, there could be *forfeiture* of the Bond Springs lease ('forfeiture' was another word I heard often, which meant the *end of everything*, which seemed as bad as all the three wars put together, if not worse). And if that happened, it would be caused by a species called *bloody bureaucrats*.

They were a group of men in white shorts and long socks, carrying clipboards and often sporting beards, who arrived from the government to tell bush people what they could and couldn't do on their properties.

Dad believed bloody bureaucrats had no understanding of the land or what was required to work it; the difficulties and the risks. They weren't open-minded to opportunities or helping stations have a go. They were only interested in playing God, shutting stations down, and making it as hard as possible for those 'working their guts out'.

Dad would thump the table. 'We're here to make Bond Springs viable, not just for ourselves, but to circulate money into the economy and give people work,' he would glare around the room, daring anyone to disagree. 'And where do they think they get their food from, anyway? Milk, bread, meat. Bloody desk jockeys. They've never lived in the real world, never had to try to make a living. They take their wages from my taxes.'

For Dad, bloody bureaucrats only brought problems, never solutions or anything good.

Dad's view on business was shaped by his conservative past.

'Private enterprise is the foundation of a successful society,' he'd argue. 'Anything that takes away the freedom of the individual to create ends up in disaster. Destroys the individual. And then the society. Small business is the backbone of this country and we should be supported in creating jobs and opportunities, not penalised for trying to make something out of nothing.'

———>•<———

It was only many years later that I learned that the Pecks' real name was Pecanek, and that they were Czech and had suffered during some of those terrible wars Dad talked about.

I sometimes wondered what the Pecks thought, coming all this way to Australia, only to find there were probably just as many bloody bureaucrats, communists and socialists here as back in their original country.

———>•<———

In the lead-up to our first Christmas with Miss Clarke, Mum said, 'We're going to a Christmas party!'

M'Lis and I fell over Mum, filled with questions. Where? When? A real party? Brett trailed behind us, echoing our questions.

'We're going to fly out to Harts Range next weekend,' she said, and explained that it was a small police station community about a hundred and sixty kilometres to the north-east.

'A police station?' Brett's eyes widened.

Mum added, 'Father Christmas is coming too!'

'Ooooooooooohhh!' We couldn't believe our luck. Father Christmas was really coming down from the North Pole early to meet with us? And other bush kids, too? What would he bring us? Would he get lost?

'It's a long way to come,' I said to Mum, anxiously.

'He's very clever,' Mum reassured me. 'He'll see Harts Range from miles away. They're very big. He'll know exactly where to land his sleigh.'

Saturday morning dawned, and with Miss Clarke, we all climbed aboard DQG. Dad took off into the bright blue sky and headed north-east. The flight seemed to take forever, but finally a long line of red ranges came into view. As Dad banked the plane, we all shrieked with excitement, as we usually did.

'Quiet!' Dad roared, as he usually did, too.

We shrank back into our seats, looking through the windows to see a Land Cruiser heading towards the dirt strip—it was the Goreys, our friends from our next-door station, Yambah.

Mr and Mrs Gorey were a glamorous couple. Mr Gorey was tall and handsome with a blond crew cut; Mum said he looked like the actor Paul Newman. Mrs Gorey was tall and beautiful with dark hair and always wore elegant clothes. She looked just like Sophia Loren (whom I had seen in photos in Mum's *Women's Weekly*). As they climbed out of the Toyota and shook hands with Dad and hugged Mum, I stood, awed, gazing at them both.

Three children stood on the back of the Land Cruiser. They stared down at us, and we stared up at them. Their eldest was Aaron, Brett's age, a small replica of Mr Gorey, and before long the two boys were entangled in a happy wrestle. Natalie and Jordie stayed close to Mrs Gorey's skirts. M'Lis and I did likewise with Mum and Miss Clarke.

The Goreys drove us all to a big tin shed set against the beautiful, rugged ranges. The shed was filled with bush people milling around, the men in their best hats and polished boots for the occasion, the women in their best summer dresses, and lots of children. The intense December heat poured down onto the corrugated-iron roof. The men drank warm beer, and the women took the chance to chat and catch up. No one else seemed to be in agony except for us. How long would we have to wait? We were too shy to talk to any of the other children. But when we heard a shout from behind the shed—'He's here!'—we rushed out.

Heading towards us was a battered white ute. Behind the wheel was the local policeman, and in the back, standing up and waving at us all, was—yes, it truly was—Father Christmas! He was resplendent in a woollen red-and-white outfit, with white hair and a huge white beard. I could not take my eyes off him. He really looked *just* like the pictures in my picture book.

Then I noticed something missing. 'Where're his sleigh and reindeer?' I asked Mum anxiously again.

'Oh, Father Christmas had to leave them at the police station so they would be safe. And the reindeer can have a rest and a drink.'

I digested this. It was very disappointing not to see a real sleigh and reindeer.

Meanwhile, Father Christmas was shouting lots of 'Ho-ho-ho!'s to all the kids swarming up against the ute. One of the local men passed the great man a beer, as he was probably thirsty. Luckily, Father Christmas didn't seem to mind the heat. He cracked open the beer and took a big swig with a wide grin. Then with more 'Ho-ho-ho!'s he pulled out a big red sack from behind him and called us to gather around. One by one, we were allowed to go up and meet him.

By now, however, we three kids had completely lost our nerve, and Miss Clarke and Mum had to lead us up there. When I stood before him, all I could manage was to hop from one leg to the other and gaze wordlessly at this beaming apparition from the North Pole.

'Ho-ho! What's your name, little girl?'

'I'm Tanya. From Bond Springs,' I finally said, after several nudges from Mum.

'Ho-ho! Here you go, little Tanya.'

Father Christmas handed me a parcel wrapped in red sparkly paper.

'Thank you!' I looked up at him shyly, then ripped it open. Inside was a pack of coloured pencils. I stared at him in delight. How had he known?

Father Christmas was very clever because he gave *both* M'Lis and me coloured pencils and Brett a tiny plastic car. Aaron got a plastic car too and before long the two boys were racing them in the dirt. I longed for a piece of paper that I could start drawing and writing on. But there wasn't one, and I'd have to wait till we got home, said Mum, as she put the pencils into her bag to keep them safe.

After the presentation, we all went into the hall where it was even hotter, and there were cups of warm, red cordial and plates of lollies. The men drank beer, except for Dad, who flew according to the motto: *Eight hours from bottle to throttle*. His war-pilot instructor had told him that 'safety in the air comes first', and we often quoted those expressions to each other. We thought they sounded very grown-up.

The day was broiling by now but a fire roared out the back onto which steaks were thrown. Father Christmas even had a go at turning the steaks.

Mum and Miss Clarke talked non-stop with the other women as though they hadn't had a good conversation in months, and they probably hadn't. I couldn't believe they were more interested in each other than Father Christmas, who seemed really quite good at barbecuing.

Then, with a piece of steak wedged between two pieces of damper in one hand, and yet another beer in the other, the great man finally headed back to the ute. He jumped onto the tray and the policeman got behind the steering wheel, and they drove off in a cloud of red dust. He waved at us until he was just a speck in the distance. We waved back at him until our little arms were tired.

'Do you think we'll see him fly off in his sleigh with the reindeer?' I asked Mum.

She shook her head. 'He'll have a little rest now too and then fly at night-time when it's cool. Too hot for the reindeer at the moment.'

But not for us. Filled with sugar and adrenaline, we clambered back into DQG, and flew home, tired but ecstatic. I sat on Miss Clarke's knee next to Dad all the way home and was as close to heaven as I'd ever been. Because of the heat, the plane bumped up and down the whole way, and everyone got sick. But I didn't care. I'd been to my first Christmas party!

'Can we go next year?' we chorused over and over again, until Mum said if we weren't quiet, she might forget Christmas next year altogether.

8

Thank You, Adelaide Miethke

When the drought finally broke in Central Australia, I learned what true happiness was.

I learned that rain was the most beautiful sound in the world, especially when it drummed on our corrugated-iron roofs, and splashed wildly into the gutters. The most beautiful smell in the world was the sweetness of rain hitting the dry earth. And the most beautiful sight was water teeming down from the skies, drenching the wide, open landscape.

Rain was precious and brought everything back to life. Everything about rain was a cause for celebration. Rain brought relief and happiness to everyone's faces.

Rain bought sweet-smelling freshness to the gum trees. It brought the joyous chaos of frogs singing, and gushing, swirling, brown water in the creeks. In the house creek we jumped and swam, and Mum drew water from it for her precious green patch of kikuyu lawn. The water tanks were filled. Nothing made Dad happier than full tanks. He strode around, inspecting everything, grinning, his hat collapsing under the weight of the rain,.

We ran out in the rain, raising our hands to the sky in joy, feeling its light touch, then its heavy pounding, and licking its wetness from our lips. We raced around in the puddles, and jumped up and down in them, and shrieked. Mum didn't stop us—she didn't care—she was just so happy herself, that she sparkled like the drops on the trees.

Even after just one day, the desert leapt back to life. Little green shoots shot up along the side of the roads. Soon carpets of bright wildflowers wove their way across the plains. Out of the tough earth, clumps of wild daisies sprang, and the tiniest round, yellow flowers that we called 'billy buttons'. Delicate purple flowers on plants called 'native tomatoes' emerged, and the red earth was soon covered by vibrant, shining, luscious green grass.

That grass grew, and the cattle got fat.

Fat cattle meant good sales.

Good sales meant survival.

And we knew that life did not get any better than this.

———— ⋙•◆•⋘ ————

But Hanrahan knew better.

'*We'll all be rooned*,' said Hanrahan, '*before the year is out*,' which meant that just as life got good on the land, problems would emerge. Droughts, floods and fires were forever lurking, ready to ruin us, and Hanrahan knew, in his laconic, depressive way, we needed to be prepared.

Miss Clarke first read the famous poem 'Said Hanrahan' aloud to us, and we learnt it off by heart, as not only was it funny, we related to it in every way.

'Hanrahan's got it right,' Dad nodded, grimly. 'You've got to be ready for what comes next. After something good, like rain, you'll have lots of feed, it will dry off, and then you'll have something bad, like bushfires.'

As Dad spoke, he searched the horizon as if smoke and flames might pop up any minute.

Could life ever be safe? I wondered. It didn't seem so. Hanrahan certainly didn't think so either.

Story books quickly became my place of comfort, security and cheer. In them, magic did happen, dreams could come true, and good always won out over bad. If books could take me to such lucky places, I thought, I wanted to spend all my time there. Luckily, Mum and Miss Clarke let my imagination soar and encouraged my hunger for stories. The ones that I wanted to hear and read.

My life was taken to a whole new level one winter's night when Miss Clarke came into the sitting room holding an old, musty book.

M'Lis, Brett and I were sitting around the log fire in our pyjamas, almost ready for bed. She sat next to us and said, 'Now I'm going to read you a story before bed. Your mum brought it home from the School of the Air library for you today.'

She opened the first, slightly yellowed, page.

'Chapter one of *The Enchanted Wood*.'

Enchanted? What a glorious word!

I was in love with everything about that story from the first chapter on that first night. A magical tree, children, fairyfolk and a ladder at the top of the tree you could climb up to find magical lands. Mostly, their adventures had a happily-ever-after ending, which was very comforting.

To our joy, Miss Clarke read one chapter of *The Enchanted Wood* each night before bed. Before long, she progressed to the second and third books, *The Magic Faraway Tree* and *Folk of the Faraway Tree*. Along with School of the Air, these readings were the best part of my day. One of the things I loved about the story was that it was set overseas, that place on the other side of the world. The stories filled my imagination to overflowing. The Lands came with castles, rivers, lakes, snowy mountains, woods, witches and wizards, queens and kings, princesses and princes, gold and silver.

I spent hours imagining living in the worlds I read about. There, I was safe and happy, cycling through soft woods of bluebells, climbing leafy green oak trees, and lying on my back in grassy meadows, looking up at a snowy mountain. Oh, joy!

But, just like real life, climbing up the magical tree and exploring the Lands came with Big Risks. You had to be careful when you were there, and remain constantly on your guard.

One evening, Miss Clarke took us to a particularly terrifying place. The children and their fairyfolk friends had ended up by mistake in Dame Slap's school. The chapter ended just as the children realised they were trapped and would have to spend the rest of their lives being slapped by the cruel Dame Slap.

'Noooooo!' we shrieked in terror on behalf of the children. 'No, this can't happen. How will they survive? What about their mum and dad?'

'We'll find out tomorrow night!' said Miss Clarke. 'Come along! Time for bed.'

'Noooooo!' we continued to shriek. 'Pleeeeeease, just one more chapter, Miss Clarke! We can't leave the children there by themselves. Surely they can find a way to escape and get off that Land?'

'I'm very sorry,' said Miss Clarke, herding us towards our bedrooms, 'but it's bedtime. Off we go now.'

As we cleaned our teeth and climbed into bed, I wondered if
Dame Slap had anything in common with bloody bureaucrats,
communists and socialists. She sounded as bad as them.

⎯⎯⎯⎯⎯⎯⎯

In addition to my Correspondence School lessons with Miss
Clarke each day, I spent thirty minutes on School of the Air, where
I spoke to a teacher over the two-way radio. Mum called School of
the Air a 'daily supplement' to my ordinary lessons.

When at Witchitie, I tuned into Port Augusta's School of the Air
with Miss Jolley. While I never laid eyes on her, her voice well and
truly lived up to her name. And when we moved to Bond Springs,
we tuned into the Alice Springs branch of the School of the Air.

To Mum's delight, and mine, Judy Hodder became my Alice
Springs School of the Air teacher. She was the wife of Rod Hodder,
who had managed Bond Springs for us in the first year. She was
also Mum's great friend from her early days in Orroroo. The
Hodders had settled in Alice and Mrs Hodder set about bringing
the School of the Air to life for me.

'But how did School of the Air start?' I asked Mum one day.

She was peeling potatoes at the kitchen sink, so I thought it was
a good time to ask her. With the large bowl of potatoes next to her,
she'd be in the one spot for a while.

'It came about because a lot of people with a lot of great ideas
and a lot of courage made it happen,' said Mum, zipping the peeler
up and down the potato. Long strands went into the bowl next to
her. 'Get another peeler and help me, and I'll tell you the story.'

I pulled up a stool, got the peeler and sat next to her. I loved
being with Mum. I always felt safe and secure with her. She also
usually knew the answer to every question in the whole world, and

if she didn't, she'd say, 'Ask Dad.' So, one way or another I usually found answers to the interesting questions that were always going around in my head.

'You know about John Flynn, who we call Flynn of the Inland?' she said, and I nodded. 'A long time ago he set up the Royal Flying Doctor Service, which as you know sends little planes, with doctors and nurses, into the bush to save people's lives.'

I did. I also knew John Flynn called it his 'Mantle of Safety'.

'But when he set it up, he had one big problem: there was no two-way radio back then, no communication. So, if you lived in the middle of nowhere, how did you tell John Flynn and his people that you had a broken leg or had just been bitten by a snake and needed help?'

I thought about this. I couldn't imagine life before the wireless or our two-way radio.

'John Flynn found a man called Alf Trager, who was very clever. Alf built a pedal radio for him and they trialled it and it worked. He could talk to people in the bush and they could talk to him.'

But not everyone had a pedal radio, so John Flynn started pushing for them to be made available throughout the outback. 'He said that if the sick person could talk to the doctor and the doctor could give advice over the radio, the sick person could take that advice and the doctor wouldn't need to come.'

'But what's that got to do with School of the Air?' I asked, peeling inexpertly.

'Well, the pedal radio is the important first step of the story. The next part is about an amazing lady, a retired teacher called Adelaide Miethke. She was ahead of her time, filled with vision.' Mum shook her head as if still amazed by what she was about to tell me.

'Adelaide Miethke wanted to work for John Flynn and help spread his word. She wasn't young but she went into the outback to see how she could help families in the bush. It must've been very tough for an older lady from the city, who had no idea what awaited her: heat, snakes, isolation.'

A vision flashed before me. I saw a tall, brave lady, marching about, doing good things, wearing high-necked dresses, stockings and sensible shoes, fanning herself as she went deeper and deeper into the hot, dry, dusty, fly-ridden outback.

What must she have thought of it all?

'When she got there, she got a shock because the children were too terrified to speak to her. They'd never seen anyone like her. They ran away and hid. Some of them were doing lessons by Correspondence School, but that wasn't enough to help them talk to a stranger.'

I thought about this, too. M'Lis, Brett and I were also shy when we met new people.

Imagine not having met *anyone* before.

Mum went on.

'Apparently, Adelaide went back and told John Flynn that something had to be done about these children. And on her next trip to Alice Springs, it came to her. She was at the Royal Flying Doctor Service and heard mothers calling in over the radio to talk about medical problems with doctors at the base. Then she had a brainwave—why not also use the radio to *teach children*?'

Now I could see how it all linked together.

Mum's pile of potatoes was reducing but she kept talking. She told me that it took Adelaide four years to make it all happen, but that she was helped by three men in Alice Springs, who did all the necessary practical things. The head of the Royal Flying Doctor Service loved wirelesses, so he got involved in buying some, building some, and then he got them out to stations. And two headmasters of the first Alice Springs school, called the

Hartley Street School, worked out all the lessons and teaching side of it all.

'How do you know all this, Mum?' I was amazed.

'Well, I'd never heard of School of the Air, or seen a pedal radio, until I went to Hamilton Downs, and Aunty Dawn told me all about it. I thought it was the most wonderful story. I really admired this amazing lady, Adelaide Miethke.'

'So, what happened next?'

Mum went on to tell me that School of the Air was officially launched in 1951. There was a huge opening, hundreds of people came to Alice, and it was reported in newspapers internationally as 'the largest classroom in the world'.

Very sadly, John Flynn died before the launch, but I just hoped he was happy with the outcome.

Mum said, 'What *is* sad is that Adelaide Miethke had the vision and pushed so hard for it to happen. But today, if you ask anyone about Adelaide, they've probably never even heard of her.'

I stared at her.

'So yes, if you ask anyone about John Flynn, they'll say, "Yes we know him, wonderful man". That's because lots has been written about him. But Adelaide, I'm afraid not as much.'

She paused. I knew she loved John Flynn because she always talked about him and what he'd done for the bush. I was a bit confused. 'But *why* don't people know about Adelaide as much as John Flynn?'

'Because Adelaide was a woman and John was a man. And it's that simple and that complicated. I have to tell you, Tanya, the world is not always fair to women.' She scraped at the potato a little more roughly.

I gazed at Mum, trying to understand what she was saying. It sounded very confusing. But I didn't want her to get distracted from the story. 'What happened after the opening?'

'In the early days, the lessons on School of the Air went for half an hour, a couple of days a week. The teachers from the Hartley Street School wrote scripts and read them out aloud to the children. Then they decided they needed to encourage the children to talk. Some were too frightened to speak at all. It was called "mic fright".'

Really? I stared at Mum. I couldn't imagine it. I already loved holding the microphone in my hands and chatting away, in play or for real.

'So, the school got a teacher up from Adelaide, called Molly Ferguson. Molly was young and gorgeous. Everyone loved her. The children talked with her, she sang them songs, she wrote them plays, and she remembered their birthdays.'

'How wonderful!'

'But the next bit is not so wonderful. Molly only taught for four or five years before she was whisked away to be married, and had to retire.'

'But why?' I demanded. 'Mrs Hodder is married and she teaches.'

'Things were different back then,' said Mum, darkly.

We'd peeled all the potatoes and Mum picked up a sharp knife to chop them. She chopped very hard and I watched, moving away just a little bit.

'There *is* one good thing,' she said, looking up over her knife. 'The Queen gave her a very big award called an MBE, so perhaps that might have helped.'

I had an image of the Queen in her glittering crown and golden gown handing over a grand award to Molly. But I guess that wouldn't have helped the children in the bush, who probably missed Molly terribly, forever. It would be like losing Miss Clarke.

I went away, thinking hard about all these things. So much about life just didn't make sense. Why did men get more praise than women? Why were men rewarded for their great works, while wonderful women like Adelaide almost forgotten?

I didn't understand.

But one thing I did understand. School of the Air was the best thing, ever.

Thank you, Adelaide Miethke, I said to myself that night. *Thank you.*

9

No Mic Fright for Me

Every day Mrs Hodder would say brightly, 'VJD calling, this is Mrs Hodder here. Good morning, everyone! Are you receiving me? Over.' And then she'd start a roll call, calling out the international radio code for every student in the class.

Every child would scramble to switch on the handheld microphones on their two-way radios.

'Good morning, Mrs Hodder. Nine Sierra Victor Uniform, Tanya speaking. Receiving you loud and clear. Over!' I would join the jumble of voices boomeranging back to greet the Queen of the Wireless from cattle stations spread far and wide.

No mic fright for me! I couldn't *wait* to tune into class each day.

All the voices talked one over the other, some louder than others because they had better reception, some almost lost in the din. None of this was a problem for Mrs Hodder. She took the chaos in her stride.

'Good morning, everyone!' Her tones, crisp and cheerful, always sent a thrill through me. 'Well, we are going to learn some new and *big* words this morning. Please open page three of your book. Over.'

'Yes, Mrs Hodder,' we chorused and waited for her next round of instructions. Sometimes I would tremble, such was my wonder at what I might be able to do next.

Each grade received half an hour each day on air on a different topic. There were questions and answers on maths and social studies, spelling tests, lots of reading aloud from books, reading from our own compositions when we got older, and being read to by the teachers, which I especially loved.

Best of all was Monday, which was Assembly Day for all the students.

'Now, girls and boys, it is time for the National Anthem. So, please stand up next to your radios and sing along with us here in the studio.'

Mrs Hodder belted out 'God Save the Queen' on a piano in the studio, while a roar of children's voices bellowing over the top almost obliterated the static. The chants crashed and dipped and melded one into the other.

We couldn't see the other children but we could hear them. Our imaginations put faces to them, hair and eye colour, freckles and grins, riding boots and hats.

And Mrs Hodder was our binding glue.

Once we finished, she clapped her hands. 'Wonderful singing, everybody. Keep up the good work! Over.'

To me, Mrs Hodder was our Queen. She spoke so beautifully, unlike anyone else I knew, and she sounded like she could be royalty. Not that I'd ever heard the actual Queen speak, or knew what royalty sounded like, but it was just what I imagined.

Being on the radio with Mrs Hodder was like a play, like theatre, and I loved it.

It never occurred to me that this wasn't the way most other Australian kids did school. I never thought for a moment it was anything but the normal way to learn.

———>•<———

The headmaster of the School of the Air was Mr Ashton. Mrs Hodder taught us younger ones, grades one to four, and Mr Ashton taught grades five to seven. They often did 'patrol', which meant every now and then they shut down School of the Air and headed out to meet students on stations.

On their first visit I counted down the hours as Mum plaited my hair and I donned my best shirt and trousers and boots.

Of course, I'd met Mrs Hodder when I was very little, but I had scant memory of it. It was like I was meeting her anew.

When the official entourage finally pulled up in the yard, amid dogs barking and lots of dust, I clung anxiously to Mum's leg as Mrs Hodder descended from the vehicle, fresh in a smart frock, leaning over me with a big smile.

She and Mr Ashton looked at our schoolroom, *oohed* and *ahhed*, and then after a cup of tea and scones they were gone in another shower of dust, whisked away to the next station. It was just like a visit from the Queen and her consort, and we talked about it for months afterwards.

———>•<———

Then there was the School of the Air 'Get-Together' in Alice Springs.

Get-Togethers were introduced as a way for children to meet not just their teachers, but each other. They were held in the

August school holidays and lasted three days. And they were chock-a-block full of activities: meeting the firefighters, visiting the police station, and going to lots of races and picnics out at the Old Telegraph Station and Simpsons Gap, where there were wide, dry areas of creek for us kids to run and play in.

I was overwhelmed by a mixture of shyness and eagerness at the prospect of meeting all the faces belonging to the voices. It was a freezing August week with vast blue skies and winds off the desert. Mum dressed M'Lis, Brett and me in matching jumpers, warm corduroy pants and boots. M'Lis and I also had a little poncho around our shoulders. We looked terribly smart.

On the first day, Mum took us to the School of the Air for roll call, this time face-to-face. As we walked through a wide glass door, with Mum on one side and Miss Clarke on the other, I thought my legs might give way with the enormity of the moment.

We found Mr Ashton and Mrs Hodder inside, meeting and greeting all the children. Mr Ashton was very formal and smartly dressed in a shirt and tie. He held a large clipboard, which was the roll call sheet. I gazed up at Mrs Hodder, and yes, she remembered me! As she bent over me and said, 'Well, hello Tanya!' I thought I would melt into the floor.

But there were more thrills to come. The School of the Air was a magical theatre—a large room with a wireless full of knobs that Mr Ashton and Mrs Hodder pushed and pulled and dialled and twirled. In the corner was the piano on which Mrs Hodder played us her songs. We gazed in awe at the room and the equipment that our teachers used to speak to us each day.

But best of all, just off to the right of the entrance foyer was a small dark room, slightly musty, lined with shelves that in turn were crammed full of books. I stared into it, my heart beating fast.

'This is our library,' Mrs Hodder said. 'It's where your books came from. Your mum tells me you are enjoying them, Tanya?'

My heart now tripled in speed. I nodded up and down, looking at Mrs Hodder and my feet in rapid succession, unable to find words.

'Would you like to go in, then?'

Would I?

She led me in there, smiling. 'I think you'll like this room, Tanya.'

I was allowed to stay in there for what seemed a very long time. It was heaven. I didn't want to join the rest of the School of the Air children when they went off to see the firefighters and the police station. I wanted to stay in the library, to spend hours soaking in that magical world of words. I stood, gazing at the spines of the stories, tentatively opening the covers, smelling the beautiful musty pages, and I knew in that moment that words would always have the power to transport me to other worlds.

———⊷∗⊷———

We saw another side to Miss Clarke and Mum at the Get-Together.

They had a marvellous time!

They met up with other mothers and governesses from around the Territory and exchanged stories, surviving-life-on-a-station tips, and also put faces to names. They laughed a lot and wore their best clothes. Mum had long boots as well, and had grown her hair a little, which she curled every day before we went out.

M'Lis, Brett and I remained hopelessly shy. We had no idea how to talk to other kids. All the other children seemed as scared as we were, so the first day was like a Mexican stand-off, all of us hiding behind our mother's skirts, clumped with their siblings for protection, not knowing what to do or say. Dogs, cattle, stockmen—yes, all bush kids knew what to say and do with them. But other children? Other children were an entirely different race from an entirely different planet.

Eventually by day three, overdosed with sugar from cakes and jelly at the CWA Hall, most of us found the courage to talk to one another. M'Lis, Brett and I were helped by the fact we stayed throughout the Get-Together with Mum and Dad's friends the Braitlings.

The Braitlings had four kids, and we became very good friends with them, right away. Shane and Denis were older than me, and seemed very adventurous. Jacquie was blonde and slim and M'Lis's age, and they were in the same School of the Air class. They quickly became close friends. Matthew was slightly younger than Brett; he was full of energy and cheek, and he and Brett became great mates, too. They also had a governess, Miss Gabby, who was very kind to us all.

The Braitlings owned what we called a 'town house'—that is, a house in town. Lots of families who lived a long way out bush had a town house. We thought they were very lucky. Grandma Braitling lived in the house fulltime, and the Braitlings stayed there when they came in from the station.

Grandma Braitling was an extraordinary woman. She'd lived in the toughest conditions in the middle of nowhere all her life (mostly in the stock camp, on a horse) and took no nonsense. She still didn't.

The Braitlings' town house was big and brick, with a large, wild garden and soft-pink walls inside. There was a big kitchen and eating area (important given how many people always seemed to be visiting), a sitting room where the grown-ups sat, and a long, L-shaped passageway leading to many bedrooms and a bathroom.

A glass door with elaborate scrolls and swirls—the first I had seen—opened onto the passageway from the front garden. I thought it was amazing.

One of the exciting things about the Braitlings' house was that it contained an endless supply of comics. They were piled in corners and under beds and on shelves. We devoured them at night after the Get-Together activities.

I'd lie in the passageway, tongue sticking out as I concentrated on reading the words with the pictures. Best of all was *Richie Rich, The Beagle Boys* and *The Phantom.* The first two were American and I was completely absorbed by all the things the characters got up to. They were different to the characters in my English books, too. Funnier, wilder and naughtier, perhaps. *The Phantom* was exotic and mysterious. I traced my fingers over Diana's beautiful face and tiny waist and wondered if I could ever look like her.

There were also Cowboys-and-Indians comics, which the boys not only read but re-enacted up and down the corridor. The noise of whooping and spear-throwing and gun-shooting would drive Mum and Mrs Braitling to their feet. They'd fling open the door and shout, 'Enough of that *noise!* We can't hear ourselves *think* in here!'

But it was difficult keeping a group of bush kids quiet, especially inside. We were so used to running around making noise in our own wide open spaces that we didn't know how to contain ourselves inside a regular house. So, the grown-ups would send us outside, where we'd play Cowboys and Indians in their back garden, dying wildly and extravagantly all over the lawn.

On our last night, Miss Clarke and Miss Gabby got dressed up and put on lipstick and went out to dinner with all the other governesses. It seemed so grown up. I wanted to grow up and go out to dinner too. I also felt sad that the Get-Together would be over tomorrow. But at least on Monday we would be back on to School of the Air. That thought prompted a discussion.

'Aren't we lucky to have School of the Air?' I asked the assembled six, after the governesses had left.

Nobody really looked up. Brett and Matthew took no notice at all because they weren't yet on School of the Air (although they were allowed to go to the Get-Together). I repeated my question, and finally someone said, 'Perhaps'; I think it was Denis.

'Only perhaps? But it's so much fun,' I said, enthusiastically. 'We can pick up the microphone and talk to Mrs Hodder and she can talk back and we can sing and we can read aloud and . . .' I trailed off. Nobody seemed to be listening. 'It's better than just school,' I said lamely.

'Yeah,' Shane and Denis emerged from their comics. 'It's better than school, because we get out of the schoolroom for half an hour.'

I folded my arms. 'Well, I can't think of anything else I'd rather be doing than being on the School of the Air.'

'We can,' came back the general response. The group rattled off things like being outside playing and working with the men and being with horses and cattle and tinkering with the Land Rover and driving it around.

'Even you, M'Lis?' I said, a bit desperate now.

'Especially me,' she giggled.

I gave up. I was the only one who absolutely loved School of the Air, it seemed. The only other things I'd loved as much was reading and writing, but I got to do all of that, and more, with Mrs Hodder, for half an hour each day.

It was strange. Not only did I *not* have mic fright, ever, I couldn't wait to get that microphone in my hand, and start talking to it, singing to it, laughing in it, and hearing the voices come back to me. I adored everything about the magical way of the wireless.

All thanks to John Flynn, Alf Trager and Adelaide Miethke.

I thought about how different I was to the others. I was drawn to the overseas lands of my storybooks and dreamed about visiting them. Why was I the only one who felt like this about all these things and longed to spend more time with them? I took that puzzling thought home with me but couldn't make sense of it.

It didn't stop the seven of us having fun together, though. In that big, stone house on Babbage Street, with lots of space to play and consume comics, the Braitling and Heaslip kids became firm friends.

10

The Importance of Being Strong

We were tired when we got home from the Get-Together. A week away with other kids in town had been fun but we weren't used to that much excitement. It was good to return to our own routine, to games in the dirt and, for me, books and writing. The nights were peaceful again—there were no cars whizzing down the streets with bright headlights waking us up—and the mornings were filled with the usual glorious colours in the sky and birds and the fresh smell of gum trees.

After a week our energy had returned. Most days we yelled, raced around, walloped each other with sticks and fists, both in games and when we got sick of each other. We were like a six-legged trio, bound to each other, unable to separate. Most days, Mum would shout, 'I'm at the end of my tether with you kids! You are driving me up the wall!'

Miss Clarke had a way of stepping in just in time to avert disaster. She was calm and capable in any crisis, which was lucky, because Brett especially tested the patience of the grown-ups. He was full of energy and cheek.

'Go and run around the lawn twenty times until you get rid of your energy!' Mum would say despairingly, directing him out the door towards the garden. 'Go on, run, run!'

But even if Brett ran twenty times (and sometimes we'd all have to stand there and count until he finished), he would run back with exactly the same amount of energy, plus a flushed face, big grin and sparkling eyes.

Bath time was the worst. Miss Clarke would have just got Brett undressed, when he'd run outside, completely naked, and jump on his little bike (a Christmas present from Papa Heaslip) and ride flat-out up the driveway towards the cattle grid and beyond. We girls watched from afar as Mum and Miss Clarke chased him, Mum with wooden spoon in hand. Both of them shouted threats that he didn't seem to hear. Then they would chase him all the way back down the other driveway until finally he'd be caught and thrown in the bath. His little body would be frozen but he'd be laughing with glee.

One bath time, Brett decided to run naked towards the chook house instead. He fell over a big stone as he ran. Screaming out in pain, he pointed to a bleeding toe. Mum was on his heels, her face red with exasperation and frustration, wooden spoon in hand. She yelled out, 'Don't think that'll help you!'

Brett's other trick was to climb up on the corrugated-iron roof just before bath time. He'd leap around, whooping like a wild American Indian, and refuse to get down. He gave Mum and Miss Clarke near heart attacks. His favourite trick was to shout out, 'I'm going to fly down, Mummy!' and then spread out his arms like a bird. A stark-naked bird. He'd laugh wildly and hop about on the roof, making a tremendous war-like noise. If Mum and Miss Clarke couldn't get him down, Dad was called for, which would always end with the belt and tears.

But the problems didn't end there.

M'Lis, Brett and I had to share the bath because water was so precious. There was about two inches of water between us. Just as we girls would get in, Brett would stand on the edge and pee into the water, laughing as he did. M'Lis and I would scream furiously as we'd jump out and chase Brett, and the race would begin all over again.

Teatime became a battle of wills between Brett and Mum. After the bath, we'd all troop into the kitchen to sit up at the table to eat. Mum always ensured we were fed and in bed well before the adults arrived. But Brett was a skinny kid and didn't like food much. He especially refused to eat his vegetables. He drove Mum crazy. When things got really bad, he'd chuck his vegetables off his plate. Then he'd be threatened with, 'If you don't eat anything, I'll have to send you to Dad's office, Brett.'

That was the worst threat of all. I would have eaten three lots of vegetables if it meant avoiding being sent to Dad's office. But it didn't deter Brett. Sometimes he would have to sit there all night until bedtime, as well as receive a belting. He must have really hated vegetables.

Physical punishment was the norm in Dad's world. He'd grown up with tough love and it was all he knew. He'd spent his own childhood being thrashed by well-meaning uncles, not to mention his father. He told us it was how he'd learnt right from wrong.

For that reason, he carried his stockwhip about and used it, or the belt, when we stepped out of line. M'Lis and I were too scared of Dad to play up much, but Brett had no safety mechanism in his brain to tell him when it was time to stop.

One winter, M'Lis, Brett and I came down with the flu. Each night we coughed and shivered with fever and cried for Mum. On the second night, Dad's silhouette loomed in our doorway.

'If you don't stop that coughing, I'll smack you all.'

We huddled under the sheets, trying to swallow our spluttering. Finally I croaked, 'But Dad, we *can't* stop.'

'There's no such word as can't,' roared Dad.

Dad didn't carry out his threat (which was probably driven by exhaustion and lack of sleep, anyway), but he was forever instructing us against the perils of self-pity or personal weakness. He admired people who pushed through and never gave up.

How else do you manage droughts, fires, cattle dying, low prices, high costs, big overdrafts, staff troubles and isolation?' he'd ask us, fiercely.

We'd nod meekly, wondering if we could ever be as strong as him.

Mum was always stuck in the middle and tried to keep the peace.

Whenever one of us was pushing Dad too far, she would assure him that she would fix things, and would then hug us and tell us she knew we were doing our best, and that she loved us.

Mum's love was healing for us all—especially for Brett.

Brett loved being with her, and he couldn't bear it when she went away, even just to town to get the stores. That would be a whole-day trip, and when we were young, she'd leave us at home with Miss Clarke. She thought the trip was too hot and long for us. So, a few times Brett would head out after her, walking down the dusty road to town, following her car tracks, determined to catch up to her.

The worst of Brett's treks took place on a broiling summer's day. It was mid-January and over forty degrees by 11 a.m. Dad came home from doing a bore run and found Miss Clarke, M'Lis and me looking everywhere for Brett.

'He's gone missing again,' said Miss Clarke, her forehead creased. 'Jan's gone to town, so he's probably followed her. It's so hot. He'll have no water . . .'

Dad didn't respond, just flicked a thumb to M'Lis and me. 'In the Land Rover,' he ordered, striding towards it. We huddled in the back of the vehicle, silent in the face of Dad's anger, gulping in swags of dust as he lurched off down the road towards the turn-off to the bitumen.

We didn't know why we had to go with him. Perhaps Dad thought he needed our eyes to help. He told us to keep a lookout. We watched the grey mulga whizzing past, wondering if Brett had taken the road or had got lost, and was somewhere inside the mulga. It was *so* hot. How could he still be alive out here?

We drove and drove, all the time fearing the worst: that Brett had perished. We always feared the worst when it came to Brett. A sinking feeling sat in our young stomachs as Dad drove like a demon.

Just before the turn-off, just when we'd almost run out of hope, we saw a little figure ahead. It was Brett, walking determinedly. He had covered nearly eight kilometres. No shirt, just shorts. Bare feet, no shoes. He was dehydrated, with swollen lips, but undeterred. He didn't even stop as we drove up next to him.

Dad screeched to a halt. M'Lis and I looked at Brett, hardly able to bear what we knew was about to happen. Dad jumped out and Brett finally turned around, his big blue eyes wide and defiant.

'*What* do you think you're doing?' Dad asked, his voice very low and scary.

'Looking for Mummy.'

Dad pointed to the edge of the scrub. 'Go and get a stick. A big one.'

Brett knew what was about to happen. He bit his lips defiantly but walked towards the edge of the road.

Then he picked up a stick.

'Not big enough.' Dad was relentless.

Brett poked around in the scrub and picked up another one. Dad nodded and held out his hand. Brett took it to him.

'Bend over.'

Brett obeyed.

M'Lis and I put our hands over our eyes and ears, desperate to muffle what was happening.

Finally, it was over. 'Get in,' Dad commanded Brett. 'In the front. Next to me. And *never* do that again. Otherwise you will *perish* out here and *die*.'

Brett crawled in the front. He didn't speak. He was defiant to the end.

He was four and a half years old.

Dad only knew how to show anger when he was fearful. And Dad was truly fearful that day. Those temperatures and conditions could have killed a grown man, given enough time. A little boy with no shoes, hat or shirt didn't stand a chance.

The fact Brett hadn't died was a miracle.

M'Lis and I thought *he* was strong!

Dad recorded Brett's death-defying trek in his diary, and wrote in capitals, 'BELTED BRETT'. Under his anger and fear was relief, but poor little Brett didn't know that.

The next big thing in our little lives was that Mum started growing a tummy. When we asked about this, Miss Clarke explained that Mum was 'pleasantly plump'. We used to run around gazing at Mum's expanding tummy and shrieking out this delicious new phrase, 'Pleasantly plump!' Eventually Mum couldn't bear it anymore and told us she was going to have a baby. That was the most exciting thing we had heard in our entire lives.

Mum became very sick in her last few months of pregnancy. We didn't know what was wrong with her. But she became sicker and sicker and had to keep going to bed in the afternoon. That was not our mum.

Things became worse when we flew to Witchitie for Christmas and the New Year mustering and shearing. Christmas was always the fun part—we got to see Nana and Papa Heaslip at Glenroy, and Nana and Papa Parnell in Orroroo, and Aunty June and Uncle John—and we loved the Flinders Ranges country. But mustering and shearing were not fun. It was stinking hot and Dad worked non-stop, gone before daylight and not home until after dark. M'Lis, Brett and I helped in the sheep yards a bit but in the early days we were too small to be of much use. During the shearing, Mum just looked incredibly miserable all the time, still trying to feed Dad, us and the men he had helping him.

In the second week, M'Lis and I were sent to stay with Nana Parnell in Orroroo. That was wonderful. We were treated to swimming lessons at the local pool, which was amazing, because we'd never seen, much less been in, a big swimming pool. We got to eat lemonade ice blocks afterwards and then take trips up to the main street to buy the most delicious thing we'd ever eaten in our whole life—apple and apricots tarts from the bakery called Benziks. The pastry was thin and scattered with icing sugar and real sugar and the fruit fell out in large, sweet clumps. We ate those tarts for breakfast, lunch and dinner, until Nana Parnell put her foot down.

Meanwhile, Mum kept getting sicker and sicker. She visited the Orroroo doctor, who said there was nothing wrong with her. She spent all day dribbling water over her arms and legs, which had swollen to twice their size. In desperation she said to Dad, 'There's a new doctor in Alice. I've got to go home and see him. I'll die here.'

Dad couldn't leave shearing to fly Mum home, so he flew her and Brett down to Adelaide (which was a short trip in comparison), where an Elders GM representative put them onto the TAA flight to Alice and arranged for another Elders representative in Alice to pick them up from the airport and drive them to Bond Springs.

Brett went with Mum because, at five, he was too young (and naughty) to leave with the grandparents.

No doubt Dad then thought his duty was done. The rest was 'women's business' and out of his domain. It would never have occurred to Dad to stop shearing and go with Mum. Not that that was unusual. That's how all men we knew thought. Dad looked after the business outside the house, and Mum looked after the business inside the house, and everything else—including pregnancy.

Besides, Dad wouldn't have thought he had any choice. Shearing the sheep at Witchitie was his priority and it couldn't wait. The sheep's woolly coats had to come off before they became too thick and hot for them in the summer heat; otherwise they'd die. The shearers were lined up and ready to work. Once the sheep were shorn, the wool then had to be sorted, graded and sent away to sale so Dad could afford to keep Witchitie afloat.

Once back at Bond Springs, Mum and Brett spent the next three weeks alone. Our stockman, Ross Coop, was caretaking the station for Dad, but he was of even less use to Mum than was Dad.

He spent every day out on the run, checking bores and fences, and eating corned beef he cooked himself. He didn't go near Mum, as that wouldn't have been 'done', with Dad away.

During those weeks, Mum lay in bed and slipped in and out of consciousness. Alone in the homestead in the summer heat, with no one to look after her, she was so ill most days she could hardly get out of bed. Her feet, ankles, face and hands were swollen to blue, she was dizzy and nauseous, and struggled to breathe. She draped wet flannels over her face and feet and forgot to eat or drink. The isolation of the outback held her captive; she was too weak to call for help and nobody was near to see or help her.

Brett didn't know what was happening. He spent the whole time sitting at the foot of her bed, pulling Mum's toe whenever she started to doze off, and gazing at her with increasing anxiety. There was no one there for him to play with—no Tanya or M'Lis or Miss Clarke as a distraction—and his mother was feverish and delirious most of the time. He was hungry and lonely and scared.

One morning, he found some matches in the bathroom. He took them, then crouched under Mum's bed (so he could still be close to her) and practised striking them until one flared up. Then he struck another one. Then another.

Mum finally came to when she smelled the smoke. She pulled herself up on her pillows, confused.

'Brett?' she called out, looking around. His little face poked out from under the bed. She looked down and saw him holding the matches in his fingers. They burned bright and orange red in the gloom of her curtained room, colouring his face.

'Oh my God!' she screamed.

Somehow, she managed to pull herself up further, then leaned down and grabbed the burning matches out of Brett's fingers. She smothered them between the sheets and the blanket on the floor, just in time before her bed went up in flames. Not to mention her, and Brett, and possibly the whole house.

Once Mum had put out the matches, she collapsed back against her pillows, white-faced and shaking. She could barely move. She and Brett were alone on the station, no one for miles, nobody to contact, with Ross away all day.

Mum finally realised she was in serious trouble.

Staggering out of bed, she made her way down to the kitchen, where she pulled out the two-way radio and contacted her great friend Barb Braitling at Mount Doreen. Even though Mrs Braitling lived nearly five hundred kilometres to the north-west of Alice Springs, she poured her children, Shane, Denis, Jacquie and Matthew, into the car and hit the road, arriving in a hot haze of dust eight hours later. Then she took charge.

Why hadn't Mum thought to call the RFDS? She was so ill that she was beyond dealing with authority and anything complicated.

'Barb, I just needed Barb,' she said. 'She would know what to do.'

And so Barb did.

Barb gently got Mum into her car, put Brett in too, then headed straight to Alice Springs to the doctor, Ross Peterkin.

Ross's wife, Lynne Peterkin, was due to have a baby about the same time as Mum, so the good doctor's hands were full. He did, however, put Mum straight into hospital. Barb took Brett into their Alice town house, and between them all they probably saved both Mum's life and Brett's.

Then they sent a telegram to Dad.

Dad finally finished shearing and flew home with us girls and Miss Clarke.

His diary entry reads, '*Flew Witchitie to BST. 0600 hrs—1400 hrs. Jan still in hospital. Did bore run to the west. Bendy Bore to be fixed. Country dry, feed turning.*'

Dr Peterkin diagnosed pre-eclampsia, and we were told we were lucky Mum was still alive. She was eventually able to come home, once Dr Peterkin said it was safe for her to do so.

We now knew that death was ever present in our world. Many things could kill us in the bush; but even more dangerous than pre-eclampsia, snakes, redbacks, heat, lack of water or a death-defying trek to the turn-off was fire.

Fire was a killer, burnt into our psyche, laid across our fear lines like red-hot grids. Fire could destroy everything. All Mum and Dad had slaved for, our home, our livelihoods, our lives. People in the bush talked about fire all the time, especially in summer.

So when Dad heard about the 'matches' episode, he called Brett into his office. He lit a match and held it over Brett's palm. Then he lowered it onto the tender flesh and burnt it.

'I am doing this so you will know what fire feels like,' Dad said. 'So that you will know what matches can do. And so that you'll never light matches again.'

Mum was called in. She took Brett to the storeroom and put lotion on the burn. Then she nursed Brett until his tears stopped.

M'Lis and I were traumatised, unable to speak. It took months for us all to recover and for the scar on Brett's palm to heal.

But Brett never played with matches again.

Would Dad have taken such drastic steps if we were still living at Witchitie, where life was kinder, softer, more gentle than in the wild outback? Had the pressure of our new life pounded him, moulded him and altered him, making him now as hard as the land? Turned him into the Boss, not Dad? Sometimes we didn't recognise the man who had once thrown us up into the air at picnic teas on the Witchitie lawn, and grinned a lot. But we knew, even if we didn't have words for it, that Dad's form of discipline was the only way he knew how to teach us right from wrong. And his whole focus was on protecting us. It was the man's job in the bush to be the tough one and to do what was needed to limit or prevent disasters.

And we were lucky. We had Mum.

She couldn't control or change Dad. But she could love us all 'to the moon and back', which is what she told us she did, kissing us 'all better' and making us happy again whenever we needed comforting and cheering up.

<hr />

Finally, the great moment arrived.

The baby we had longed to see and hold and have in our family was nearly here. Mum went back to hospital and was gone for over a week. Nana Parnell came up to look after us, given Miss Clarke was so busy teaching us. The waiting was horrible, but Nana Parnell spoiled us as she always did, and Miss Clarke kept us in line.

Finally, one day Dad came home, and for the first time in a long time, he *was* grinning.

'You have a baby brother.'

'When can we see him? When can we see Mummy?' we chorused, desperate to meet our new baby brother and see Mum. We were missing her so much, especially Brett.

Dad drove us in to the hospital the next day after school. We were so excited, we could hardly breathe. The maternity ward was breezy, bordered by a large veranda. Mum met us on the veranda wearing a beautiful lemon nightie and housecoat, with lace all over it. She was smiling and threw her arms around us all.

'You look so beautiful, Mummy,' we said. 'We miss you. When are you coming home?'

We crowded around her, smothering her face with grubby kisses, and then begged to see the new baby. But he was sleeping in the ward full of babies and we were only allowed to peep through a gauze screen. It was hard to make anything out but lots of little lumps under blankets in cots. So, we trudged home again, desperate for both mother and baby to join us.

The waiting became even harder, but then the day came for Dad to drive in to pick up Mum and the new baby. We had to do school that morning, and the hours ticked by so slowly until finally we were free for lunch and then, just as we'd started eating, we heard Dad's Land Rover. We rushed to the back door, abandoning plates and cutlery, and there were Dad and Mum, carrying a white bassinet.

They put down the bassinet by the back door. Clutching Mum's legs, we peered in at the soft little face under a blue satin rug.

'His name is Benny,' announced Mum. 'Short for Benjamin Frank Heaslip.'

We all drew in breaths of awe and admiration.

Brett was the first to speak. 'Hello, darling,' he said gently to the baby.

Then he looked up at us and announced, 'I'm going to call him darling.'

Benny was a wonderful arrival for us all, especially after the past few months. Having a new baby in the house was like having our very own puppy or kitten or poddy calf to play with. Only much better, because he was one of us, and didn't have to go out at night into a kennel or yard. We loved him, and adored him, thought he must be the most wonderful baby in the whole world, picked him up constantly, kissed his cherubic cheeks, and took him everywhere with us in his bassinet.

'How long until he can talk?' I asked Mum one day. That was the downside of a baby, we'd discovered—we chatted away constantly to him but he didn't answer, except in burbles and gurgles, and sometimes smiles. All very gorgeous but we wanted him to *talk*.

'A while,' said Mum. 'It will take a while.'

None of us understood the concept of patience but we soon worked out that babies could communicate very well, even without words. Crying? Pick him up, cuddle him, kiss him, give him a bottle. Laughing? The same, except for the bottle. We all loved him from the very first moment and he quickly became my responsibility.

Perhaps because I was the eldest, I wanted to look after him. Once Mum recovered, she was back to looking after the mob, and glad to have extra help. After all, I was seven by now and considered responsible. I loved doing it. I felt important and useful, and it also gave me unlimited access to Benny's round cheeks, which I couldn't resist kissing.

We loved *everything* about our new arrival.

11

Loss

By now, I was regularly getting gold stars for my reading and writing. I spent every spare moment learning to write cursive, making up my own stories, and reading adventure tales.

Mum brought home more and more boxes of books from the School of the Air. Every time she went to town, she and Mrs Hodder would put together a compilation for me. As well as the *Magic Faraway Tree* books, Mrs Hodder introduced me to the *Famous Five* and *The Secret Seven*. Every time Mum arrived home from town, I would rush to greet her, struggle to carry the boxes to the back veranda and dive into them. It was like Christmas.

There would be beautiful hardback books, with drawings of children on the cover in wonderful English-looking clothes (hats, scarves, gloves), with equally exciting titles—*The adventures of . . . The mystery of . . . The hidden/secret of . . .*—and each promised hours of breathtaking, page-turning wonder. When I opened the books, the pages were yellow and smelled deliciously musty.

I couldn't wait to devour them, impatient to finish school so I could escape. I read everything I could get my hands on.

Miss Clarke encouraged both my reading and writing, which included composition stories. These were a peculiar blend of English and Australian-isms, and Mum started to worry when I refused to write *paddock* in stories and used *field* instead.

'Tanya, my darling,' she would say. 'We live in Australia. In the outback. We have *paddocks*. That's the proper word.'

But I didn't agree. I thought *paddock* a particularly ugly word, denoting areas that were usually dry, stony, red or brown, and dusty. *Fields*, on the other hand, suggested stretches of soft, green landscape, golden with daffodils, bordered by green woods. And in those places, there would likely be children and fairyfolk and exciting adventures. I happily blended my two worlds of reality and imagination and saw nothing strange in that at all.

The more I read and dreamed of England and Europe, the more they seemed as real to me as my own home. My images were as vivid as if I were there. The old Aboriginal women had taught me the pleasure of walking through the bush, and I'd been wandering around and telling myself stories since I was a little girl. I could spend hours in my imagination, because it was where I was happiest.

Dad spent lots of time in the bush, too, but for different reasons.

He was busy building a good herd of Poll Herefords, and they required constant checking. He couldn't have too many cattle, because drought was always just over the horizon, or too few, because there had to be enough to breed in order to sell. A bit like Goldilocks, the numbers had to be just right.

But before long, he was talking about another problem.

'Pastoral leases in the Territory don't give us enough security,' he said, firmly.

He spoke in the way people did when they were completely right about something, giving no one a chance to say anything different. Besides, if Dad said it, it would be right. Dad was never wrong. He knew about these things.

'We need to borrow money to make improvements but it's hard to persuade the banks when we have such a weak form of land tenure.'

The way he used the word *weak*, it sounded like something disgusting. I always felt a bit sick in my stomach at this point.

'We need stronger lease terms in our favour,' he'd pace up and down, 'otherwise we could lose everything we put in. Yes, we were prepared to take that risk to get Bond Springs in the first place, but it's not sustainable long-term.'

I didn't understand all his words, but the meaning was clear. Yet again, we were facing big worries. Hanrahan of '*We'll all be rooned*' fame would no doubt have agreed.

'Why are we pastoral lease-holders prejudiced by such onerous, unsupportive terms, when landholders down south aren't? It's double standards and wrong.'

I chewed my lip.

'Freehold, that's what we need,' he pointed into the air, as though if he could just grab that elusive thing, every problem in the world would be solved. 'The bloody bureaucrats won't agree, but at least they should give us more control over our future. Trouble is, they just don't understand what private industry needs—a fair go.'

Dad was so worried about our future that he joined with a group of cattlemen and they lobbied the government for better, stronger lease terms.

They didn't get them, but the group went on to become the Northern Territory Cattlemen's Association and Dad was its first chairman. He worked for years to try to improve conditions for those on the land. And while he did finally get improved lease terms, freehold was 'never going to be a happening thing', as Mum would say.

Bloody bureaucrats.

Even though I understood none of the detail, to my ears it seemed that the governments were completely against us, and always looking for ways to bring us down. That meant that our life on the land was always at risk. You could never relax. You had to always be *vigilant* (another word I'd learnt from Dad), ever ready for the next disaster.

As the eldest child, I felt both responsible and powerless. I wanted to protect Mum and M'Lis, Brett and Benny from these things, because they seemed equally powerless, but I had no way of doing that. Nor did I have the words to describe my fears or what I could or should do about them.

So, I didn't talk about my worries with anyone. I stuffed them deep down inside and built a picture inside me that grown-up life was a difficult and dangerous business. And I knew I was lucky to still be a child for a while yet.

Being with Mum helped me forget my worries. She had a lightness and gaiety about her, despite Dad's many deep-held anxieties. Her eyes were so warm. She could solve all problems with kisses and hugs.

Her idea of relaxation was coming home from Alice with the latest *Women's Weekly* and *Woman's Day*, and devouring stories of 'life on the outside', with all its glamour and glitz and gossip. Under a ray of dull, yellow light, after a long day, she would sit up in the kitchen with a cup of tea and whip through the magazine pages before bed.

'Keeps me going!' she'd say with a smile, after catching up on the latest story about the Queen, or a sewing pattern, or a new recipe for beef.

———>•<———

Whenever we weren't at school, we had little time to ourselves. We were often squashed up in the back of the Land Rover while Dad did bore runs. Mum would send us off when we were driving her crazy, or when Dad needed help. M'Lis and Brett mostly enjoyed bore runs, but I hated them. Stuck in the heat and dust, getting carsick, with no books, was like a prison sentence for me. Especially because Dad could literally drive all day.

Baby Benny received real praise in Dad's diary one day: *'Benny with me all day on bore run.'* Benny was nine months old.

When M'Lis, Brett and I had time to ourselves, we continued to live in our happy imaginary world. We played chasey, ran around with the dogs, or talked to the poddy calves, or put on song and dance performances on the lawn. We lugged Benny in his bassinet everywhere and spent hours cuddling, carrying and kissing him. We were each other's best friends.

Down at the creek, the wonderful, old stone wall was falling down. It was the perfect place to play games and spend warm winter days on the old flat stones. A little further down on the other side of the creek was a deep, off-limits well. It was said that somebody had once fallen down there and died. Whether or not that was true, we were terrified and went nowhere near it.

But we spent endless hours playing Cowboys and Indians around the wall. In its crumbling form, it provided wonderful spots to hide, and then jump unseen up on top and point an imaginary bow and arrow, shouting, 'Die! Die!' to the hapless ones still below. The top of the wall was home base and it gave a wide view of the old windmill on one side and the huge gum trees lining the riverbed on the other.

Our Number One favourite game was creating little cattle

stations out of sticks and stones in the dirt and making roads with our fingers. We squatted in the sand or around the old meat house, absorbed in our make-believe world for hours. We built dams and poured dribbles of water in them (they were never full, because we had rarely seen a dam that was full). The roads were a winding maze. The stockyards were built out of twigs. There were creeks, always dry, and bores made of stones.

M'Lis and Brett saved their pocket money to buy little Matchbox cars and whizzed them around and across their labyrinth of roads. They built bridges of branches for their cars to mount and tunnels for them to drive under. Mostly, the cars got stuck in the branches and the tunnels collapsed, but nothing deterred M'Lis and Brett in their determination to beat each other to the finish line (there was always a race involved).

When I wasn't playing with M'Lis and Brett and Benny, or reading and writing, I was drawing and tracing pictures. Over time I started to put words to pictures, like the cartoons I'd read at the Braitlings' house. The options for creativity seemed endless to me. Sometimes I'd just study words I found in Dad's encyclopedias, the dictionary, Mum's magazines and any fiction books I could lay my hands on. I'd write them down and make myself spell and pronounce them off by heart.

Words were the key to my Aladdin's cave.

Being alone was a joyous thing to me. It rarely happened, because there were always jobs to complete, games to play and Benny to look after, but my idea of absolute happiness was being alone, daydreaming, lying on the lawn looking up at the big blue sky, reading my books and making up stories.

In my imagination I could soar to places of joy and limitless freedom and endless hope. I could fly into a glorious weightless space of opportunities. There I was safe.

Around this time, I also learned how it felt to lose someone you loved.

M'Lis, Brett and I had already experienced the loss of animals. Death was part of the natural cycle of life. We lost little poddy calves to dingoes, we lost our dogs to snakebite, we lost cattle to drought. We went to get a killer with Dad every month when the station needed meat.

But I'd never lost a person before. That was until Miss Clarke decided to marry a man from the Flinders Ranges, and said she had to leave us.

We were devastated. We couldn't believe she was going—we thought she would live with us forever. I think I was the most grief-stricken. I'd had the longest bond with Miss Clarke and I loved learning with her. She gave all of us support when Mum was so busy working. She was part of the routine and structure of our lives. I couldn't imagine life without her kind, calming presence.

The misery of losing Miss Clarke was slightly lessened when we were invited to her wedding. We knew that weddings were the most exciting thing in the world because the previous year our Aunty June (Dad's younger sister) and Uncle John (Mum's younger brother) had got married. Mum said, with a mischievous grin, she'd matchmade them, and M'Lis and I thought their wedding was a fairytale. So, whenever we were sad, Mum would say, 'You'll be able to see Miss Clarke in a wedding dress!' and that cheered us up.

We flew down in DQG for the big occasion and stayed at Witchitie. Miss Clarke's wedding was to be held at the tiny Cradock Methodist Church, deep in the Flinders Ranges, where we four children had been christened.

It was June, and cold. M'Lis and I wore exquisite blue velvet dresses with an equally exquisite fur collar and trim, white striped stockings and little boots. Nana Parnell had made our dresses, and we felt like little princesses (even though we were beaming through gaps in our little front teeth on the big day).

It was joyous standing next to Dad and Papa Heaslip and hearing their beautiful voices singing the old Methodist hymns in harmony. It was always surreal to be taken out of our outback bush life to rural South Australia with its long-established religious and cultural traditions. There was something about coming back to the Flinders that made Mum and Dad's faces light up, as they embraced their former life, and momentarily forgot the stresses and strains of running Bond Springs. Dad relaxed, looked young again. Mum beamed the whole time.

Miss Clarke looked so beautiful, and her new husband was incredibly handsome. When she came over after the service and kneeled before us, she was a vision in white.

'Make sure you work hard at school and be good for Mummy and Daddy, won't you?'

She smiled and wiped away the tears under my eyes, and then left our lives.

That night when we went back to Witchitie to stay, the first thing I did was rush to the schoolroom. I opened the door and fell on my knees to smell the lino, which I adored, and traced my hand over my desk. Even though I hadn't been in that schoolroom for some years, my exercise books and pens and paper were still sitting there—as though it had only been yesterday I'd started learning about 'Dick and Dora, Nip and Fluff' with Miss Clarke.

There I said my own private, sad goodbye to her.

I love you, Miss Clarke.

12

An Outback Lifeline

After Miss Clarke's wedding, we flew home in DQG with our new governess. She was also from country South Australia, and it was not a great trip.

The new governess was given the luxury of the front seat next to Dad, but that meant Mum, M'Lis, Brett, Benny and I were squashed behind in a space built for three. We were two more people than the tiny plane was allowed to carry, but there was no other way for Dad to get his family and a governess up and back from the Territory in one trip.

Not that Dad told anyone—and we weren't allowed to either.

Bloody bureaucrats.

M'Lis and Brett got sick en route. I couldn't hold on. Benny did more than his fair share of howling. Mum had to stop us all from fighting. The new governess—squashed in with all of this smelly chaos for eight hours—had despair in her eyes the closer we drew to our destination.

Things did not improve when we got home and into the school-room. We were missing Miss Clarke (and certainly didn't want a new governess). Brett was in his first year of school and couldn't bear being stuck at a desk; he was a wild bush kid who just wanted to be active and outside. M'Lis wasn't naughty, but she wanted to be outside too. While I was glad to be inside the schoolroom, I was sulky because the poor woman wasn't Miss Clarke.

After a month or two of trying to manage three cranky children in three different grades in one tiny room, our new governess said to Mum, 'I want to go home.'

Mum had to drive into Alice Springs to the Elders GM office to borrow their telephone to ring the governess's parents. There was no other option, apart from a telegram sent over the wireless, and Mum said that wouldn't be nice for the parents to receive out of the blue.

Once our governess left, Mum had to step into the teaching role for a short time. She brought Nana Parnell up to look after Benny while she taught us. But having Mum in the classroom didn't work either. She was our mother, not our teacher, and none of us managed it well. Mum was forever rushing out to pull some meat from the oven or prepare smoko or pack the tuckerbox for the stock camp. And Benny kept clamouring for her at the school room door. It was just confusing: Mum was pretending to be a teacher rather than Mum, but we could hardly say, 'Excuse me, Mrs Heaslip, can you please explain . . .'

Fortunately, before we all went backwards in our grades and Mum had a nervous breakdown, Miss Thiele came into our lives.

Miss Thiele was also from country South Australia. She had blue eyes and red-blonde hair. She also had our measure from the outset. A natural teacher, she took no nonsense. She was often cross because we drove her to it. But when she was in a good mood and happy with us, she had an infectious giggle, and her cheeks dimpled. We loved hearing her laugh.

Another South Australian girl, Helen McGilvray, came to assist Mum in the house at about the same time, so those two gave each other much-needed moral support.

Miss Thiele was wonderful for me because I was hungry to learn and she inspired me to keep learning.

Except for maths. I hated maths. I'd stare hopelessly at a page of sums and they would mean nothing. Words I could connect with but sums were from another planet.

Day after day, I'd wrestle unhappily with this subject. And day after day, Miss Thiele would hover, exasperated, eventually throwing down her pencil and shouting, 'You're not *trying*, Tanya!'

I'd stare back at her grumpily, knowing she was right, but not knowing how to make the connections to work it out.

But I would always perk up when it was time for maths on School of the Air. Perhaps that was because time with Mrs Hodder was like play, like theatre.

'Today we're going to discuss a maths problem,' Mrs Hodder would say. 'Good morning, Tanya at Sierra Victor Uniform! I'll start with you. Can you read me? Over.'

'Good morning, Mrs Hodder,' I'd respond breathlessly. 'Yes, I can read you, loud and clear. I'm ready! Over.'

I made many mistakes on air but the embarrassment of that faded completely against the joy and theatrics of being on the wireless.

———⊷∞⊷———

Mum loved the wireless as much as I did; maybe more. It gave her a connection to people and the outside world. Being a people person, she craved conversation. She found a way to be on the session nearly every morning.

First thing in the morning, Dad put the wireless on. The big, old two-way sat in the kitchen, so over breakfast we'd hear the static and crackle as people called in, trying to connect with people on other stations. Mum would lean in to hear other voices and stories and she said it 'filled her up'.

At 8 a.m., George Brown of the Royal Flying Doctor Base would take over with his morning telegram session. He would read out the list of telegrams for the relevant call signs in a booming voice, and then people would call in with telegrams they wanted to send.

In either case, telegrams mostly involved the two stock and station agents in town: Elders GM and Bennetts. There were orders for stock feed, engine and machinery parts, trucking requests and sometimes advertisements for staff. Every now and then there would be a personal telegram, but they were not as common, because everyone could listen in and there was no privacy. It was for this reason that Mum didn't want to send a telegram to the parents of our poor departed governess.

Following the official sessions were 'skeds', where station people could get back on and call one another up; women, desperate for female conversation, and men keen for updates on weather, moving stock, road conditions and cattle prices.

Mum was regularly on the sked to talk to her great friends Barb Braitling from Mount Doreen to the west, and Nancye Gorey from Yambah, our next station to the north.

Throughout, there would be bursts of static, but the conversation (mostly about children, the weather and stock work) would struggle on through it. There was a five-to-ten-minutes-only airtime protocol. If anyone spoke too long, the next lot of people waiting to talk would start calling over the top of them. And the fact that there were plenty of listeners for an eleven-hundred-kilometre radius was also a natural circuit breaker.

The only exception to the five-to-ten-minute protocol was the Bloomfield family who, on account of having so many stock camps on the go at any one time, had carved their own regular spot in the late afternoon. Everyone else basically just gave up trying to get on the air until they were finished. It was known as the Bloomfield Half-Hour. Every evening there would be a different episode, covering all the dramas and issues the Bloomfields were dealing with at any given time. I loved tuning in—it was like listening to our own radio broadcast, with all the different actors and parts in a play.

But Mum and Barb didn't have that luxury.

'Better go, Barb,' Mum would finish reluctantly, when their time was ending. 'But we've had good reception today. That's something. One last thing—when are you next coming to town? Over.'

Trips to town were a highlight for many of the women out bush. They loved the chance to dress up and meet friends for a few days. In the early years, Mum went about once a month to get stores (including heavy sacks of flour, sugar, potatoes and pumpkin) and collect mail. It was always a full-day trip, by the time she got in, got around Alice's shops, and got home again. She would wear a gorgeous frock, even though it wasn't very practical for lugging heavy sacks around, and meet as many people as she could while in town. Because she'd previously lived in Alice she had a lot of friends there, and it would take several hours just to walk from one end of Todd Street to the other talking to everyone.

But the downside now, for both Mum and for us, was that she usually took us with her. We were now old enough and, besides, she thought Miss Thiele and Helen deserved a break.

We hated everything about going to town: the long trip where we inevitably all got carsick, the sticky heat of the vinyl seats, the blazing sun through the window, the bickering ('It's my turn to be by the window!' 'No it's not!' 'Yes it *is*!'), Benny's crying, and Mum's exasperation at our constant whining and fighting.

When things really got out of hand, she would pull up with a screech of brakes and dust and shout, 'That's *it*! I'm at the *end of my tether*!'

We didn't know what a tether was but we always thought Mum got to it quite quickly.

She would turn around to glare at us furiously, her frustration spilling out in puffs and shouts, her brown eyes flashing, her curls damp on her hot forehead. 'I've had *enough* of you kids. You can *get out* and I'm going to leave you here by the side of the road *until the middle of next week*!'

We would cower, terrified, and pinch whoever we thought was the culprit.

If we were really bad, she'd pull out her worst threat: 'I'm going to *belt* you all into the middle of next week!'

Her rage invariably had the desired effect. 'Sorry, Mum, sorry,' we would cry, and eventually she would relent and agree not to carry out her threat. This time.

Throughout this Benny would chat to us all in his funny little language, with lots of smiles, and I'd squeeze him tight. The thought of being left by the side of the road until the middle of next week without Benny was unbearable.

But no matter the season or time of year, the trip to town was dreadful and did not get better for years.

The trip was in two parts.

First, there was the dirt road from the homestead to the bitumen. It was boggy, narrow, corrugated, rough and winding.

Driving it could take anywhere between thirty minutes to three hours, depending on whether we got bogged in the sandy creeks, or broke down, both of which happened frequently.

Once on the bitumen (the second part), it was equally narrow and winding, up and down through the northern parts of the MacDonnell Ranges. Driving it would take another thirty minutes to an hour, depending on how many trucks we got stuck behind, and how slowly Mum drove, which was very slow, as many people were killed on that stretch of road.

When we got bogged in the creek, or the car broke down, there was often no way of letting anyone know we needed help, especially if we were on the dirt road. It was bad enough if we were going to town, but if we were on the way home, it would be worse. Night would usually descend upon Mum and us kids trudging along wearily, and hungrily, step-by-step, on the dusty road back to the station. We took it in turns to carry Benny.

If we were lucky and Dad was home (and not in the stock camp), we would finally hear the Land Rover in the distance, when he'd realised something must have gone wrong, and came to find us.

'It's Dad!' we'd cry, as his vehicle rumbled towards us, the brightness of the headlights enveloping us, our eyes poking through dirty, tired faces. 'He's come!'

Dad would pull up, step out, put his arm around Mum (who by now was usually limping and cross-eyed with exhaustion), and make everything better. 'C'mon', he'd say in his commanding, practical way. 'Let's go.' He'd drive us all home, squashed against each other, and his strong, steady presence meant we knew we were safe again. Our tears would dry; Mum would breathe out.

There was no feeling like it.

Overwhelming relief.

———⊷⊶———

The routine and structure in our lives at home otherwise continued, unchanged. Every weekday it went as follows:

6.45 a.m.: get up, wash face and clean teeth, get dressed in jeans, boots, shirt (and jumper in winter)

7–7.10 a.m.: breakfast when Mum rang the big triangular bell outside the kitchen (it could be heard all over the station including the cattle yards)

7.10–7.30 a.m.: complete daily jobs such as watering plants, feeding the calves and emptying the chook bucket; clean teeth again

7.30 a.m.: into the schoolroom

10 a.m.: smoko

10.30 a.m.: back to the schoolroom

1 p.m.: end of school, and lunch when the bell went

Afternoon: play, more jobs, bore runs with Dad

5 p.m.: the bell went again and it was time to clean boots in the laundry, have a bath and dinner

7 p.m.: bed and lights out.

In the midst of our busy lives, Mum was always there for us. We would run out of school at recess time and she'd be waiting for us at the kitchen door, her arms open, embracing us all in a big hug. Benny would be with her and we'd all fall into each other like puppies.

She didn't like changes to the structure of our week and school life. Routine was how she coped with all she had to do every day. But Dad often came along and pulled us out of the schoolroom to help with work. This happened increasingly as we got older. When Dad wanted something done, we hopped to it, and everything else went by the wayside.

He was the Boss, after all.

The only difference in our day on the weekend was that we didn't go to school—unless Dad had pulled us out of the schoolroom earlier that week for work and we had to go back on Saturdays to catch up on school.

Miss Thiele was the stopgap for Mum and supervised many of our activities to ensure that all our jobs were done, and our boots were cleaned, and that we kept up with our lessons (especially if we'd missed school). She was strict, but kind to us, and a good teacher.

Before long, it was as though Miss Thiele had been with us forever.

13

Buckjumping on the Bond

At the start of the mustering season, Dad had to make sure he had the right men and horses. His gamble with the beautiful but expensive stallion was paying off. Foals were being born with good, clean lines and good breeding.

One of the first colts was golden all over, with dark eyes, and, Dad said, had a 'noble nature'. Dad knew the moment the colt cantered into the yards with its mother that it was the horse for him. 'He's got a heart for work,' said Dad.

Dad broke the colt in himself; slowly, gently and reverently. Then Dad threw his leg over the saddle and rode off to do his first muster.

From that moment on, it was as though they were one.

Dad called the colt Limerick, after the city in his beloved Ireland he'd never seen, and together they were a dynamic team. We loved watching Dad saddle up Limerick in the yards. We hung over the rails, agog but not allowed to say a word or interrupt Dad in any way. There was something special about the ritual for us. Then we'd wave madly as Dad and Limerick headed off. It was like farewelling a king riding grandly to his next conquest.

———⊶⊷———

Ross and Colin had moved on, as had all the Aboriginal stockmen, so Charlie Gorey came to us as head stockman.

Charlie was nineteen when he arrived, but to us he seemed to be much older because he was tough and gruff. He came from Bundaberg in Queensland, a mysterious-sounding place to the east. He was stocky, with Asian heritage reflected in his dark eyes and face, although we never had the courage to ask him about that. He spoke with the usual Queensland drawl, and added 'eh?' to the end of every sentence, whether it was needed or not.

He drank Bundy rum ('What else, for someone from that town?' Mum said cheekily), and he loved a fight.

We trailed after Charlie. Everything about him was interesting. He wore Longhorn trousers every day, RM Williams boots and smart press-stud shirts. Moleskins were for special occasions. He knew horses and stock, and had a dry sense of humour. We'd never met such a character, and we started saying 'eh?' at the end of our sentences too, until Mum stopped us.

A young Irish stockman also came to us. His name was Ray Murtagh and he was 'full of the blarney', as Mum would say. We'd beg, 'Talk to us some more, Ray!' just to hear his lilting accent.

Over breakfast during Ray's first week, Dad said, 'Ray, I hear you were a bareback rider in Ireland.' Ray looked startled but Dad continued, 'Charlie reckons you should be the number-one horse breaker. What d'ya reckon?'

Our eyes darted from Charlie to Ray.

'Well, Mr Heaslip, to be sure, I can give it a go,' said Ray, swallowing some steak and eggs in a hurry. 'T'was only on my family pony . . . on my family farm but—'

'Settled then,' said Dad, standing up.

Charlie couldn't hide his smirk.

M'Lis, Brett and I were a bit worried for Ray. We knew that breaking in horses was a big and scary job. We'd seen Ross Cooper and Colin Ansell do it. There had been a lot of horses bucking wildly, and men flying through the air and hitting the dust. Ray was neither big nor tall. He might get crushed underneath one of these horses if they turned wild.

But Dad was on a mission. Over the next few days, the brood mares and their offspring were mustered into the yards. By now there was quite a number. Once they'd settled down, Dad walked around and examined them.

'Righto, I reckon we should start with these five,' he said, pointing to some younger colts and fillies standing quietly in the morning sun. 'We start mustering in two weeks. Need these five broken in by the end of the week. Then another five after that. That'll give us a plant of fresh horses we can rotate. And we'll use our current stock horses as needed.'

Our jaws dropped. Ray would have to break in one horse per day. Was that even possible? Charlie's smirk grew bigger.

The next morning, we rushed down to the horse yards before breakfast.

Ray had chosen his colt and was already walking around him, talking to him soothingly, rubbing his mane with a halter. The horse was a beautiful chestnut with white forelocks and we thought that was a good omen.

'How's it going, Ray?' we shrieked.

The colt jumped and snorted at our voices. It skittered over towards the edge of the yard.

'Quiet, you bloody kids,' came Charlie's voice, his face like thunder, as he emerged from the side of the yards. He was overseeing Ray's first day.

'Sorry,' we said, shamefaced. We were always too noisy, we knew that. Dad was always telling us off, and not just in the plane.

We hugged the rails, keeping as silent as we could, while Ray slipped the halter over the colt's head. It felt the weight, startled, and jumped sideways. Ray had to jump too, so he wouldn't get stepped on.

'Time to hobble and side-line,' instructed Charlie.

We knew Charlie wanted to stop the colt from kicking or bucking, so Ray had to hobble it, then slip a leather belt from the hobbles through to the back legs, which was the 'side-line'. All the while, trying to avoid being kicked in the head. Not easy.

The breakfast bell went, so we had to leave. Then we had to go to school. On our way there we ran past the horse yards for one last look. Poor Ray was still trying to get the side-line belt on and the colt wasn't liking it one bit. It was whinnying and kicking.

'Oh, to be sure ...' we heard Ray's exasperated tones as we headed for school.

At smoko time, we raced back to the yards. We weren't sure whether Ray had had breakfast or not, but he certainly wasn't getting smoko. He was talking to the colt in Irish. Then we saw him take a deep breath, lean back then forward on his left foot, grab the colt's mane, and then jump, high up onto its bare back.

The colt felt Ray's weight and went crazy trying to buck, but the leather belt held. We stifled our cheers, and then the bell went for school again.

At lunchtime, we ran back to the yards again. Ray was removing the side-lines and hobbles (still trying not to get kicked in the head). His face was red and sweat dripped down his sideburns.

'Now, then, wee thing, we'll try a wee bit of ridin', we heard him say, as he leaped back astride the colt. There was now nothing to stop the colt's legs from moving, and it sensed freedom and went wild. He pig-rooted, with his head down and back legs in the air, and when that didn't dislodge Ray, he moved into full-on bucking all around the yards.

'Hang on, Ray!' we shrieked helpfully, forgetting we were meant to be quiet.

'Aaaoouweeeeee!' Ray shouted back, as he clutched on for dear life, the mane in one hand, reins in the other. We couldn't believe he was bareback. So brave.

Next minute Ray was sent flying in a perfect arc over the colt's head and landed face first in the dust.

'Back on,' commanded Charlie, who'd caught the colt at the far end of the yard. 'Can't let him get away with it.'

Poor Ray. He dusted himself off and hoiked himself back up on the colt, only to be chucked off again.

We had to go for lunch but could hardly eat, such was our excitement and worry for Ray.

Ray didn't or couldn't eat lunch.

But Ray was nothing if not determined.

By mid-afternoon, he said to Charlie, 'Time for the bridle and saddle, to be sure, yes?'

Charlie agreed. There was more dust and swearing, but Ray was soon astride the colt, with both saddle and bridle intact. By the time we'd left to do our evening jobs, polish our boots, have a bath and go in for dinner, Ray was now the boss of the colt. He rode him around and around the yards and stayed on.

When Ray staggered in later that night, he could hardly walk. But Dad slapped him on the back and Charlie grinned like a proud parent.

'Only four more horses to go this week,' said Dad. 'And lucky we've got these good colts, not the brumbies.'

Ray nodded weakly.

'How about a bit of guitar before we have to go to bed?' we begged Ray.

Mum stepped in. 'Ray's tired enough,' but Ray's eyes lit up. He didn't move far without his guitar. Even though he was sore and tired, he pulled it out and strummed a few songs. He was a beautiful guitarist and with his lilting accent we felt transported to what we imagined were the green hills of Ireland.

'Bed time,' ordered Mum, eventually. 'Ray's got a big day tomorrow.'

'And the day after that and the day after that,' said Charlie, still grinning.

'I'll play yer all "Nobody's Child",' Ray offered, unexpectedly. 'Just as a goodnight lullaby. One I learned back home.'

Ray started singing about an orphan who wasn't wanted by anybody because he was blind. He didn't have any kisses from his mother or smiles from his father. He was just like a plant growing wild in the field. It was about the saddest song I'd ever heard, and I felt tears filling my eyes.

'To be sure, it is sad,' Ray agreed, as he put away his guitar and Mum packed us off to bed. I hoped going into such a sad space in his heart and head wouldn't put him off his breaking-in program tomorrow.

Luckily for us, Ray was good-natured and cheerful, and was in good form by the morning. He went on to break in horse after horse for Dad and helped build his plant of horses for the stock camp.

But Charlie still had some mischief up his sleeve. One morning at breakfast he said to Dad, 'I reckon we should give Ray a go on Big Mac. The horse has come in with some of the other plant.'

Dad frowned. 'Nobody can ride Big Mac. He's just a mad buckjumper.'

We knew Big Mac, too. He was a huge bay horse, sired by a brumby stallion to a brumby mare. He was terrifying. Dad and many others had tried to break him in and failed.

'I reckon our Ray might have a chance,' persisted Charlie.

All eyes turned to Ray. Yet again he swallowed his steak and eggs so fast I thought he might choke.

So, Ray was given his next big challenge, which we thought was very unfair, and we rushed down to the horse yards with Dad and Mum, who'd come out to watch in case things went wrong. Charlie put the bridle on Big Mac and led him over to Ray. We all held our breath.

Ray lifted up the saddle he was holding and put it straight on. Big Mac stood there calmly, tail flicking back and forth against the flies. He didn't even seem worried. Ray patted him and put his foot in the stirrup a few times to indicate he was about to mount. The big horse continued to stand there quietly, unperturbed.

'Maybe he knows that Ray is the big horse breaker from Ireland!' M'Lis said excitedly.

Ray put his foot in the stirrup one more time, and swung aboard.

'Yay!' we yelled.

Ray got into the saddle, put his other foot in the stirrup, and after a long moment, Big Mac looked around, tossed his head— and then went wild. We couldn't believe it as we watched him buck and buck and buck so high and so fast that Ray was thrown to the other side of the yards. Then Big Mac stopped, and went happily back to eating some chaff on the ground.

'I think he just likes to buck,' said Ray, despairingly, staggering back across the yard.

'Have another go,' said Charlie. We couldn't work out if he still had the glint in his eye.

Ray approached Big Mac again. The big, old horse looked as though butter wouldn't melt in his mouth. Once more, he let Ray climb aboard easily. But once Ray was aboard, he started to buck. He bucked and bucked. This time, Ray held on, knees bent, like a true buckjump rider. In fact, Ray held on so hard that he looked stuck to the saddle. We were amazed, but then we realised what was actually happening: Ray couldn't get off. Big Mac wouldn't stop bucking long enough to let him.

We could see the desperation on Ray's face. As Big Mac approached the rails, Ray decided it was now or never. He let go of the reins, grabbed the rails with both hands, kicked his feet out of the stirrups and leaped onto the rails. He swung from them, high above the ground, as Big Mac took off down to the end of the yards, saddle and stirrups flying. Ray clung to the rails, his knees bruised and his fingers scraped, his hat scrunched on the ground. When Ray realised it was safe, he climbed down like an old man. We all cheered.

'It's just a game to that horse,' said Ray disgustedly, as we took him up to the kitchen for a strong cup of tea. Ray was pretty bow-legged by now.

Ray gave up on Big Mac but he still kept on breaking in horses for Dad. Soon there was a good plant of horses available for the stock camp. More stockmen arrived and Dad had what he needed: a strong group of men and horses to muster cattle for market.

But no one was allowed near Dad's beautiful horse Limerick. No one ever dared consider riding him, much less handle or even touch him. All the other horses on the property were interchanged between musters and the men took whichever horses were fresh and available. Limerick, however, was hands-off.

14

Learning to Ride

It was time for M'Lis, Brett and me to learn to ride. All kids on cattle stations rode horses and joined the stock camp as soon as they could. We wanted to be like everyone else, especially Charlie and Ray.

But I was the 'nervous nellie', to use a phrase I'd read in a book.

I'd seen what happened to the men, and I knew what came with riding. *Pain*. Lots of it. Horses were beautiful, noble, strong—but also dangerous. You got hurt. You were thrown off, trampled upon and suffered. Life seemed hard enough without deliberately adding pain to it. Dreams of being left to die in the empty desert courtesy of Big Mac who had just bucked me off (and was now galloping wildly into the horizon) consumed my already overactive night-time imagination.

But Dad said it was time, so it was time.

Dad had a lovely Shetland pony called Pinto down at Witchitie, and I thought, *If I could just ride him, I'll be all right*. Pinto was old and quiet and lived in the paddock near the Witchitie house. When we were down there, Dad would lead him up onto the lawn for us. We'd climb onto his broad back and pat his mane and breathe in his sweet, horsey smell. Sometimes we'd feed him carrots or apples. When we felt brave, we'd stand up on him. He never minded, and just munched the lawn. We loved him.

Pinto wasn't at all terrifying, unlike the sixteen-hand stock horses or bucking colts and fillies we had here. But Pinto wasn't here.

Mum, fortunately, decided another Shetland pony would be perfect for us to learn on. So she and Dad bought a little grey Shetland pony from Alice Springs.

We called her Lesley (after Miss Clarke, of course). Dad's lovely sister June came up to teach us how to ride, and she brought her friend Robyn. Both were expert horsewomen and their job was to transform us from wild bush kids into expert riders too. Dad and the men were too busy to do it.

'Learning to ride is simple,' Aunty June and Robyn chorused. 'First, you have to learn to walk, trot and then canter bareback. Once you can do that without falling off, you can have a saddle.'

Two old, bony stock horses that had been put out to pasture were brought in to rotate with Lesley for us to practise on. As it turned out, Lesley was the most difficult of the three horses to ride. She was unlike Pinto in every respect. She was cranky and didn't like having us little ones on her. The minute we would hop on, she would bolt, and we would clutch on, screaming. Her favourite trick was to then prop, coming to a sudden stop and sending us sailing over her head. We didn't have helmets—nobody did in the bush—so we just had to hope we didn't land on *our* heads.

It wasn't much fun learning on the two bony, old horses either. Trotting meant bumping up and down on their bony backbone, clinging on with our little knees, and then holding on for dear life once the horses broke into a canter. We had so many falls and scrapes and near misses that I almost gave up before I started.

'You can't give up,' Aunty June told me firmly, when I came to her with a quivering lip and bruised bottom. 'You need *ten falls* off a horse before you can be called a rider. And that's ten falls off a *saddled* horse. You've got a way to go, yet.'

Aunty June and Dad were of the same mould. There was no surrendering on their watch. And given what our Irish Ray had been through, we didn't dare complain. Ray and Charlie would sometimes come and watch us learning to ride and I always hoped they didn't think me too hopeless. Brett and M'Lis were much better at it than I was. And nowhere near as nervous.

Finally, we became good enough to be given a small saddle to use on Lesley. In truth, it could barely have been called a saddle— more a piece of leather on Lesley's back with clogs for stirrups that we could put our feet inside and cling to—but it did give us a bit more grip. Lesley still bolted and tried to chuck us off whenever possible, but the saddle gave us a bit more security, and our falls became fewer.

Eventually, the great day arrived when we were allowed to graduate to a proper saddle. By this time, Aunty June had returned to South Australia, so we were in the hands of Charlie, Ray and Dad. On the basis that *there's no such word as can't* (Dad's favourite retort to any of our feeble complaints), we were then sent out to join the stockmen for our first muster.

'Here we go!' shouted Brett, as the three of us rode out of the house gates for the first time. Our destination was a mob of cattle up near the yards. It wasn't a long trip but it was our first one, and hugely important to us all: me at age eight, M'Lis seven, Brett and six, all grown-up. Mum stood and waved goodbye from the gate, just as we had done when we were younger, when waving to the stockmen heading out to the stock camp.

My stomach was full of butterflies and my hands were sweaty. But Brett and M'Lis were happily whistling Slim Dusty songs. They couldn't wait to get to the mob and be part of the stockmen's world at last.

'And here they are!' shouted M'Lis, pointing towards the group of cattle in the distance, with a big grin on her freckled face. Ahead of us were red dust and bellowing bullocks and the sound of stock-whips. We could smell the bulldust, smell the cattle. I could smell my own fear.

Dad had drilled us beforehand so we knew the rules of approach. Come behind the mob slowly, take up a position on the tail, don't get in the way of the lead, let the men take the wings. Our job was to learn how to keep the cows and their calves moving along from the rear. Once we knew what we were doing and became better at the job, we would be allowed to take the wings, and maybe even the lead. But today just being on the tail was a huge responsibility.

That event was a rite of passage for us. We were leaving behind childish things and becoming little men among big men. It never occurred to us to ask why we had to do this. It was life in the bush and that's just how it was.

M'Lis and Brett felt proud and honoured to have come so far.

Me—I felt that in snatches, but mostly I just had knots in my stomach.

Dad, who showed no fear about anything, was now spending a lot more time in the air. He flew low over fences and gates, to see if they needed fixing before and after a muster. He checked outlying paddocks where cattle might be stuck and perishing, and yards after trapping to make sure there were no cattle left inside. And he practised his dives and swoops again and again. He became deadly at scaring away dingoes swarming around a bore and attacking calves. He flew harder, lower, faster.

Of course, Dad didn't tell the aviation authorities down south what he was doing with his plane.

'Need-to-know basis,' he'd say firmly.

Bloody bureaucrats.

———⋙◆⋘———

So, while Dad practised his flying, M'Lis, Brett and I practised our riding.

One day after school we all saddled up to go out into the horse paddock. M'Lis was on Lesley, because she was the best at controlling that difficult little pony. I was still on the old, slow stock horse, because I was still the least adventurous (my heart was always back at the homestead with my books and stories, where I felt safest and happiest). Brett was considered good enough to ride Bundy, a rangy, cranky stock horse the stockmen used in the stock camp; Bundy was short for 'Bundaberg Rum', so that should have said everything.

We had a good ride and headed home along the north side of the creek. We were feeling happy with ourselves and our progress; me, especially. But just five hundred metres out from the yard, Bundy slyly rolled his head and jumped over a ditch. In that strange and deliberate movement by that cunning old horse, Brett was thrown to the side, and M'Lis and I watched in disbelief as he sailed downwards and his head smashed into a rock.

'Brett!' We jumped off our horses and rushed to him.

Brett didn't move. He lay crumpled.

'Brett!' We tried again.

Still no answer. His eyes were shut.

M'Lis and I stared at each other, stricken.

'Quick!' M'Lis finally had the presence of mind to act. 'Get Dad. I'll look after him.'

I pulled my old stock horse behind me as I ran frantically towards the yards. Locking the gate behind me, I tore up to the house, screaming, 'Mum! Dad! Brett's fallen! An accident!' I nearly said, *Brett's dead*, but didn't dare, just in case I was wrong, which would have made things worse.

Fortunately, Dad was home and in the shed. He came out at a run, as did Mum, her eyes wide with horror. We all raced across the gravel and through the yards and up the hill. We could see two tiny figures in the distance, one slumped on the ground. The two horses were standing obediently with M'Lis (Bundy had now decided to behave himself). Dad looked down at Brett and carefully lifted him into his arms. As he did, Brett moaned and moved, and we all uttered sighs of relief.

'Just knocked out, that's all,' said Dad, carrying him to the house. Mum and I followed, panting, while M'Lis brought the horses.

After some ice and a soothing flannel placed on his forehead, Brett came to. He hadn't been knocked out for long. And luckily for him, he got the next day off school.

But his reprieve was short-lived. The day after that, Dad took Brett, M'Lis and me back to the horse yards.

Bundy stood there, looking at us nonchalantly through lowered lashes.

'Saddle Bundy up,' Dad instructed Brett. 'Got to get back on. Can't ever let a horse think it's won. You must be the boss, always. Have to get back on and keep going.'

Brett swallowed hard. He went and got his saddle and bridle, put the bit in Bundy's mouth, did up the girth and climbed on. Bundy snorted, but let him stay there. M'Lis and I watched, frozen.

But Dad hadn't finished.

'You girls next,' said Dad. 'Get your horses. Saddle up, too. Then I want you three to go out and join the mob that Ray and Charlie are bringing back in from Palmer's Camp. By the time you get there they'll have reached the hills. They'll need some extra hands.'

There was no opportunity to shirk or be a wuss on Dad's watch. Every difficulty was just another learning curve to be overcome. And just like Ray had done with the colts and fillies, Dad was breaking us in, too.

Aunty June's 'ten falls'—and even the number suffered by Ray—faded into comparison with the number I managed as I learned to ride.

One of the worst came from a tall chestnut stock horse I was riding called Back to Front. We'd just finished pushing a mob into the cattle yards. I was on the tail and went to close the gate, but something startled Back to Front—maybe a bird—and he reared backwards. Shrieking, I fell backwards too, and thudded onto the dirt, flat on my back. It was a hard landing, which left my back badly bruised. I could hardly walk for days, but Dad said briskly, 'You didn't break anything, so you're okay.'

I had another fall chasing cattle. By then I'd become confident enough to chase cattle at a flat gallop if need be. So, there I was, leaning low over my horse's neck, trying to stop the getaways. One of the greatest sins of mustering was to let cattle get away; I couldn't let that happen. Even if I didn't always feel confident inside, I couldn't let anyone know, or let the men think I wasn't up to the job. The rule was clear and simple: you always brought the cattle home.

But this time, I was after two heifers who were fast and heading towards thick scrub. As my stock horse and I gained on them, my heart was thumping so hard I thought it would explode through my ribs. We hit the scrub and the heifers dived into the thicket, lost to sight. As we raced in after them, my horse hit a rabbit hole and stumbled. It was so unexpected and we were going so fast that I simply sailed straight over the top of his head.

This time I did break something—my collarbone—and by the time I got back to the homestead, and Mum got me to the hospital, it was hours later. Hospital was a place of white lights and beeping sounds. Mum was only allowed to return during visiting hours. I cried in loneliness for the first day.

My visit lasted a week, and to distract myself from the pain I asked Mum to bring me in a dictionary and a pen and paper. Then I spent my time in hospital teaching myself new words. M'Lis couldn't believe her eyes when she came to visit me.

'That has to be the most boring thing in the world to do!' she spluttered.

'Oh, no,' I said, carefully lifting the dictionary and paper filled with words. 'Look how many exciting words I've taught myself!'

One of those words was *interminable*.

Before long, I quite liked hospital. Despite missing Mum and everyone at home, it was exciting being somewhere new. I got to eat jelly and ice cream. Mum brought me books, which I could read without being told to go to bed, because I was already in bed. And I didn't have to get up to go to work or school, because I couldn't. Instead, I spent my time gazing admiringly at the nurses in their uniforms and made up stories in my head about life in a hospital. Plus, I knew I was getting out of a big, hot muster on the western side, which I knew would be *interminable*.

Over the years, I went on to break both wrists and ankles and numerous other body parts. But I wasn't lucky enough to get back into hospital.

———————

M'Lis broke no bones during her childhood. She was an excellent rider and managed her horses well. Brett did break bones, but that's because the stockmen and Dad thought he was up to riding the most difficult horses. Brett was a natural daredevil, so he relished the challenges, but nor was he given any choice. 'T'wasn't' easy for Brett, to be sure, as Irish Ray would say.

———————

On one of our trips to Witchitie where Dad now had an interim manager, we discovered that our beloved Shetland pony, Pinto, had died. Pinto was very old, and had passed away in the paddock, as we knew horses always did when it was their time. But we were bereft. M'Lis hid in our bedroom and sobbed, inconsolable, and wouldn't come out. Mum couldn't do anything with her. Finally, Dad came home from a bore run and went in. He sat down on the bed next to her and put his arm around her little shoulders.

'Now, Lis,' he said, in his calm, direct way (Dad always called her Lis, which was the family's special name for her), 'This is what happens. Animals and people die. It's part of life. We have to expect this to happen.'

M'Lis wiped her eyes.

He stood up and turned to her with a slow smile. 'It's how you love them when they're alive that matters.'

———>•<———

Dad certainly loved Limerick.

One year, he was persuaded to enter Limerick in the Stock and Station Horse Race at the Alice Springs Cup. It was to be held at the old racecourse, on the northern end of Alice. The event drew people from all over the bush to either watch or compete, and no one wanted to miss out. It was the annual chance to showcase the stock horses that formed the backbone of the stock camp and enabled the cattle stations to function. It was also a day of great pride as all the bush men paraded their favourite horses.

Dad would have the chance to show Limerick to the world. We knew he was the best horse ever, and that together, he and Dad could do anything. Dad trucked Limerick in the night before. He stabled him at a set of yards some way from the racecourse over a large hill, Mount Nancy. It was too big a risk to leave such a valuable horse alone in Alice Springs, so Dad took his swag and slept close to Limerick that night.

We all stayed at the Braitlings' town house that night, so we didn't have far to go the next day. We couldn't wait to meet Dad and Limerick at the racecourse for the big event, which took place at 11 a.m.

There were no jockey uniforms or caps for the participants of this race. Instead, Dad and the other bush men were in their usual attire: stock hats, Longhorn trousers, work shirts. At the starter's call, they mounted their horses, and cantered slowly down the racecourse to the starting blocks. It took about ten minutes for all the horses to get into place. Many of them were stirry and flighty, not used to people or town, and some were shying and pig-rooting.

Fortunately, Dad kept Limerick calm. When the starter's gun went off, Dad and Limerick streaked out to the lead. We hung over the fence, cheering Dad on, with Brett, and his great mate Aaron Gorey from neighbouring Yambah Station, leaning over the rails and cheering the loudest.

It was a fast and dusty race, the station men spurring their favourite steeds along the dirt track towards the finish line with grim determination. Those bush men were hugely competitive. Which horse would be the best? To our joy, we saw Dad keep the lead and then fly over the finish line in front of the others.

We grabbed each other and yelled, 'Limerick is the winner! Limerick is the winner!'

After the horses had slowed, turned and then cantered back towards us, the starter grabbed Dad's hand and raised it in the air in a triumphant salute. We kids were beside ourselves as Dad returned to the yards. He leaned over Limerick, patted him and dismounted. His face was covered in dirt, but a big grin shone through it. Limerick was sweating hard, his head and nose jerking up and down with the adrenaline of it all, but he looked like the happiest horse there ever was.

People were slapping Dad on the back and pointing him towards the bar where celebration awaited. Still grinning, Dad handed Brett Limerick's reins.

'Take 'im back to the stables, Brett. Give him water and hay and settle him down.'

But Brett was in bare feet. As was Aaron, who was hanging by his side.

Aaron never wore boots unless he had to. He'd grown up with a big group of Aboriginal kids on the station, and so his feet were as tough as leather. And while Brett's feet were pretty tough, they weren't at the same level of Aaron's. So, why Brett thought to remove his boots on race day made no sense, but presumably Mum hadn't discovered what Brett had done (she was trying to keep Benny from being trampled underfoot), and Brett wanted to show Aaron he was as tough as him.

Dad hadn't even noticed Brett's bare feet.

Brett went to protest—but nobody protested to Dad. So, he obediently took the reins and just hoped Limerick wouldn't step on him.

Besides, this was a big honour. Dad was allowing him to walk his precious and beloved Limerick back. It was no easy task, either, because Limerick was flighty and buzzing after the race.

Brett never forgot that walk. It was a long, long way, and the hike over Mount Nancy seemed even higher, bigger and longer as Limerick snorted and jumped and sidestepped and was hard to hold. He kept knocking Brett, and Brett had to keep jumping into the prickles to avoid being stepped on. The soles of his feet became increasingly swollen and pierced the further they walked.

Brett vowed he would never, ever take his boots off again. Aaron cheerfully marched beside him, unfazed.

15

Bush Art and Animals

Mum loved having visitors from 'down south' to stay. She would always take them out to show them our local history. We kids would have to go too, but we didn't mind, because there was lots of room to play and fun things to do, and we never got sick of hearing Mum's stories.

We would start at the Old Telegraph Station, a beautiful area of old stone buildings on the banks of the Todd River, just north of the town.

'This is where the town of Alice Springs really began, back in 1871,' she would say crisply, as though a tour guide. 'Although of course the Arrernte people were here for many thousands of years before then. Alice Springs is known as *Mparntwe*.' She would pause, then go on, 'And you know of John McDouall Stuart, of course?'

The visitors would usually nod politely, but she'd explain anyway. 'He was the famous explorer who travelled all the way from South Australia to the top end, where Darwin now is. Do you know', she'd pause again, 'the explorers back then hoped they'd find inland seas in the centre of this country? What a shock they must have got to discover it was mostly arid desert!'

The visitors would invariably nod politely again at this point, and Mum would sail on. 'Stuart was a very brave man. He opened up the inland, got scurvy, went blind, but thanks to him the Overland Telegraph Line was finally built from south to north. That meant Australia could be connected from end to end at last, and then to England through cables under the sea. They began relaying messages here by Morse code in 1872.'

Morse code! Cables under the sea! It sounded like something from one of my adventure books. We were so fascinated by it all, probably even more so than the visitors were, because it was *our* history. We loved exploring the old buildings where they still had some of the Morse code machines.

'Can you imagine', mused Mum, 'they only got supplies up once a year. You wouldn't want to miss out something in your order, would you? Ha-ha!'

Ha-ha, indeed!

The next beautiful place on Mum's tour was Pitchi Richi, a sanctuary just south of Heavitree Gap, built by an inspired man (we thought), Leo Corbett, in the 1950s. Its name meant 'gap in the ranges'. To us, it was a wonderful place for adventures.

The sanctuary was filled with birds and plants and red earth, shaded pathways, bushy hide-outs and turkey nest dams (just without the water). The dams were covered by huge athel pines in which we could play hide and seek.

Just like at the Old Telegraph Station, there was an area set up as though the pioneers were still living here. There were old leather bags and saddles, an old wooden wagon (complete with the name *Overlander* painted on the side), which we could climb and play on. There was a rusty bush oven set up in a round fireplace with an iron tucker box, iron water container and copper pot. Swags were dotted around, so we sat on them and pretended to make dinner camp like we were pioneers.

There was also a dark cave filled with what we thought were precious stones. When we peered in, gold and silver sparkled through the dim light. Mum told us they were actually local gem-stones, and even though we were disappointed they weren't like the kind of stones in *The Magic Faraway Tree*, we loved their colours.

But perhaps best of all, the bush garden was dotted with fasci-nating statues. They looked to us like they'd been made out of red earth and water mixed together, coming straight from the Dreamtime. Aboriginal faces and people were interwound with wildlife and plants and trees. Some were tiny busts. Others were large works, taller than us.

The creator's name was William Ricketts, and I thought he must have been deeply in touch with God, because some of the statues really looked like angels with flowing hair and their faces turned up to heaven.

———————

One day a tall, bearded man turned up in a battered Land Rover pulling an old trailer piled high with camping equipment.

'I'm a painter,' he said simply. 'I've been wanting to paint the space and light of the Centre for a long time. Hate bitumen roads. Would you let me camp by one of your creeks for a couple of weeks?'

Normally Dad would have sent somebody like this on their way. He was wary of strangers being on the place. It meant gates left open, fences cut, cattle disturbed and—worst of all—in some instances, his precious cattle killed.

But the owner of the Alice Springs Arunta Gallery, a formidable woman named Iris Harvey, had sent the painter to us with a character reference. He had a name—Brian Nunan—and he was a renowned artist in his home state of Victoria. Mrs Harvey already sold his works and wanted more from him.

So, in an unusual fit of benevolence, Dad said the painter could camp down near the Todd for a couple of weeks to paint, as long as he kept his fire under control at all times—'And make sure you shut the gate.'

Brian headed off happily and, on the way, met Mum. She was driving home from doing a bore run for Dad—with us in tow—and had a flat tyre. In true pragmatic style, she was just about to start changing it. Brian couldn't believe the sight of this slight figure of a woman carting a huge tyre around, a gaggle of children at her side. He jumped out, introduced himself and changed the tyre for Mum—immediately charming her in the process.

M'Lis, Brett and I were intrigued by this new arrival. We knew what it was like to be out in the stock camp for a couple of weeks, but we were never on our own. How did the painter survive out there, all by himself? And what did he do? We'd never seen a painter before. Was he like the man who made the statues at Pitchi Richi? Perhaps he really *was* him in disguise?

Over the first week Dad went down several times to check that everything was in order, and soon we started to beg him to take us with him, to see the painter in action. After a week, Dad relented, and we all, including Mum, piled into the back of the Land Rover and headed towards the creek. It was about a half-hour drive from the homestead but utterly idyllic—big, sandy bed, huge old gum trees, birds sailing above, peace and quiet.

As we arrived, we saw the most extraordinary sight.

Brian's Land Rover and trailer were neatly parked in a semicircle, around a small fire and Primus stove and swag. In the middle was the bearded artist himself, looking a little like the pictures we had seen of Moses in the Bible. Unlike Moses, though, he was splattered in paint from head to toe, sketching the creek bed onto a large exercise book with big bits of charcoal. Several easels stood around and paint tins were scattered at his feet. A billy was boiling.

'Love charcoal,' he said, simply, pointing to his current work, his big hands still flying over the page, black everywhere, even smudged onto his nose. 'Cuppa?'

We crowded around, mystified by the drawing and fascinated by the smell of the oils and paint. It was hot and there were plenty of flies, but the painter didn't seem to notice.

He didn't have a generator, or any kind of power, so he lived very simply. Lots of root vegetables—carrots, potatoes, pumpkin— some tinned fish, powdered milk, flour for damper. Foodstuffs he could keep in his tucker box that wouldn't go off.

Mum had brought a cake, so we had a feast around the fire.

'I love your animals,' he said, as he poured us tea in pannikins from the bubbling billy. 'They have a real sense of humour.'

He told us the cattle would wander up to his camp, congregate and gaze soulfully at him for hours. They had all sorts of facial expressions, many of which Brian was able to capture on paper and would go on to use as the basis for cattle paintings in the future. It was the same with the horses. They'd sneak up behind him and lick the charcoal off his pages. As he turned and yelled, 'Oi!' the horses would jump away, flicking their tails. They kept him amused and intrigued.

'They're very intelligent,' he said. 'It's a game.'

We were sorry to leave Brian and go back to the homestead. But he stayed with us for three weeks. And then for another three.

And another three. Towards the end of his stay, Dad invited him to come and watch some of the yard work with the cattle.

When Brian finally left, he said, 'Would you mind if I come back next year? I'd like to do some paintings for you.'

Brian came the next year, and the next year, and the year after that. We finally discovered he had a wife and children. And that alcohol was one of the demons he'd had to fight. So, he went bush to survive. Some years he brought his wife, who was a lovely, strong woman named Pat. But we learned that he needed to go away to paint on a regular basis and live in solitude.

'I have no choice,' he once said simply. 'I have a terrible feeling of frustration if I can't paint and draw. I am happiest when I'm alone in the bush doing what I need to do. I lose myself.'

Not only did he go on to paint beautiful paintings of Bond Springs, he infused his paintings with stockmen on horseback, working cattle, Dad and his beloved DQG, the hills and the flats and the bores and the dams. His powerful, rich ochres and blues perfectly portrayed the red heat and dust of our daily lives.

We loved the painter. He knew us. He *got* us.

On his third trip, Mum and Dad asked him if he would paint portraits of us kids. He agreed, no doubt reluctantly, because that meant he had to stay at the homestead and deal with live human subjects.

M'Lis and I were terribly thrilled, though. We were let out of school to go for our sittings in the—of course—sitting room, where Brian had set up easels, paints and charcoal, and Mum had sensibly put sheets all over the floor. Brett wasn't as excited and insisted on being painted wearing his bush hat. Benny came last and of course, being just a youngster, couldn't sit still for more than a couple of minutes. He'd jump up and run outside and go back to playing under the pepper trees. Brian got in the habit of simply following him with his sketchbook and sketching Benny under those pepper trees.

'Not so happy with this painting of Benny,' he sighed, after Mum hung all the portraits on the sitting-room wall. 'He was just too hard to capture, always being on the move.'

That was our Benny. And that was our Mr Nunan, as we kids called him, a wondrous spirit for us all.

And he came to us every year for over forty years.

———⊰⊚⊱———

In the meantime, Dad kept building opportunities.

His father had taught him to never put all his eggs in one basket, and he was ever conscious of locals saying that Bond Springs was unviable on its own, so he set about 'diversifying our interests'.

To start with, he decided to link Bond Springs with other properties to ensure its long-term viability. He'd seen how others had successfully done this, and with the support of Elders GM and yet another increase on the overdraft, Dad bought another cattle lease a hundred or so kilometres north of Bond Springs. It was called Singleton, and was larger than the Bond, with rich grassy plains and excellent water. This gave Dad flexibility, meaning he could move cattle between the three leases according to the seasons. When it was dry on the Bond, we could truck cattle down to Witchitie, which had high-protein saltbush, or up north with its green, grassy flats and soft water. Singleton was an excellent fattening block, unlike Bond Springs and Witchitie, both of which were marginal country and mostly dry.

But juggling the workload of three properties became a big problem.

Dad was constantly moving people from one station to another—sometimes by truck, or Land Rover, or in his Cessna 182—depending on what was required according to the different times and seasons. Everyone kept in contact via the two-way radio but that was unreliable. You could only talk at certain times, information was always delayed, and you couldn't always speak openly. In the end, Dad was in the air almost more than he was on the ground, and he was often away from the homestead more than he was there.

One night, we heard the familiar drone of DQG approaching, and rushed outside, on full alert, as we always did.

'I spend my *life* waiting for that man to come home!' said Mum, as she stood at the back gate, gazing up into the sky. Her tone was a mixture of wistfulness and exasperation.

The familiar outline of DQG was silhouetted against the darkening sky. It dived and swooped with a roar over the homestead. Then it turned, and came in to land quickly.

I looked back at the sky. The sunset colours that had filled it moments ago were dying. Five minutes more and Dad wouldn't have been able to see the airstrip. But that was Dad. He timed his flights—in fact, everything in his life—so he didn't waste a minute.

But by now, even Dad knew he was stretched. So, he went searching again for people from the area he knew and trusted—the mid-north and Flinders Ranges of South Australia.

Before long he found a full-time bore man and mechanic for Bond Springs. Then he persuaded his great friend from Elders GM, Malcolm Roberts, to take his family up to Singleton. Finally, he employed a couple, Mike and Margaret Kimber, who had four young girls, Jane, Sally, Kate and Margot. They took over the full-time management of Witchitie.

The house at Singleton was no more than a huge corrugated-iron shed with concrete floors. It was tough living up there and unbelievably hot. Mum constantly said, 'I don't know how Malcolm and Jan and the kids are coping.'

Malcolm and Jan and their two children, Grant and Andrea, coped amazingly well, and went on to develop long-term business partnerships with Mum and Dad.

Down at Witchitie, Dad brought in a large demountable for the Kimbers to live in, because otherwise they would have had to live in our house, and that would have been a bit squashed when we went down. The demountable was some distance from the main house, and Dad built verandas around it, and plumbed in water and sewerage.

On our first visit to meet the Kimber family, we crowded into the demountable kitchen for smoko. The girls were younger than us and stayed close to Margaret, undoubtedly wary of us. Suddenly Brett looked over to the corner and shouted.

'Mum, snake!'

In front of us a large snake slid across the room. Everybody froze, then screamed. With one move, Mum scooped us all up onto the table. I clutched Benny tight.

'Stay there, stay there,' she ordered, before she and Margaret raced after the snake. Margaret must have wondered what kind of wild place she'd arrived in as she and Mum pulled the house apart. We kids sat frozen on the table, and as the search went on and on with no result, we became fidgety. 'Can we get off now?' we begged.

'Not yet,' said Mum, her face set with determination. No snake was going to get away on her watch. You couldn't let it go; if it disappeared into your house, you'd never feel safe and you couldn't risk your children being bitten. Snakes did not belong inside.

On a hunch, she tipped over the linen basket, and all the clothes fell out—along with the snake. It came out slithering through the garments amid more shrieks, until Mum killed it with a broom handle.

We were so proud of her. She had protected us from possible death.

What a brave mother.

Then we climbed off the table and went safely back to play with our new friends.

16

Bush Music

Dad had a beautiful voice and he had sung the old Methodist hymns at church with Papa since he was a little boy. During our early years at Glenroy and Witchitie, I had soaked in these melodies and harmonies on a weekly basis. Whenever we returned down south for holidays and Christmas, I would soak them in all over again.

The little country churches at Cradock or Hawker or Carrieton would ring with 'When I Survey the Wondrous Cross', 'How Great Thou Art', 'Guide Me O Thou Great Redeemer', and 'The Lord is My Shepherd'. Being part of the singing of these hymns connected me with something far bigger than myself. It always brought goosebumps to my skin and tears to my eyes.

Sometimes Dad sang 'Danny Boy'. Every time, a lump would reach my throat as his voice transported me into the green and beautiful vales of Ireland where Danny Boy had once roamed and would never return. I would wait for Dad to hit that exquisite high note, and he always did, pitch-perfect, holding it for just as long as was appropriate, and finishing the last note with his eyes lowered, as if in prayer.

Dad had grown up with family singing around the piano, as well as singing hymns all weekend, so singing was normal for him, and a legitimate way to express his deep emotions, which he usually kept hidden. Singing always made him smile, right up to his eyes. It always made us feel close to him and so happy.

Mind you, he never sang in front of the stockmen—just us.

One day, when Dad was in a slightly philosophical mood, he let slip that his God was in the trees and the landscape, in the bush and the skies. Dad didn't say that his God *wasn't* in a church, but we instinctively knew his deep connection was to the land.

But in every other way Dad was a Methodist to his core. For him, his religion was found in hard work, never giving up and always being grateful. Dad always said grace before dinner, and the whole table, stockmen included, had to bow their heads and give thanks for what we were all about to receive.

Mum taught us prayers and was very spiritual, in her wild, Irish way.

When we were being particularly naughty and fighting, she would shout in despair, 'And you children are meant to be Christians!' We knew that meant Mum was very angry and we should feel great shame. I spent a lot of time on my hands and knees praying and repenting and longed to be back in Mum's good books and be called a Christian. It meant that life was easier and better if we behaved in a way that made Mum happy.

Mum loved music too and she ensured we were exposed to it from a very young age. Dear Mum was tone deaf but that didn't stop her from singing to us constantly—nursery rhymes when we were little, which taught us words and repetition, and undoubtedly helped grow our neural pathways—and teaching us songs and their meanings.

One day, Dad brought home a huge surprise for us: a tiny, bright-red record player, with an LP called, 'The Ugly Duckling'. It was a very sad song, but we played it over and over, until we could sing the words in our sleep.

Dad might have been tough on us with station work, but when it came to music he was generous and kind-hearted.

Of course, Slim Dusty and Charley Pride were the most famous of all singers for bush people, because they sang ballads about our lives. We loved them. Even though Charley Pride was American, we still felt he sang for us. All bush songs were a mixture of the funny and sad and inspirational. They were played on the local radio station and sung by the stockmen and became the soundtrack of our lives.

We knew by heart the words to Slim Dusty's poignant 'Saddle Boy', 'Rusty, It's Goodbye' and 'Leave Him in the Long Yard'. We often cried when we sang them. Losing horses, dogs and people in the bush was something we now all understood. It was heartache for all of us when we lost them. But perhaps Slim Dusty's most profound song was 'Hard Hard Country'. It reflected perfectly what we already knew to be the case: that the bush was an incredibly harsh environment, and to live and survive in it you had to be an incredibly hard man or woman.

Slim Dusty was lucky to share his musical life with the beautiful and talented Joy McKean. Not only did she play the fiddle, she wrote many of his great songs. And best of all, they were married, but Joy always kept her maiden name—presumably because she was an entertainer with that name before she even met him.

She was my first pin-up gal for independence.

We loved the fact that Joy and Slim sang deeply spiritual songs set against a bush background. 'The Old Rugged Cross', 'Heaven Country Style' and 'When the Golden Sliprails are Down' were always reverently played. Given our Methodist upbringing with Wesley hymns, we connected unconsciously to such ballads. We had sliprails on the edge of the trough paddock next to the horse yards, so I always imagined Slim and Joy walking together hand in hand towards them, watching them glow brighter the closer they got, until they were completely illuminated in a blaze of gold.

M'Lis was lucky enough to get *Slim Dusty's Greatest Hits* for her birthday, which meant we could play the songs over and over whenever we wanted to rather than wait for them to come over the radio. Next in line was Brett's birthday and so we got *Charley Pride's Greatest Hits* as well. We were ecstatic. 'The Crystal Chandeliers' and 'Me and Bobby McGee' got a huge workout.

Now we had our two favourite records, there was room for just one more.

The Bangtail Muster by Ted Egan.

We loved Ted Egan like he was our own national hero, which in a way he was. Ted lived in Alice Springs and wrote and sang songs about the characters of the Territory, of which there were many, and accompanied himself on an empty Fosters beer carton. He played it like it was a guitar crossed with a drum and called it a Fosterphone. We thought he was the most marvellous musician in the world. Whenever there was a chance to see Ted perform, we would plead for Mum to take us, and she always would. Ted had twinkling eyes and lots of time for us kids and let us sing along with him. Our favourite song was 'The Drinkers of the Territory'. It was beyond outrageous that we could legitimately sing, 'Oh, they've got some bloody good drinkers in the Northern Territory' at the tops of our voices and get away with it. We learned all his songs and could sing them anywhere at the drop of a hat. So, for my birthday, I received the large LP, *The Bangtail Muster*, and we were set.

———✦———

Our good-natured Irish stockman Ray Murtagh continued to play guitar and sing with us. Our favourite nights were when we were out in the stock camp, sitting on swags, watching the crackling flames flicker up into the air and light the darkness as we listened to Ray sing to the stars. Someone would lift the billy off the fire with a long piece of wire and we'd all drink sweet black tea. Ray's gentle lyrics and guitar playing transported us to different times and places.

We desperately wanted to play guitar like Ray. And we told him, again and again, until finally he said to Mum, 'To be sure, these kids need to play the guitar, Mrs H.'

So, to be sure, Mum lined up weekly guitar lessons in town. Of course, we hated the trip in and out but we loved the lessons. A quiet young man with greasy hair taught us the guitar in a little studio next to the general store, which sold lollies, so there was always an incentive to go. We all learned earnestly and practised our chords determinedly. We might have only been three-chord-wonder kids, but before long we three were playing together and singing every country song we knew. As Benny grew up, he would join in banging a stool, and go on to become a brilliant drummer.

———✦———

One day Mum said that she and Dad would take us on a big outing.

'We're going to see *The Sound of Music* at the Alice Springs drive-in,' Mum enthused. She seemed very happy about this.

We'd heard about the drive-in from Ray and Charlie, and we could hardly believe that Dad was going to stop work and come on an evening outing with us. We didn't know what the movie was about, and we didn't really care.

'It's about music, so you'll love it,' promised Mum.

It was a Saturday night. Mum packed beef sandwiches and a thermos of tea, and a thermos of cordial for us as a treat. We all piled into the car; Benny was on my lap, of course. Dad drove in his usual fast manner, and before we knew, we were heading through the Heavitree Gap towards a vacant paddock, at the end of which sat a huge screen. We shrieked and Dad roared his usual 'Quiet!' but even he didn't seem as cross with us as usual tonight.

We followed a long line of tail-lights, Dad stopping to buy tickets from a man at the gate, and then drove in to where there were lines and lines of parked cars. Dad chose a good spot, near the centre, and arranged for a speaker to be put inside the windows on either side of the car.

'When will it start?' we pestered Mum as she distributed the sandwiches, until Dad roared again and we really were quiet then for a while, until Mum whispered, 'It's starting!'

To my amazement, the sounds of an orchestra floated through the speakers, and before us emerged Julie Andrews running across her Austrian meadows, twirling in her pinafore, arms outstretched. I leaned forward, utterly enchanted.

I'd never heard anything so glorious. The music filled the entirety of the car in surround-sound from the two speakers. For nearly three hours I barely breathed. (In the same way I'd become entranced by *The Magic Faraway Tree* from the very first reading, I was entranced by *The Sound of Music* from the very first viewing.)

I didn't really understand the scary bits or the dangerous bits or the sad bits. Dad later said that it was important for us to understand them when we grew up, because they were about the war. But none of that dimmed the star quality of the show for me—the music, the romance, the love, the glorious setting—the magic of it all. The scenes depicted exactly where I imagined all my Enid Blyton and Heidi storybooks were set. Snowy mountains, beautiful lakes, chateaux and mansions, green fields and dark woods.

To cap off the wonderful evening, when we got home Dad carried us all into bed. We'd fallen asleep as the car rocked its way towards Bond Springs and were groggy when we pulled up. Mum gathered Benny in her arms and Dad picked up Brett, and they both whispered, 'M'Lis and Tanya, wait there'. We were happy to obey, snuggling up to each other and pretending to be asleep when Dad returned. We both longed for him to carry us too. And he did—M'Lis first, and then me. I burrowed into Dad's strong arms and felt so safe as he strode over the gravel.

We were all given a special treat from Mum. 'You don't have to clean your teeth tonight, it's too late. Just quickly get into your pyjamas and hop into bed and I'll kiss you goodnight.'

We did, our heads and hearts filled with visions of the evening— and snatches of Dad humming 'Edelweiss' as we drifted off to sleep.

From that moment I longed for the record of *The Sound of Music*. Luckily, Christmas was close, so it was a joint present for us on that special day, and we played it until the needle nearly rubbed through the record. I had found a place and a story where I knew I belonged.

It was made all the better by Dad singing 'Edelweiss' along with us whenever he strode past.

17

DQG in Full Flight

Once we began mustering, our lives changed. We were away almost as much as we were home during the mustering season. There was school, obviously, but Dad would regularly crunch over the gravel up to the schoolroom door and order us out to work if he needed help.

Stockmen, including Charlie and Ray, came and went. That was the reality of trying to hire and keep staff on a cattle station in Central Australia. Many were drifters or nomadic or simply wanted to try different places to work. Dad found it hugely frustrating every time a stockman left, often with little notice, because it messed with his tight schedule.

So it meant we quickly became good at what we had to do, because, as Dad told us, we were 'the core' of his workforce.

Each muster would take a similar format.

We would walk our horses all the way to our destination stockyards, which usually took a day, depending how far the paddock was. Once there, we would feed and water and hobble the horses, set up camp, light a fire, cook the steak and boil the billy, then head to our swags. By dawn, we'd be up to bring in the horses, saddle them up and head out for the muster. That would usually take all day. Sometimes it would take several days if the paddock was very big and we'd have to set up mini stock camps throughout the paddock, with different people camping at different spots.

We didn't use packhorses anymore to carry food, as the Land Rover was more efficient (assuming there was someone available to drive it). The tucker box would be filled with corned beef, cold roast beef, tomato sauce, flour, tea, sugar, and enamel plates, knives, forks, spoons and pannikin mugs. Steak was only for the first night (it wouldn't last long beyond that, with the heat, flies and ants). But there was lots of bread (rarely time to make damper) and treats like apricot jam and strawberry jam to put on the bread (which quickly became dry, so we mostly toasted it over the coals). The biggest treat of all was rice-cream and little tins of peaches in juice, which we'd take for something sweet after the evening meal if we were away for a long time.

On the day we left, I was reminded of the days we used to watch the stock camp heading out, when we were just little kids and holding on to Mum's hand. Now it was just Mum standing there waving us off. It was like watching ourselves inside an old movie. By now I was nine, M'Lis was eight and Brett seven, and we were practically grown up.

Dad started to fly the musters as well, which made them more efficient.

We'd ride out at daylight and listen for the hum of the plane in the distance, flying towards us. I always felt a huge sense of relief as the speck in the sky grew closer—*Dad's here. Everything's all right.*

The early part of the muster was my favourite. Dad would be diving and weaving in his plane, looking for cattle hiding along the

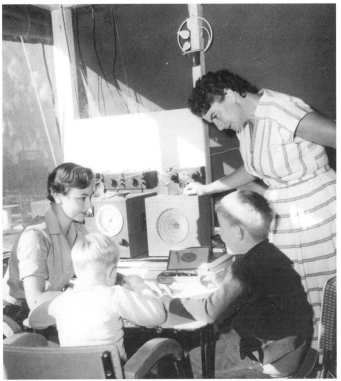

'Governess Mum' on Hamilton Downs Station, overseeing School of the Air lessons with (from right to left) Aunty Dawn and Gary and David Prior.

Mum and Dad's wedding, 1961—'the happiest day of my life,' said Mum. As a wedding gift, Dad made her a kangaroo skin blanket, which she kept on their bed their whole married life.

Brett on an old stock horse at the Bond Springs stockyards, aged eighteen months. He was a natural-born horseman.

Brett, with Dad's hat and stockwhip, aged three, ready for action!

Brett and Mum (in one of her many gorgeous home-sewn frocks) and Dad's beloved horse, Limerick.

A hot day at Singleton: (*from left to right*) Me, Benny (with Dad's hat), Dad, Mum, M'Lis and Brett, 1969.

Homestead horse yards—horses saddled and ready for mustering. As soon as we kids could ride, we were off to the stock camp.

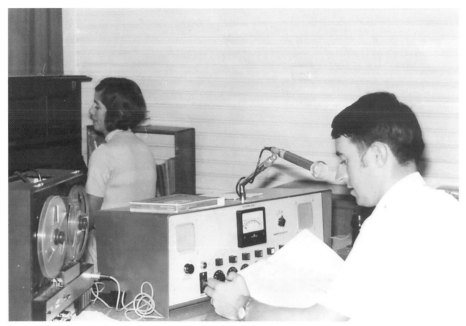

Some of my best memories are of my time learning through the School of the Air. Here, Mrs Hodder plays the piano while Mr Ashton reads the news in the School of the Air studio. (Courtesy S. Hodder)

Bore runs were a daily part of life, and the whole family would squash into Dad's Land Rover and head out: (*from left to right*) Me, M'Lis and Brett (peeking out from the trough). As Dad checked the bores, we made our own fun in the dirt and dust.

The whole family, with our baby Benny, 1969.

Me in the homestead horse yard, nearly eight, in 1970. Having horses as friends was one of the best parts of every outback kid's life.

'The open shirt shot'—my first visit to Everard Park Station to visit my friend Jane Joseland—riding her beloved Lucy.

'Young rodeo rider' Brett, at age six, with Dad in the cattle yards. Stockman Ross Coop is in the background.

Janie Joseland doing School of the Air lessons in the stock camp. It was the School of the Air that allowed my friendship with Janie to build, until we could finally meet in person. (Courtesy J. Joseland)

Mrs Hodder and friends making music in the School of the Air studio for us kids out bush 1971. (Courtesy S. Hodder)

Miss Clarke, our much-loved governess, with Benny on a pony, Midge, outside the homestead, 1970. Miss Clarke was like a younger sister to my parents, and welcome company for Mum. And of course, she kept us in line!

From left to right: Brett, me and M'Lis at Miss Clarke's beautiful wedding. We loved her so much and were very sad to say goodbye.

From left to right: M'Lis, me, Mum, Brett (with hand wrapped, ever ready for combat) and Benny, on the homestead lawn, 1972. Mum was forever busy, but she always found time to give us lots of love and hugs.

Me on our beloved Pinto on the Witchitie lawn. We all had to prove we could ride bareback before we were allowed to graduate to a saddle.

Dad, Brett and the Land Rover, at 'dinner camp' during a muster. Hot, dirty, exhausted—but still a grin from Dad. Working with cattle out bush was our life.

Drafting wild cattle in red dirt, red dust and mulga scrub. We all worked hard during drafting, which often led to some near misses and heart-stopping moments. (Courtesy B. Braitling)

Such glamour! My beautiful Mum and my handsome Dad at an Alice Springs Ball, 1971.

Gorgeous Aunty Jill and Uncle Pete Gemmell, dancing at Bond Springs, 1973.

Mr and Mrs Gorey dancing on the Bond Springs patio, 1973.

Mrs Braitling and her beloved 'Echo Foxtrot Whiskey'. The pilots were mostly men, and so we kids greatly admired women like Mrs Braitling, who took to the air. I loved her ready laugh; she and Mum were like sisters.

From left to right:
Dad, Mr Crowson and
Mr Braitling playing
'wild bullocks' at the
Dalhousie 'Fly-in', a
rare moment of fun for
these hardworking bush
blokes.

Brett and his best,
bootless buddy Aaron
Gorey, having breakfast
out bush, 1971.

From left to right: Brett,
M'Lis, Benny and me, in
the homestead stables,
1971. Always together.

From left to right: Me, M'Lis, Brett and Benny, on the homestead lawns.

From left to right: Me, Benny, M'Lis and Brett, swinging on the horse yards gates.

From left to right: Brett, Benny, me and M'Lis, outside the kitchen, ready for horse action at the Alice Springs show. It was always such an adventure to go to the show!

Our schoolroom, where
I spent many of my
happiest moments.
I loved every bit of
school, except for maths!

From left to right: Me,
M'Lis and cheeky Brett
with our new wonderful
governess, Miss Thiele,
in the schoolroom.

Me, concentrating hard, during
School of the Air on our two-way
radio. Oh, the joy I felt every day
talking to my teachers and on-air
friends! It fostered my love of
learning for life.

Dad in front of his beloved DQG; Mum (on the right) in a 'pantsuit of the day', with friends.

M'Lis and Brett, ready for the Alice Springs show, with our legendary Head Stockman Charlie Gorey, 1972.

Me on Sandy at the Alice Springs show, when I won my first-ever ribbon. I trained so hard and was so proud to come third in 'Quietest Horse and Pony'!

Janie Joseland on her beautiful horse Lucy, with Benny.

Dad and stockman Barry Elliott, at 'dinner camp' during a long, cold, winter's muster. Both men silent, thinking, in the way of bush men.

Our much-loved Head Stockman Mick Schmidt, leaning up against his swag in the stock camp, blackened billy in front. Mick had such a cheeky grin and laugh!

Barry Elliott, leading his camels down the railway line through Alice Springs'
Heavitree Gap, early 1970s. We called Barry the 'camileer'.

From left to right: Benny, Robbie and Rhonda Schmidt, and Eeyore John Wayne, on Mum's precious lawn. That donkey was a menace, but Benny loved him.

The orange typewriter Mum and Dad gave me for my tenth birthday—my most magical present ever. I wrote many stories on that typewriter and escaped into exciting new worlds.

From left to right: Brett, me and M'Lis in our best jodhpurs with our governess Miss Thiele celebrating her twenty-first birthday. She was a natural teacher and didn't put up with much mischief from us, but we loved her.

Alice Springs School of the Air camp—Lea Turner (on the left) and me (on the right), with Eric Turner, Jamie Turner, Grant Roberts and others.

M'Lis and me at School of the Air camp, 1974. These camps were a great opportunity for us to spend face-to-face time with our on-air classmates.

M'Lis and me playing our guitars around the campfire at School of the Air camp, 1974. We loved to sing and play whenever we had a chance.

From left to right: Benny, me and Janie Joseland after a game of 'cattleduffers'. This was our favourite way to spend a day—crouched low over our galloping horses, fighting off 'baddies' and protecting Dad's precious cattle.

From left to right: Brett, me, M'Lis and Benny in the homestead horse yards, some years on.

Dad on his beloved Limerick. We rode many horses growing up, but we were never allowed on Limerick (except M'Lis—once). He was Dad's pride and joy.

boundary or in scrub, where they weren't very visible to us. We'd all split up to make the best use of resources, galloping fast to meet him. Some would head towards the plane and some away, trying to cover the entirety of the paddock.

Dad of course couldn't communicate directly with us on the ground, so he would dip his wings and roar over the top of us when he wanted our attention. After a while he started opening the window of the plane and yelling out instructions as he dive-bombed us. That rarely worked because we couldn't hear a thing over the roar of the engine. It did impact the stock, though, which would flee in terror.

To avoid this, Dad started scribbling notes and dropping them out the window, which was a nightmare because the note would flutter off and be lost in the wind before we could get to it. Or if it simply fell to the ground, it was always a challenge to follow it with our eyes from the plane window to where it landed. A lost note was a terrifying thing. As often as not, we couldn't find it, and Dad would furiously scribble another one. His writing was almost indecipherable on a good day, but when he was trying to fly and scribble a note, it was almost impossible to read.

We all became as telepathic as possible, trying to intuit what a turn of the plane or a dip of the wing meant. Sometimes it worked and sometimes it didn't. The person who actually found the note, picked it up and read it was the hero of the hour. We'd all race to hover around, anxiously, trying to decipher Dad's instructions. We always feared Dad's fury if he was forced to land in the middle of nowhere to give those instructions in person.

One day, when Charlie was still with us, we were mustering Bendy Bore on the west side. We quickly learned to hate that leg of mustering more than anything. Flat, red earth and thick scrub provided a perfect place for unwilling cattle to simply sit down in and either hide or not move. It was an endless trek. It was always stinking hot and because it was such a long route, we would have to go without water for hours. The water in our water bags was precious and was kept for emergency sips.

We had camped overnight at the aptly titled Mob'o'rock Dam, and in the early light we started our long trek to Weii Ben Dam, named after the birth of Benny. The plan was for us to pick up cattle from that dam and paddock and move them on to Bendy. Dad flew over us and dropped a note. As usual we all rushed to get it. M'Lis got there first, jumped off her horse and grabbed it, climbed back on again and read it out to us all, triumphantly. *'Cattle in the Round Yard in dam.'*

We were all confused. The round yard was back at Mob'o'rock, which we'd just left. We didn't know what to do. Did that mean Dad had run the cattle back to it? That didn't make sense. However, we were too scared to disobey orders, so we turned around and galloped back towards the bore we had just left.

We were secretly hopeful. Perhaps this meant we didn't have to do the long, dreadful trek to Weii Ben after all. But as we galloped back from where we'd just come, Dad's plane hurtled towards us. The next minute he dive-bombed us with another note.

We hammered to a halt, our stomachs sinking. This time Charlie jumped off and grabbed it. He read out loud, slowly. *'Can't you read? Cattle in Weii Ben Dam.'*

Charlie shouted to M'Lis, 'Gimme that first note, eh?'

M'Lis fished it out from her pocket with dirty fingers and Charlie did a lengthy comparison. Charlie rubbed his forehead under his hat.

Then he read out, 'Cattle *in and around* yard *and* dam.'

Dammit—we were off to Weii Ben after all. Turning our horses back, we galloped again to try to catch up to the plane.

Dammit. Dammit.

Eventually, Dad realised the notes weren't very successful, so he had a loudspeaker fitted to the plane. We all hoped that would help, though we were nervous it would frighten the cattle. There was still the roar of the plane engine too, so we could rarely hear more than half the message. His jumbled voice would burst in and out, and we'd all turn to each other, shouting, 'What did he say? What did he say?'

When it was obvious that we didn't understand Dad, he would dive-bomb us again, even closer and more terrifyingly, yelling harder. Sometimes it worked and sometimes we were none the wiser. In the latter case, we raised our hands to him, hoping he'd realised we hadn't understood. Then he'd fly off and we'd be forced to follow him, hearts in our mouths, hoping what he was saying was 'Follow me' and fearing the consequences if it wasn't.

Once, we were out at New Well Bore. It was wintertime, 6 a.m. and one degree. We'd camped out the night before and were in thick jackets, our hats pulled low, our fingers blue in the frosty morning as we rode out. Our breath froze on the chilled air. Then we heard the familiar drone and finally saw the plane, with Dad swooping over the top of us. We made out the words, 'Cattle . . . behind . . . hill. Follow me.' Or at least that's what we thought he said.

After a quick, frozen discussion, we all agreed it was.

M'Lis and Brett turned to each other and grinned. Then they offered up what would become their standard response: 'And good morning to you, too, Dad.'

———◆———

When Dad did have to land—usually because he needed to give instructions we hadn't understood—it was risky and I always felt sick to the stomach. Would there be somewhere safe for him to land? Would we incur his wrath for forcing him to land? Then, assuming he did land safely, could he take off again?

The ground was invariably rocky and pitted with rabbit holes and spinifex tussocks, or sandy and scrubby. Light aircraft were built to land and take off on airstrips, not in wild bushland. Landing and taking off were also the most perilous part of flying, according to Dad. 'Easiest part is when you're in the air,' he'd say. Our innards would twist whenever we saw him roaring towards the ground.

One New Year's Day Brett was out at New Well Bore helping Dad put in a dam. Brett was on the ground, driving the Land Rover (he'd started to drive it when he was five so was pretty good now), and Dad landed to give instructions. Dad only had a short distance in which to land but Brett watched him get the plane down, skidding to a fast halt. Dad got out, gave his instructions to Brett, then got straight back in the plane. Brett looked in concern at the space in which Dad had to take off—at least half that of the airstrip at the homestead—but Dad simply kicked the propeller into life and roared off, pulling the plane up into a U-turn in order to get the wheels off the ground. Brett watched, stunned, convinced Dad would crash in the middle of the U-turn. But the next thing, Dad pulled the plane up and was soon just a speck in the sky.

Another time, Brett and Charlie were out mustering at the greatly misnamed Tanya Dam (it took in water for a couple of years and then dried up, becoming completely useless after that). Dad landed on a small flat with his usual skidding stop, met with the team and gave instructions. Then he climbed back into the plane. However, due to recent rain, the small flat now had a huge ditch in the middle. While Dad had been able to put the plane down, there was no room to take off. Undeterred, Dad kicked the engine into life, upped the speed, put on second-phase flaps to the wings, and got just enough speed to 'leap' the plane over the ditch, before touching down on the other side and then pulling the plane up into the air. It was a miracle. Brett later explained it to me like this: A one-phase flap is used in aircraft to create speed, while second and third phases slow the aircraft for landing. Dad had worked out that second phase also got DQG's wheels off the ground quickly, without the plane climbing upwards, which meant he could use it to jump over ditches, logs or big rocks in the way. So in effect, DQG clawed itself off the ground to a height of a couple of metres for a distance of about fifty metres, until it was safe for Dad to increase speed, after which he'd climb upwards. Yes, it was absolutely a miracle!

Brett was once in the Plant Paddock mustering, with Dad overhead. Dad nose-dived over some cattle, then pulled the plane up high, arcing back onto the cattle with a turn so sharp that the plane should have stalled. But to Brett's disbelief, Dad dived again, pulled out and flew over the nearby Bushranger Yard with aplomb.

Over the years we got to see firsthand Dad's skill of twisting the plane around, descending low over cattle or fences and then pulling up with the stall button flashing and beeping furiously. *Beep beep beep beep beep beep!* In the end Dad got so sick of the button flashing and beeping that he got some thick black tape and stuck it over the top of the button. It still beeped, but at least he couldn't see the flashing, which he said was distracting.

Mum was horrified, and said we weren't allowed to tell anyone about *any* of this.

Charlie refused to go up with Dad unless he absolutely had to. Indeed, most people avoided flying with Dad when he was mustering—he flew like one of the 'Dambuster' pilots, low over bridges and dams, ready to bomb them—but Brett and I loved going with him in the early days.

Dad could have been a war pilot, Mrs Braitling confirmed admiringly. 'He's a natural—flies by the seat of his pants!'

The daredevil aspect of it sent a rush through me like nothing I'd ever experienced, not even galloping flat out on a horse. There were, however, scary moments, especially when Dad came up out of a dive. Gravity pushed me back into my seat and tightened my ears and contracted my chest. I could never breathe properly until he levelled out. My body felt like it had been through a compressor. But it never stopped me wanting to go flying with him.

Sometimes Dad would take us if he needed a cattle spotter. I wasn't a very good spotter, given my tendency to daydream, so that job would often fall to M'Lis or Brett. Brett saw what an aircraft could do in the right hands and it instilled in him a passion for flying.

———————

Dad had an uncanny way of flying his plane all morning and issuing instructions and then, once the cattle were moving forward steadily, disappearing. We'd watch him fly off and think, furiously, *Lucky Dad, he's going home, where it's nice and cool, and he can have a drink of water.*

But Dad usually flew home, dived over the homestead (which was a message to Mum to saddle up Limerick and have him ready and waiting) and then landed fast, put DQG in the hangar, and rushed back to the homestead to take Limerick's reins from Mum. Then he'd ride out to help us out near the end, at the most crucial moment of the muster. We might have been going for five kilometres or fifty kilometres, but the final half-hour when we had to get all the cattle through that last gate and safely into the yard was the riskiest. If they broke away at that stage, we could lose the lot, and the whole muster would have been wasted.

So, it was always like a miracle when Dad arrived fresh and took the lead. We—along with our horses—would be hot and exhausted, but Dad would walk the cattle into the yards through that last gate like a hero.

Dad's arrival was a gift from God to me. If Dad and Limerick were there, and they took the lead, we'd be right. I had as much faith in Dad as I did in God.

He was the be-all and end-all.

———⟞⟐⟞———

Dad was always giving us instructions. They were varied, but mostly revolved around the welfare of his stock.

Make sure you check and double-check cattle after you finish trapping them, because often you'll find some left behind by mistake.

Make sure you check and double-check where your cattle are all the time—never let cattle run out of feed or water.

Make sure you check and double-check bores and tanks and pipes all the time.

Always put your stock, your animals and your equipment before yourself.

Vigilance is everything. Water and feed are everything. Water is absolutely everything.

Dad would only tell us something once, so we had to listen carefully. He had learned his lessons the hard way, and expected us to do likewise. Asking him to repeat or explain anything a second time was something you'd only do once. So if for any reason we didn't quite understand his orders, it was safer to simply pretend we did, and hoped we were heading in more or less the right direction.

When Dad wasn't giving instructions or asking us questions, however, he could go for hours, if not days, without speaking. Mum said it was because he had to concentrate so hard on so many difficult, complicated things at once, which left no time or energy for talk. We knew most bush men were like this, and rarely dared break his silence.

Nor was he a man to give praise. He thought it weakened people.

Challenges, he said, strengthened them.

He would say, 'It's like DQG. You have to take off into the wind, against the wind, because it lifts you higher. You need the obstacles because they push you higher.'

To the best of our recollection, he made an exception to his no-praise rule only three times.

One day, he said to M'Lis, 'Right, you and I are going to muster Palmer's Camp, and Brett and the others can go straight to Hijack Dam.'

'On our own?' M'Lis was wide-eyed.

It was a huge responsibility for M'Lis. It was a very large area to muster between the two of them—there would be no back-up. However, she felt such a sense of importance riding out with Dad. It was a long day but they got all the cattle, which M'Lis then described as an amazing feat. They met up with Brett and his mob and brought the combined mob in. A successful end to a muster, which wasn't always the case. Everyone was happy.

Once the cattle were in the yards, and they were unsaddling, Dad turned to M'Lis and said, 'You and I did this, just the two of us, Lis.'

M'Lis swelled with pride. It was perhaps the biggest compliment she had ever received in her life.

Brett's moment came when Dad told him he had to muster Todd Dam, on his own, and Dad would assist from the air. It was a vast area to muster, and with no back-up, a big job. But Dad was on a deadline, no one else was free, and our two stockmen had just left.

Dad helped Brett saddle up at 3 a.m., and sent Brett off in the darkness. By now Brett was eleven and considered capable of doing a man's job. Dad would fly out at daylight to meet him.

Brett, like we girls, was no more than twenty-five kilos, wringing wet. We were strong but tiny. Brett was riding a 16-hands-high and very flighty horse called Blueberry, who could easily toss him off, but could also gallop all day with someone as light as him on her back. That *was* lucky because Brett and Blueberry did have to gallop all day to bring home the mob. Dad rode out on Limerick to meet them, joining him just before the homestead hills. Both Brett and Blueberry were done in by this point.

When they finally got the cattle in, just before dark, Dad tilted his chin towards Blueberry.

'Blueberry did sixty kilometres today.'

He nodded again at Brett.

Hot and dirty, thirsty and hungry, Brett never forgot that nod. A sign of acknowledgement from Dad.

And once, when I got a mulga stake in my leg, but continued mustering all day despite it, and made it back with the cattle rather than giving up, Dad said three words that I held precious for years to come.

'Good job, Tanya.'

18

Characters

The Territory was renowned for its characters, especially in its stock camps.

One of those characters was Tommy Burrows. He'd once been an excellent horseman and brilliant with stock, but he'd had a bad horse accident and never quite recovered, mentally or physically. At some point he was taken in by the wonderful Ted Egan, the famous Alice Springs musician. When Tommy wasn't staying with Ted, a number of station people shared him around. Mostly it was the Braitlings on Mount Doreen, the Goreys on Yambah, and us on Bond Springs. Tommy had to be shared around because he could only stay in one place for so long, both for his own mental health, and ours.

Tommy would arrive for his stint with us, complete with camp oven and swag. Then he'd find Mum and kiss her, slobbering as he did.

'Hello, Mother darling!'

Mum endured Tommy as part of her Christian duty—but only just.

Dad didn't think much of Tommy hanging around Mum, always wanting to kiss her, so as soon as he arrived Dad would pack him off to the stock camp to cook for us. But once there, we had to endure him, watching, terrified, as Tommy marched about in his wonky way, waving his arms, his eyes slightly askew.

We'd been told of his accident, and felt sorry for him, but that didn't stop us avoiding him whenever we could, which was not easy given he was in charge of our meals in the camp. And worst of all was Tommy's cooking. He often made rabbit stew from rabbits he'd caught. It wasn't too bad if he'd caught the rabbits that day. But mostly he'd had the dead animals lying in his pot for days on end. The stew was, therefore, mouldy and tasted disgusting. The bubbling smell made us feel sick. Almost everyone in the camp refused to eat it, which really said something, because at the end of a day of hard physical work, everyone in the camp was exhausted and starving. Then Tommy would chase us because he was so angry, waving his pots and pans in the air.

When we finally got home, he'd march straight to Mum.

'Those buggers of kids, Mother darling,' he'd shout, angrily. 'They won't eat my rabbit stew.'

Then he'd tried to kiss her in his slobbery way.

Tommy Burrows reminded us of the character in a poem called *The Drover's Cook*, taught to us by a wonderful, wild bush man named Bill McKell, who was a local stockman and spent a lot of time out at Mount Doreen. We loved the poem so much we learned it off by heart.

'Remember teaching us *The Drover's Cook*?' we'd ask Bill breathlessly, whenever we saw him, and we'd start reciting it there and then.

Images of a cook with a bloodshot eye, the fly on his trousers open, and saliva dripping into his terrible cooking were hysterical to us. And they captured everything we thought about Tommy.

Of course, Tommy did his best, and looking back, we were cruel and unthinking, but we were always so relieved when he left. We just never felt safe with him around. There was always a chance we'd get belted by pots and pans, and it wasn't much fun surviving on an empty, rumbling belly given how much hard, physical work we did.

On another occasion, we had a stock camp cook who looked like Moses, complete with flowing white hair and white beard.

He went to sleep every night on the ground without a blanket or swag, so that the cold would wake him up at 3 a.m. and he would be ready to cook the camp breakfast. We thought it incredible that the snakes, ants and dingoes didn't get him. He wasn't quite as terrifying as Tommy Burrows, but he was not to be messed with.

Another time, Mum's Uncle John came to us. His wife, Aunty Eileen, had died after a long illness, and he was very sad. 'How about a stint as cook in the camp?' Dad asked him, and we couldn't believe our luck when he said yes.

We called him 'Mon Oncle', which we thought was terribly amusing, and pronounced it 'Mon On-*cluh*', which we thought even more amusing. He had an enormous stomach and an enormous snore at night, which would shake the ground around us.

We loved Mon Oncle because he was so much fun to be around and had a great sense of humour. This was unusual for a camp cook; in the bush, cooks had the reputation of being drunken and grumpy, and very often both. Mon Oncle, in contrast, would be up at 4 a.m. to prepare breakfast every day, cheery and bright, and over our steak, bread and sauce, he would give the camp 'a thought for the morning', usually something like 'Be brave' or 'Respect others'.

Mon Oncle was very strict about his camp. He set it up perfectly, everything in its place, and we were not allowed to touch anything—he ran it like Fort Knox.

One night, there were so many cattle we had to take turns night-watching them. Dad had brought in a few extra stockmen to help out, and at 2 a.m., a couple of the new boys snuck across to Mon Oncle's camp and stole the billy to make a cuppa. They built a little fire under the fence, tied their horses up with the reins looped over the fence and their arms, and then sat back and relaxed, waiting for the brew to boil.

Suddenly, an apparition appeared out of the blackness. The apparition kicked the billy over, shouting furiously, and water from the billy spurted onto the fire.

'Ahhh!' the two young stockmen screamed, thinking it was an Aboriginal Kadaitcha man. They leaped to their feet and the horses pulled back, whinnying in fright.

One of the horses pulled back so hard he dragged one of the blokes under the fence, with the reins still wrapped firmly around his forearms. That bloke was scraped and bloodied quite badly.

No one messed with Mon Oncle's camp again.

Mum and Dad vetted anyone who came onto Bond Springs. Grog was forbidden in the stock camp. My parents had been scarred by the problems alcohol had caused in the late sixties and Dad was determined to take total control over who came onto the property and what they did when they were there.

Dad didn't have a bookkeeper. Despite not having been good at school, and now self-taught in pretty much everything, Dad did all the books himself, right down to the last cent.

'If we're not in control of our life, someone else will be,' he'd say, 'and they won't have anything good in mind for us.'

Bloody bureaucrats, communists and socialists.

But one day I discovered there was an even worse type of person to be worried about, when Dad marched in to lunch after a long bore run. His face was set, his lips tight. Instead of sitting at the head of the table as he usually did, he headed straight to his office. He didn't look at any of us, not even Mum.

We panicked. Had we done something wrong?

'Is everything all right, Grant?' Mum rushed after him. 'Don't you want lunch?'

They were gone a while. Eventually they came back together. Mum looked at her feet. Dad stood with his hands on the back of his chair. We sat at the table in silence, too scared to eat.

'The stallion's been shot.' He cleared his throat. 'In the Corkwood yards.'

Knives and forks clattered onto plates. Our beautiful thorough-bred stallion? Who'd sired Limerick and the other beautiful colts and fillies now making up the stock camp plant?

Dad pursed his lips. 'Stallion obviously went in for a drink. Some low-down, stinking, mongrel bastard's got to him.'

That was about the worst swearing we'd ever heard from Dad.

Who? *Why?*

Dad shrugged, helplessly. 'Somebody trespassing on the Bond, thought it would be fun, who knows the mind of evil?'

Then he picked up his hat.

'There goes our future colts and fillies,' he said, and walked out.

Low-down, stinking, mongrel bastard.

I started adopting a serious disposition whenever I was with Dad, steeling myself for news of what latest disaster was about to explode. I realised early on it would never do to appear frivolous or disrespectful about life. There would always be something hanging over us like a ticking clock and we constantly had to be on our guard, could never truly relax. I certainly knew that we were to be grateful for what we had, while we had it, and to show it where possible.

Every now and then I overheard Dad and Mum argue about money.

It was a juggle for Mum to ensure that all the staff were properly fed to her standards within Dad's ever-tightening budget. One day, when the money argument seemed particularly heated, that old deep, dark anxiety started churning away inside my stomach again.

Eventually I grabbed Mum and whispered, 'Mum, we can live on Vegemite sandwiches, no problem. Will that help?'

She laughed and ruffled my hair. 'It's all fine, my darling,' she said. 'Don't you worry about things like this.'

I ran away relieved, hoping that was the truth. Because it was just too hard to be a grown-up, and I didn't want to think about all those things anymore. So, I returned to my books and my place of happiness.

Not long after that discussion, Mum came home from town and said, 'I have a record that I think you'll like, Tanya.'

She handed me a brand-new LP and I stared, agog, at the cover. There was a picture of a beautiful ballroom with shining floors and high ceilings. Around the ballroom, young women in long, blue gowns adorned with sashes were in the arms of handsome men dressed in what Mum told me were 'black tie and tails.'

'These pieces of music are called "The Viennese Waltzes",' said Mum, as she put the record on. 'And Vienna is the capital of Austria, where *The Sound of Music* was set.'

I thought my heart might leap out of my chest as the record introduced me to Strauss waltzes, particularly "The Blue Danube". Its sweeping, soaring violins and the thrill of its falls and crescendos transported me back to *The Sound of Music* and its ballroom scene.

'Come on!' said Mum with a smile, and took me in her arms. 'You and I are going to dance.'

The kitchen was so hot that I resisted at first. I could smell a roast cooking in the oven and flies were buzzing angrily at the window. Mum's curls frizzed at her forehead, but she wasn't taking no for an answer.

'Okay,' I said, hoping I could match her steps.

Mum was in fact a wonderful dancer. She and Dad were dynamite together on the dance floor, but they rarely had the opportunity to dance anymore. Not in the same way they used to when they were young, in their life before Bond Springs with all its responsibilities and worries. So, Mum appeared determined to make up for lost time. She whirled me up and down the kitchen, turning me around and under, laughing as we dipped and twirled. Swept up in the violins, I was transported to another time and place.

By the end, my beautiful mother was shining all over and her eyes were sparkling. I hadn't seen her look like that for a long time.

'There!' she said, smiling softly as she took off the record and put it back in its cover. 'There!'

And even though I wasn't sure what 'there' meant, I was filled with childish happiness at witnessing Mum's joy, and thought it could only be a good thing.

Mum and I would continue to dance to Strauss's waltzes. M'Lis joined in, too. She loved the music as much as I did. Mum, M'Lis and I would dip and curtsy and swirl. We tried to get Brett to dance with us but he wasn't interested. He was a bush kid at heart, happiest outdoors, driving in the Land Rover, walking up to the cattle yards, watching the stockmen break in the horses, and riding.

It didn't occur to me that it was perhaps odd that I connected as strongly with *The Sound of Music* and Strauss's waltzes as I did with Slim Dusty and Charley Pride, not to mention our very own Ted Egan. They represented completely different worlds. But I felt utterly at home in each. It was as though I had a foot in each camp and such a thing was utterly normal. It gave me yet another happy place to go to in my heart and mind.

Stories, books, daydreaming, music—and now dancing.

19

Mrs Hodder and Tall Tales

Mrs Hodder continued to encourage me on School of the Air. She was very clever and thoughtful, and constantly surprised us with her knowledge of our bush life. As far as we were concerned, she just knew *everything*.

She was also good at dealing with unexpected and scandalous tidbits from students. There were always quite a few: stories about the governess and the ringer, or the bookkeeper who'd got on the grog in town and hadn't been seen since, or whose racehorse had been swapped with whose to win the next bush race meeting.

Mrs Hodder knew that a lot of parents were listening in. Bush people were so isolated that any kind of gossip was seized upon and enjoyed—some adults wouldn't go back to work until the stories were over, if they were very good.

'Good morning, Jacquie, at Romeo Juliet Papa,' Mrs Hodder would commence cheerfully. 'What exciting things have happened at your place on the weekend? Over.'

'Good morning, Mrs Hodder,' Jacquie's voice from five hundred kilometres away dropped in and out through the static. 'Dad's very cross . . . we lost the cattle . . . we were late for the trucks . . . and Dad said that . . .'

In the background was more noise. It sounded like Dad was still cross.

'Poor Jacquie,' M'Lis said. 'It's hard to hear her. Reception's always so bad out at Mount Doreen.'

But Mrs Hodder could hear Jacquie better than we could, with her big wireless in Alice, and knew just what to say. 'Oh dear,' she said, quickly restoring order. 'I hope things get better for Dad very soon. Now, let's quickly move to, say, Robin and Stephen at Phillip Creek . . .'

I'm sure some of the adults were equally sorry they couldn't hear more of Jacquie's story. Grown-ups were always *very* interested in what cattle were being mustered where on what station, how many cattle were being trucked off to market, prices received, and comments from the stock and station agents who oversaw the sales.

Children would happily share what they'd heard the Elders agent tell their dad, or what the Tanami Transport road train driver reported to the head stockman, or what the Dalgety agent whispered to mum as he thanked her for the special cake she baked for his arrival.

These stories would lead to Mrs Hodder coughing discreetly and moving the conversation on as soon as the student had stopped speaking.

'That's marvellous, Johnny,' Mrs Hodder would say, brightly. 'Thank you for telling us the story of Mum wearing her new bikini at the dam. I think we'll now hear from Simone out at Amburla. Eight November Hotel, how is your horse today, Simone? Over.'

Sometimes there was no way to cut a student off if they were really letting loose with some tasty news, like the next time that Johnny reported that Mum's bikini actually fell off at the dam.

'Goodness me, Johnny, that must have been chilly for poor Mum. Now, Tanya at Nine Sierra Victor Uniform, you're next. How are M'Lis, Brett and Benny? Over.'

Benny used to toddle in with me when I was on School of the Air. He was fascinated by the sound of the voices and the music coming out of the radio. Often he would try to join in, and when Mrs Hodder heard him, she would exclaim, 'And an extra special clap from the studio for Benny Heaslip out at Bond Springs! Well done, Benny.'

Then, of course, there was the weather, the most important topic of station life. Rains, floods and fires were talked about endlessly.

One of the great events for bush people were the annual camp-drafts, gymkhanas and bush race meetings. We waited impatiently all year for these weekends to come around. People for hundreds of kilometres gathered in the middle of nowhere to camp for several days and compete against each other on horseback.

The campdrafts allowed horse and rider to show off their mustering skills by cutting a beast out of a mob and working it through a difficult course in a very short time. Gymkhanas were all about horse and rider skill over different courses. And the races allowed the best horses to gallop around a dirt track, like Dad had done with Limerick back in Alice Springs. Throughout, people drank huge amounts of rum and VB beer (all hot), danced all night to Slim Dusty on a concrete slab under the stars, and played the odd game of cricket on the dusty flat.

And that was just the men.

These weekends led to fights, romances and too much grog, all of which we bush kids watched in fascination. Then we happily reported everything back to Mrs Hodder after the weekend.

'Yes, Mrs Hodder,' Sally reported enthusiastically from three hundred kilometres away to the east. 'Our housekeeper is getting on the first mail plane out, she says, because the stockman from north that she had her eye on got full on Bundy and went off with a governess from somewhere else. She hasn't stopped crying since we got back. Mum's cranky and Dad's headed for the stock camp, because he said things were a bit chilly at home. Over.'

'Oh, dear,' said Mrs Hodder in her best deadpan voice. 'Well, you'll just have to be a very helpful girl, and help Mum with all the housework, won't you, Sally? Over.'

Mrs Hodder would quickly try to steer the conversation out of dangerous waters, keenly aware that half the Territory was tuned in to this conversation about the housekeeper's demise.

After each campdraft, gymkhana or bush race meeting, there would always be colourful events to report. You take a handful of people living isolated lives for months on end, put them together with a group of other people living equally isolated lives, mix them up for a rocket-fuelled weekend, and Mrs Hodder was guaranteed great stories.

And these stories could go on for several weeks, as children reported stories of their mums trying to get the dads and the 'rest of the useless staff' dried out and back onto the straight and narrow.

———>•<———

The School of the Air was where I met Jane Joseland from Everard Park Station, more than six hundred kilometres of corrugated dirt road to the south of Alice. We were in the same School of the Air grade and quickly became best friends over the air.

The first time I heard Jane was when she called in one news morning to proudly report that she had come third in a gymkhana event at the Finke race meeting.

'Splendid effort, Jane,' said Mrs Hodder, encouragingly.

There was some noise at Jane's end until she added, 'Dad said to say that there were only three of us in the event.'

Mrs Hodder didn't miss a beat. 'How splendid for *everyone*, Jane. Well done!'

I thought Jane's achievement was the cleverest thing ever. I hadn't yet started riding in bush events and couldn't imagine being so brave as to do so. I conjured up in my imagination Jane as a fearless young warrior. As it transpired, that described her perfectly.

<hr>

When we were not telling stories over the air, we made them up at home.

Best of all were our night-time tales. M'Lis and I shared a bedroom at one end of the passageway, and Brett and Benny shared one at the other end. After lights out, Brett and Ben would sneak down to our room and squash into our beds and I would create stories of outback families (whispered, of course, because we were meant to be asleep).

The families of my stories were always fighting blazing bush-fires, fixing broken-down bores, worrying about droughts, scrub-bashing in old Land Rovers to find a wild bullock, work-ing with drovers under starry skies or calling in the Royal Flying Doctor Service to save the life of someone who had been crushed in the yards by a mad scrubber bull.

M'Lis and Brett were a rapt audience and I was very strict. If anybody spoke or interrupted my stories, they had to go back to bed. Benny was only little (still wearing plastic pilchers over his nappies) and he made the most noise.

'Shh, Benny!' we'd all hiss. 'If you're not quiet, *they'll* hear us.'

'They' could have been Mum, Dad or Miss Thiele. Any one of them meant trouble.

'Snuggle in with me, Benny, and be quiet.' I'd pull him in close, and off we'd go again.

Best of all were our School of the Air night-time plays.

Being the eldest, I bagged the right to play Mrs Hodder. (I'd learned the word *bagged* from *The Secret Seven* and liked it very much.)

And so I would begin: 'Good morning, everyone, this is Mrs Hodder. Now, today we're going to hear from Brett at Bond Springs. Good morning, Sierra Victor Uniform. Brett, are you there? Over.'

Brett would gallantly respond: 'Good morning, Mrs Hodder. Yes, I can read you loud and clear. Over.'

After a while, we all changed roles. Brett was cast regularly as Mr Ashton (the headmaster), or Mr Walker (a new and very funny School of the Air teacher) or Dad. M'Lis and I played everyone else, including School of the Air classmates, Mum and governesses. Sometimes M'Lis and Brett played our neighbours; the Gorey kids from Yambah Station, or the Hayes kids from Undoolya, or even Simone out at Amburla, two stations to the west.

There was always some sort of Hanrahan-type problem to fix.

'VJD, this is Sierra Victor Uniform, do you read me?' M'Lis's voice would cut through the static urgently. 'We have a problem out here with a bushfire burning out of control towards the boundary of Yambah Station. Over.'

M'Lis rarely got to play Mrs Hodder, though. I claimed the right as the eldest child and storyteller.

'Come along!' I'd respond in my best, bright, no-nonsense Mrs Hodder voice whenever M'Lis complained. 'Buck up now, everyone!'

Our plays and stories would continue until we heard the door open at the other end of the outside veranda next to the kitchen and we knew someone was coming to check on us.

If it was Mum, we knew she'd be cross, but she would forgive us. If it was Miss Thiele, she'd just be cross. However, if we heard Dad's boots clomping down the outside veranda, we'd be galvanised into terrified action.

Brett would flee back to his room, with Benny struggling along in tow, his pilchers squish-squish-squishing all the way until Brett pushed him safely into bed. M'Lis and I would dive under the covers, hearts beating wildly, heroes and heroines of our stories to the last.

20

Jane Joseland—My New Friend

I longed to meet my School of the Air friend, Jane Joseland, in real life. But she lived hundreds of kilometres south of Alice Springs, so it seemed impossible.

However, when Mum and Dad were invited to the Oodnadatta races to stay with the Greenwoods, I knew I had my chance. Jane would be there—competing in the gymkhana, no less!

Benny would go with Mum and Dad. So, I begged to go, too.

'But what about M'Lis and Brett?' asked Mum. We'd never been apart before, except in emergencies.

'Yes, what about us?' echoed M'Lis, her big eyes wide with dismay.

I felt a wrench in my stomach. 'It's just for a weekend,' I said, lamely.

It showed how much I wanted to meet Jane that I was prepared to leave M'Lis. Indeed, I was torn. I couldn't bear to miss this opportunity, yet I felt bad about M'Lis and Brett. In the end Mum made the decision for me. She called Mrs Joseland on the sked, and with me hovering at my end, and Jane at hers, both mothers agreed we could do this.

Looking back, Mum was incredibly kind to give me this chance, especially because I was receiving an opportunity that M'Lis and Brett weren't. Mum was always determined that no child should be treated differently to the others, but I think she realised I needed to start meeting people and developing friendships beyond my own home and family. I didn't realise that, of course. I just knew I wanted to meet Jane.

The night before we flew to Oodna, I could hardly sleep. The next morning, we took off and the wings of DQG glinted in the sunlight as we soared south. I sat at the front with Dad. I felt so lucky to be up there in the air with him, and to have him all to myself. Mum sat in the back with Benny, no doubt relieved to have most of the back to herself, too. By the time we landed on the gibber stones of Oodna mid-morning and headed to the race-course, my sense of anticipation was at fever pitch.

It was bedlam at the racecourse. Hundreds of people gathered around an enormous dirt track. Dust rose in the air, and underfoot. Horses galloped around and around; there were so many kids and adults. The bar was doing a busy trade. I even spied a fairy-floss and toffee-apple stall.

My heart pounded as we headed towards the stables to meet Jane. I'd never been so nervous in my life. Jane and I had talked every day on School of the Air for several years and we'd declared each other our best friend, but would we know each other in real life? Would I even recognise her?

Mum said I needn't worry. She had plaited my hair, and attached red ribbons on the end of each plait, and said I looked smart. Of course, I was wearing my best press-stud shirt and trousers. And I'd polished my riding boots until they shone. Mum held my hand.

Next minute, a girl with a shock of blonde hair emerged from a mob crowding around the stables. She had a snub nose and freckles scattered across her face, plus the cheekiest grin I'd ever seen. She was wearing riding clothes covered in dust and strode along with complete confidence, leading a bay horse. It had to be Jane! She was followed by a slim, glamorous woman with blonde hair swept back into a French roll, leading a grey horse. Jane's mum, I was sure of it.

'Jane?' I squeaked.

'Tanya?' the girl giggled.

She giggled some more and we had a quick hug, after which I looked down awkwardly at my embarrassingly overshined boots.

Jane's mum smiled at me and said hello to Mum. She was wearing a soft pink blouse with a bright-pink scarf at her neck, moleskins and riding boots. How impressive to have a mother who was competing in the events and still looked so glamorous!

Jane introduced her bay mare, Lucy, to me. 'We've just won the Bending race!' she enthused, handing me a blue ribbon to look at. I admired it and patted Lucy's nose.

'Come on!' Jane grabbed my hand. 'I have to get ready for the next event. Let's go!'

I looked at Mum, who nodded, smiling, and I trotted after Jane. I still could hardly believe I had finally met my best friend from School of the Air, and how self-assured, brave and successful she was in real life!

As we reached the rails, two young Aboriginal kids ran past, waving and speaking to Jane in their language. She grinned and spoke back to them.

I stared at her.

'Yeah, I speak Pitjantjatjara,' she said, as if it were an everyday thing. 'Mum said I could speak Pitjantjatjara before I could speak English.'

'Are they your friends?'

'Yeah. Those are the kids who live on Everard Park with us.'

I took this in. I knew Jane had three older brothers. Two of them were already at boarding school. She was much younger than them all. So, her playmates were the Pitjantjatjara kids? My playmates were M'Lis, Brett and Benny. And I was the eldest, not the youngest. Jane and I were different in so many ways. She seemed so clever, so free-spirited.

I was star-struck. And it didn't take long to learn that Jane had stardust in her veins. Her glamorous mother, Helen Grieve, was actually a film star.

As a young girl, Helen had starred in two iconic Australian movies: *The Overlanders* and *Bush Christmas*. The first was with Daphne Calder, a local celebrity in Alice Springs, and the famous Australian actor Chips Rafferty. *The Overlanders* was partly filmed near Alice, where they drove a huge mob of cattle across the MacDonnell Ranges.

I longed to see the movie, and Jane promised me that we could some time.

But even more thrilling was learning about the second movie, *Bush Christmas*. Helen played the eldest child in a horse-duffing movie set in the Blue Mountains, again with Chips Rafferty. Mrs Joseland, as I called her, later lent me her book of *Bush Christmas*. It was crammed with photo stills from the movie. There were black-and-white photographs depicting her, the other children and the horse-duffers either galloping across ravines or camping out at night, trying to keep warm and eating cooked snake. Helen was twelve when the movie was made. She had long blonde plaits and an oval-shaped face. Jane looked just like her, only younger, with wilder hair.

By the end of the Oodna weekend, Jane and I were inseparable. We'd persuaded Mum to let me stay with Jane at her house for the whole weekend. This was a big thing—I'd never spent a night away from Mum, except with family. But I couldn't get enough of this free-spirited bush girl who spoke two languages and was funny and fearless. Perhaps three older brothers and a stock camp of Aboriginal kids had made her that way.

She proudly showed me her half finger. 'It got chopped off by the meat mincer when I was a little girl,' she explained. 'Mum was making rissoles and I got too close. Look, it looks like it's got a little face on it!' Indeed, the indents of the mincer had created a little smiling face on the stub of her finger.

Over the weekend Jane rode her way determinedly to 'Best Girl Rider' and won blue ribbons in almost every gymkhana event she entered. And if she didn't come first, she came second or third. She'd come a long way since coming third in her first event!

As we walked along between events, she held the reins of her horse in one hand, and rested the other elbow on my shoulder. I was so small, it was easy for her to do so, and seemed to me a wondrous display of affection. Every time she mounted her horse with ease and cantered off to her next event, I stood on the rail, gazing in awe. She was a natural rider and gripping to watch.

Staying at the Joselands' Oodnadatta house was eye-opening. A seemingly endless procession of people stayed or visited and the little weatherboard house overflowed with laughter and parties. Mrs Joseland wore pink lipstick and silver jewellery that jangled in a grown-up way. She seemed equally at ease entertaining guests as riding a horse. I longed to ask her if she missed being in the movies but didn't dare.

Mr Joseland was a big, kind man with a great moustache and even greater laugh. Both he and Mrs Joseland seemed like relaxed parents; Jane didn't have to ask permission for much and never seemed to be in trouble.

I curled up with Jane in her swag at night, next door to her handsome older brothers. I'd never spent time with older boys and was tongue-tied in their company. Mostly I twiddled my fingers and looked at my boots if they came near. John, the eldest, was kind and serious; Chris, next, was cheeky and charismatic; Tim, handsome and gentle.

I quickly realised, however, that living with older brothers came with many challenges. Jane had to defend herself against Chinese burns, big brother tricks of all sorts and constant teasing. Perhaps being the youngest was not as easy as it looked.

On the Saturday night, a family friend turned up. He and Mr Joseland took a bottle of rum up onto the roof, where they sat on the rusted-out corrugated panels in their riding boots, happily drinking and telling stories. After a while they started calling out for everyone to come and join them. Then they started dancing. And finally, they fell through the roof. Luckily, they landed right in the middle of the kitchen table, which broke the fall. They dusted themselves off and kept on dancing.

I couldn't imagine anything like that happening at my house.

By the time we flew back to Bond Springs, I was worn out but elated. For the first time in my life I had connected with a friend outside of my family. Who had three older brothers. And a film-star mother. And a gregarious father who fell through a roof and didn't miss a beat.

All the way home I thought of my last conversation with Jane. She had said, 'You can call me Janie, if you like. That's what my family calls me.'

'Oh,' I stuttered as Mum led me away. 'Okay, thanks—*Janie*.'

It felt like a rite of passage.

As I flew home, all I could think about was my new friend. Janie was a natural extrovert and I was still used to clinging to Mum's hand or skirt. But neither of us had a friend—who was a girl—our own age, so it was an experience we shared.

It made me feel grown-up, and enthusiastic at the opportunities ahead. Maybe Jane and I could even ride together one day.

Jane and Mrs Joseland, between them, had offered me a peek into the outside world, and I wanted more of it.

21

Charlie Gorey and Bush Work

Back home, life continued. School and work, work and school.

Luckily for us, we had Charlie.

We often spent days in the stock camp with just Charlie, and from the beginning he was patient and looked out for us.

Every day, he rose at 5 a.m. to hear the start of 8HA, the Alice Springs radio station. In the stock camp we would roll over in our swags and listen to his little wireless kick off the day. It was a miracle Charlie got his wireless to work in some of the places we camped, but he almost always picked up a signal. We could always rely on 8HA to serve us up a good dose of Slim Dusty and Charley Pride early in the morning, and they were just what we needed to start the day. 'Ribs Cooked on the Coals' by Slim Dusty got us out of our swags, wishing and hopeful, and 'Kiss an Angel Good Morning' by Charley Pride always got our Charlie whistling.

When we weren't in the camp, Brett would often go with Charlie on the back of the motorbike. He was light and could jump off and help with opening gates, fixing fences and dealing with cattle; the kinds of jobs that were so much more difficult for a man on his own.

One blistering summer's day—the kind that saw the thermometer reach forty degrees by mid-morning—Brett rode out with Charlie to check a fence. Dad was worried about cattle getting stuck on the fence and perishing, so his instruction was that if they found cattle, they were to move them on towards the bore so they could get water. A routine morning's job.

They were about sixteen kilometres from the homestead when they hit a narrow, sandy creek. The wheels of the bike spun, and Brett and Charlie flew in different directions. The bike landed on top of Brett, smashing his leg in numerous places.

'I've gotta walk home and get help, eh?' said Charlie in his slow drawl, when he finally pulled himself out of the dust and the dirt. 'You stay here. Don't move, Brett.'

'No, don't leave me, Charlie,' pleaded Brett, eyes dazed with pain.

'Gotta go, Brett. I'll be back, eh,' said Charlie, limping off into the horizon.

Brett had to lie in the dirt and the dust for several hours before Dad reached him in the old Land Rover. Mum insisted on going with him, and she recalled finding a bundle of clothes on the red earth, out of which poked a dirty, tear-streaked face and terror-stricken eyes. He was dehydrated and hallucinating about the crows picking out his eyes and the dingoes eating his innards. It was a long drive home over the bumps and dirt and spinifex.

His leg ended up stuck into a thigh-length cast for six months. Dad built a dam nearby in later years and called it 'Broken Leg', so at least Brett got some recognition for his courage. And before long Brett was riding the motorbike with one leg in a cast, much to the doctor's and Mum's horror.

It took Charlie a while to recover as well, and he limped every-where for quite some time.

The Land Rover also caused Charlie problems one early December day.

It was the time of the year when storms started to develop in Central Australia. Dad said that our storms came from monsoons, usually off the coast of Western Australia, and that 'the sweet spot for us is just under Jakarta'.

I'd had to rush off and look up that new name in his *Maps of the World*.

It was important to nod knowledgeably whenever Dad men-tioned these kinds of things. I never wanted him to think I wasn't as focused and worried as he was, all the time, about the weather. After all, Dad studied the weather every day as though his life depended on it, which it did. If I drifted off, or didn't make the right kinds of comments, Dad would stare at me as though I were a dumb southerner. That was one of the greatest sins, we knew—to be a dumb southerner who had no idea what 'life was really like here'. Dad would curtly remind me of the facts underlying his weather-worry-of-the-day, before stomping off.

Dad's biggest worry was that the storms wouldn't come.

We all longed for storms, for their life-giving, much-needed rain.

But if a storm was wild, creeks would flood quickly and rise, taking everything with them like a raging bull. If it was big, you couldn't see where the creek started and ended, what tangled tree limbs and debris lay underneath, what driftwood might suddenly knock you from your horse.

We had listened to Slim Dusty sing 'Saddle Boy' over and over again, and it never failed to bring fear mixed with deep sorrow to the heart. A flash flood of foaming, brown water was the scariest thing in the world, after bushfires, and we feared it with our lives. We had good reason—it had taken Saddle Boy's life.

But on that hot December day, Charlie wasn't thinking about flash floods. He was driving the old Land Rover along the side of the Todd River looking for dingoes. They'd been troublesome around the bore and were killing lots of calves, so Dad instructed Charlie to take his rifle and find the lair. It was always deeply upsetting to see calves with their throats ripped open, and little bodies pulled into parts, and Dad was always looking to protect his herd.

The four-wheel drive function on the Land Rover had recently broken, and though Charlie was a very good driver, the handicapped Land Rover was no match for the grip of the big, sandy creek. He got bogged and had to walk sixteen kilometres home under an increasingly dark sky. He made it home just before the first large spots of rain started hitting the ground.

When the drops got bigger still, we were torn between a range of emotions: joy at the sweet smell of rain, happiness that Mum and Dad would be happy, relief that Charlie hadn't got swept away (like Saddle Boy) and concern for his Land Rover and rifle, as he mournfully described their parting.

Overnight it poured with rain, and the next day it was still bucketing down, which made everyone, particularly Dad, ecstatic. His eyes sparkled. The load of the world temporarily lifted from his shoulders. He marched here and there, checking storm waters, checking the dam, checking the creek. The house creek was 'running a banker' by now. Dad then told us, losing his sparkle momentarily, there would be a lot of damage, especially to the floodgates.

'C'mon, we've got to go and find my vehicle, eh?' urged Charlie. He hadn't slept a wink and there was no time to waste.

'Why didn't you bring your rifle home with you, anyway?' asked Brett as we clambered into Dad's Land Rover.

Charlie got into the driver's seat. 'Too bloody heavy to carry. Thought it would be right overnight. Didn't know it was going to rain like this, eh?'

Charlie put the vehicle into gear and we hurtled through the rain back to the creek. It had burst its banks and was now a raging torrent.

'Bloody hell,' said Charlie. He even forgot the 'eh'.

We looked around in stunned silence. Charlie's Land Rover was not there.

'Swept away,' we chorused, helpfully.

Charlie was beside himself with despair and rage. That day, and for the rest of the week as the rains lessened, he returned to the site and searched for it.

Eventually the creek went down and Charlie found the Land Rover. It was pushed up against a bank, several kilometres from where he'd left it, covered in soaking leaves, twisted branches and three inches deep in mud. Charlie rushed to it and pulled everything out, swearing in his special Queensland way as he did so. But despite his best efforts, it was clear his precious rifle was not there.

'Swept away, too,' he said, furiously.

Over the next few months, Charlie spent hours down there looking for it along the creek bed. But to no avail. The rifle had disappeared and was never seen again.

—>•<—

A brighter time for Charlie came when he met a beautiful redhead, a woman named Dawn.

One of our favourite songs playing on 8HA was 'Delta Dawn', and we couldn't believe this gorgeous girl had the same name. Charlie brought her out to Bond Springs, and we thought she looked like a movie star. (And our jaws dropped when we discovered that she stayed overnight with Charlie.)

We started singing 'Delta Dawn' to Charlie all the time, until he got sick of us and threatened to take his strap to us if we didn't stop. One day Dawn stopped coming, and Charlie took to the rum, and we didn't sing 'Delta Dawn' to him anymore.

As a way of cheering himself up, Charlie taught Brett to smoke gum roots down in the creek. Before we knew it, Brett was coming back from motorbike trips with Charlie with a silly grin on his face, charcoal all over his lips and smelling like smoke.

Mum took one look at his scruffy appearance and demanded to know what he had been doing. Now, all bush kids look dishevelled—and Brett was no exception—but there was something not quite right that caught Mum's eagle eye.

'Nothing, Mum,' grinned Brett, looking sillier and smelling smokier by the moment.

Charlie ducked off sheepishly at that point, as Brett wilted under Mum's stern gaze. Eventually he cracked and confessed. Mum was appalled, and told Brett—and Charlie—never to do it again or she would take the most extreme measure at her disposal: to tell Dad.

Charlie nodded obligingly, but Brett wasn't going to give up that easily. He had graduated beyond naked bike rides at bath time and, at eight years old, was pretty pleased with this grown-up form of misbehaviour. And best of all, he could do it when he was kilometres from the house, which meant that mostly Mum would never know.

————⊷⊶⊷————

Despite Charlie's occasional encouragement of our less-than-exemplary exploits, he still looked out for us. That was lucky, because we needed all the looking out for we could get.

One day we were out drafting at Bulldust Bore, where there were a lot of big scrubber bulls and cows. They were the cattle that had got away during previous musters and were always a challenge: wild, they completely ruled the mob. They could charge and kill you in an instant.

'Right,' said Dad, assessing the scene. 'These scrubbers are going to be hard to manage. You're going to have to be quick off the mark on your gates.'

Dad stood in the round drafting yard and assigned us our positions. He put Charlie on the gate for the micky bulls and young calves that led to the branding yard. Brett was in charge of the gate for steers headed to the trucking yard. A young jackaroo who came for a short time was on the gate for the young heifers. He assigned M'Lis the bush gate—that's where the old cows and mad scrubber bulls would be sent back to the bush, because they were too old to be bred from or marketed. I always thought it was the best gate, because it meant freedom for the cattle. If I were a beast in the yards, that would be the gate I'd want.

But I wasn't a beast, just a worker, and was sent to the bottom of the back yard to push the cattle up into the drafting enclosure. Normally I hated being down the back. You were in line for the bull dust; it was just like being on the cattle tail during droving. But today it brought a benefit: it wouldn't be as dangerous as being on one of the gates. We knew what could happen if things went wrong. If a beast charged the gate, you could be sent flying, especially if you were as small and skinny as we were. Worse, Dad would yell furiously at us, especially if the wrong beast got through and got away.

There was one other benefit: once I got the cattle up to Dad, I could return to the back of the yards where I was largely out of his sight for ten minutes before he called me to push up the next mob. I could do a lot of daydreaming in ten minutes. Go to a lot of places in my imagination. Create stories. Find a way to escape the heat and the boredom of the hours of drafting that lay ahead.

We all took our places for what would be a long day. It was already hot. Dad stood in the round enclosure, stockwhip in hand, hat pulled low against the sun.

'Righto, Tanya, push 'em up!' he yelled, and I set to work.

It was no mean feat getting the mad group to move in an orderly fashion into the drafting enclosure, so I pushed them in smaller groups to make it more manageable for Dad, darting in and out, trying not to get stepped on or kicked as I went. My mouth was filled with dust within minutes. My hair stuck to my head under my hat. Even thoughts of daydreaming started melting away.

Dad stood in the middle of the swirling mob of mad cattle, moving as if on a sixpence, pushing a micky bull here, a steer there, a bullock for market there, his focus razor-sharp. It was as though he never noticed the heat.

Suddenly, one of the big scrubber cows in the back broke away from my group. She stormed her way through the middle group towards the drafting yard. She was bellowing and snorting, snot dripping from nostrils, flies across her huge eyes.

I tried to yell to Dad but my voice was lost in the bellowing of the cattle. Dad saw her coming just in time and flicked his stock-whip to push her away. The cow took his hint—and headed at a gallop towards M'Lis's gate.

'Lis, scrubber to the bush gate!' shouted Dad.

But it was too late. The cow was faster than all of us. Before M'Lis could even get to undo the chain, the cow smashed through the gate.

M'Lis was pushed backwards and went flying into the dust. Through the red blur, I saw her on her hands and knees.

Dad yelled, 'Get up, Lis! You'll be right,' and turned his attention back to the mob.

The mad cow was through the gate by now, and galloping to freedom, but M'Lis was still trying to get up, dazed and winded by the knock.

Next minute there was a streak of blue.

Charlie.

He picked M'Lis up and put her on his knee. Then he gently held her while she had a little cry.

The knock had 'hurt like hell', she later told me.

But M'Lis's narrow escape led us to create a new expression: 'Block . . . [insert type of animal; my favourite was 'the red heifer'] at the bush gate!' So whenever we wanted someone or something to stop, we'd shout, 'Block 'em' (for short) or the whole expression (for maximum effect). Or if we wanted someone or something to go away, we'd simply roar, 'Bush gate!'

These became some of our all-time favourite expressions (although we never dared use them on the grown-ups).

22

Mind Over Matter

We kids had to eat first at night so we could be put to bed and the adults could have dinner in peace. However, one summer's evening we all got home late from yarding up bullocks, and we were allowed to eat with the adults.

At the time, Dad had a few extra stockmen helping out, so it was an enormous crowd of about twenty-five that trooped into the kitchen for dinner. The air was full of noise, with people chatting and laughing. M'Lis and I helped Mum dish up plate after plate of steak, potatoes, peas and beans, topped with delicious thick gravy, all cooked on the Aga stove. It had been a good day and even Charlie was grinning.

But somebody had forgotten to properly close the back door.

There was so much noise and chaos in the kitchen that a long king brown snake was able to slide in under the back door undetected. In fact, it was able to slither into the kitchen and under the table and through people's feet and up onto the cabinet where Mum's cups were laid out—all without anyone noticing.

Mum, however, was always on high alert for snakes, day and night. She either felt the movement at her feet or caught the movement out of her eye—she wasn't sure which—but through the hum of conversation and clink of knives and plates, she shrieked: 'Grant! Snake!'

Dad's head swivelled and then he jumped up so fast none of us had time to speak. He grabbed the shovel, which stood conveniently in the entrance hall next to the door, and then—although Mum then shrieked, 'Not the shovel!'—smashed its blade down onto the snake. The sound was like a *ka-chung* from one of the Braitlings' comics.

By now the snake was curled around the cups and saucers, and Dad missed. Cups and saucers went flying into the air and smashed down onto the concrete floor.

The noise was horrific and everyone finally started screaming. Even Charlie took a back step. A long king brown was not something to be messed with. One bite and we were dead (according to all the grown-ups).

Meanwhile the snake, which was slightly put out by all of this, slid onto the Aga stove next to the cabinet. It then wound its way around the plates of food piled high there.

'Not the food!' shrieked Mum, but whether that was directed to Dad or the snake, I wasn't sure. Anyway, Dad took no notice. He smashed the blade of the shovel down again: *ka-chung* and *ka-chung* and *ka-chung*.

Plates went everywhere, shattered all over the kitchen. Bits of meat and beans and gravy hit the walls and the floor. By now everyone was up on the table, except Charlie, and the hapless king brown was finally in a number of pieces, partly on the plates, partly on the wall and partly on the floor. Dad kept smashing it with the shovel while it writhed madly in its death throes.

'Oh, my God, Grant! Stop, get it out!' shrieked Mum.

That was a dinner nobody would forget. The clean-up was unbelievable, and by the time it was over, everybody had well and truly lost their appetite.

But Dad just marched out and went back to his office to continue his bookwork.

———————

Even without a snake, dinner with Dad could be a trying event.

Actually, it didn't have to be dinner. It could be lunch, or break-fast, or morning smoko. We'd hear his boots coming along the rocks and the gravel—*clip-clop, clip-clop*—and everyone would quieten down and snap to attention.

Dad always sat at the head of the table. Once everyone had taken their place quietly, Dad would say grace. And then, when everyone started to enjoy their food (and Mum's cooking was always deli-cious), Dad would start firing questions around the table. Or if it was smoko, the questions would come just as everyone had piled their plates high with slabs of Mum's fruitcake or chocolate cake.

Dad's questions would go along these lines:

Have you checked Davis Bore? (Or any other bore he felt fit to name.)

Did you weld that leaking pipe?

Did you fix that fence along the creek?

Did you get the yards ready for the trucks?

Are the horses ready for tomorrow?

Did you know the house bore has stopped pumping? (Terrified silence would generally ensue.)

Everyone would squirm, desperately hoping the questions wouldn't be directed at them. But Dad made sure he had a question for everyone.

While Mum put her heart into cooking beautiful food to ensure everyone was physically and soulfully nourished, Dad viewed mealtimes as an opportunity to find out what was happening everywhere on Bond Springs. There was so much to do, all the time, that it was the most efficient way for him to keep on top of it all. It was also his chance to then give orders, to instruct people and most of all, to keep everyone on their toes. He hated to repeat himself, so he saw his role as teaching people to think for them-selves and be proactive.

Of course, we didn't realise that. We were too busy ducking and diving and weaving and trying to come up with answers that would satisfy him, all the while our throats dry and hoping we wouldn't be next in line.

<hr>

For Dad, it was all about survival of the fittest. He'd spent years now watching and learning from the land and the animals around him, and had taken that knowledge deeply into his psyche.

We saw this firsthand at Bull Dust Bore, when we had to deal with about eight scrubber bulls that had been trapped in the yard overnight. They'd come in for water at the trough through a swinging gate, positioned so that they could get in but not out, and Dad wanted to see whether he could truck any of them to market.

By the time we arrived the bulls were stirry and angry, pushing up dust and intimidating the rest of the mob that had also come in overnight for water. At the back, one old bull stood against the rails. As we looked closer, we could see he had a huge cancer growing over his eye, which looked to be weeping, the goo stuck to his face. One leg was broken and was covered in blood. He was struggling to stand up.

We gathered around while Dad checked him out—at a safe distance.

'He's in a bad way, poor ol' fella. Can't truck him. And he'll die if he goes back into the paddock on his own. Dingoes'll get him before long, then the crows.'

Dad went to the Land Rover and pulled out his .222 rifle.

He always believed in putting animals out of their misery if it was necessary. He hated to see them suffer, and he knew just how bad it could be in the bush.

'Righto, you kids, out of the way.'

He shot the scrubber bull in the head.

Dad was a good shot. The bull went to one knee, but it refused to die. Scrubber bulls were, after all, the toughest of all tough cattle, and they didn't give up easily.

And in that moment, we were given a lesson in nature in the wild.

The rest of the scrubber bulls *charged* him.

I stood in disbelief and horror as they attacked the dying bull, knocking him again and again. Those scrubbers with horns gored him. Yes, the bull was nearly dead, but his comrades finished him off.

Don't worry about the dingoes and crows: your own kind is your biggest enemy.

The moral of that story was: No matter how big you are, the minute you show weakness, you're finished. That was life in the bush. And it certainly described Dad's attitude to life. He never showed weakness, especially to his own kind.

———◆———

Dad's toughness was tempered by Charlie Gorey's kindness, especially during those long musters. There was a particularly horrible route through a paddock between Bendy and Corkwood where a water bag had to last nearly a day. It was dry, sandy scrub as far as I could twist my head; red, red, red underfoot and seemingly even hotter under a blazing blue sky.

Dad would say, 'Get a rock and suck it. That'll help. It'll create moisture in your mouth. Take your mind off being thirsty.'

However, one particularly stinking hot summer's day there, we were almost 'finished'. We hung over our horses, our throats thick with the filth of the muster, our eyes squinting miserably at the tempting mirage on the horizon.

'Boss, these kids need a drink.' Charlie looked like he might even throw a punch if Dad didn't agree.

Dad finally nodded. 'Righto, when you get to the next trough, you can stop for a bit. Have a short spell.'

We couldn't believe our luck. When we got to the trough, we buried our faces in it, as did the horses. The water was disgusting and covered in slime, but we didn't care. Bush people drank whatever water was available, just to survive, and never thought of complaining. We were just thankful to have it. Charlie told us that he did his usual thing: he dipped his hat in, swirled the water around, threw it over his face and had a small sip.

Dad didn't have anything. Not a drop. He didn't even leave the cattle. He was in the lead, focused on his destination, leading the cattle onwards, undistracted by human weakness.

Dad was the toughest man we knew.

Even Papa Heaslip, who was notoriously hard, wasn't as hard as Dad.

Papa and Nana Heaslip came up to visit us during September one year. When we came down to the house for lunch, covered in dust after a morning of drafting cattle in the house cattle yards, we were exhausted. As usual, it was hot, and we'd been up since daylight. As soon as lunch was finished, Dad stood up and collected his hat. Then he turned to us and said, 'Righto, you kids, we're back to the yards.'

We got up wearily. Wouldn't have dared protest.

Papa said, 'You work these kids too hard.'

Silence filled the kitchen. Mum looked shocked. I was stunned.

But Dad simply said, '*Now*,' and we got up out of our chairs and followed him.

M'Lis said afterwards that she'd never previously thought about our heavy workload. And when she did, she felt her chest swell. 'I just felt so proud that we worked so hard and helped Dad.'

I wasn't sure my heart swelled like M'Lis's did.

Dad had changed a lot since he'd taken over Bond Springs. Once Papa was the top dog, but not anymore.

For example, when Dad grew up, there was no work on Sunday. Not even sport was allowed. Good Methodist rules.

Dad changed all that: Sunday became a work day, just like every other day. He had more work to do on Bond Springs (and elsewhere) than he had staff, resources or days in the week to do it all, so he didn't have time to rest. And if he didn't, nor did we.

Nor could we ever feel sorry for ourselves.

If we got hurt when riding or working out bush, Dad would use salt or kerosene to clean our wounds—it was usually the only thing he had handy to kill germs—and then pronounce his usual prognosis: 'You'll be right.' And we knew we had to use 'mind over matter' to manage the pain.

Dad said to M'Lis, 'The mind has no sympathy for the body'.

He seemed to view his body as something separate to himself and always referred to it in the third person. He also saw it as something under his control, and something that he drove forward, as he drove all of us forward.

———⟫•⟪———

The one creature Dad didn't ever push beyond his limit—and he might as well have been a person, given how much Dad loved him—was his golden horse, Limerick.

He and Limerick would gallop up hill and down dale in the toughest of conditions and always make it seem effortless. Even as Limerick got older, neither of them slowed down, and Limerick seemed happy to be wild and free under Dad's hands.

It was, however, a different story if someone else was involved.

One day, M'Lis was given the privilege of riding Limerick. Only one other person had been afforded this honour—Miss Clarke, who was allowed to walk around the horse paddock and feel how beautiful Limerick was to touch and ride. This was a mark of respect and a farewell gift from Dad before she left Bond Springs.

There was a different reason for M'Lis being offered Limerick.

Dad needed to muster Junction Waterhole. The landscape was hilly and scrubby and it was a difficult muster, always. The cattle were usually wild and prone to escape, especially because they knew all the little valleys and gullies and areas to hide, and once hidden, they were incredibly difficult to find and get out.

Limerick was considered perfect for the day because the team needed a really strong horse who was good in that kind of country. Limerick was *born* for that kind of country. But Dad couldn't ride him because he had to fly. So, we all stood in awe as M'Lis lifted her small leg up into the stirrup, and swung herself up on the back of the most important horse on Bond Springs.

We headed off as usual at daybreak. It was several hours before we reached the Junction. We followed the creek beds but it was still a long, rocky ride. Ahead of us, we heard and saw Dad in the distance, a speck of white and red dipping and diving, as he found mobs and pushed them along the creeks for us to take over when we got there. Once closer, he dived over us and shouted directions for us to all split up to maximise resources.

M'Lis found a mob quickly and as soon as she had, they were off, escaping along the creek at full speed. She galloped after them at full speed too, desperate not to lose them. Limerick stretched out under her, snorting happily, loving the chase.

Suddenly she heard Dad zoom overhead and his voice shout angrily out from the microphone: 'Steady on, Lis. No galloping. He's an old horse.'

M'Lis was furious. 'Why did he let me ride Limerick if he wasn't going to let me do the job properly?' she demanded, as she slowed Limerick down.

If only he showed that kind of concern for us, I thought, huffily.

23

The Best Weekend of the Year!

In the early 1970s Dad focused on building not only the numbers in his herd, but also the quality.

Our neighbour to the north, John Gorey of Yambah Station, was passionate about breeding stud bulls to improve his commercial line, and Dad followed his lead. And with Mr Braitling from Mount Doreen and Uncle Bill from Hamilton Downs, plus some other station men, Dad and Mr Gorey founded the Centralian Beef Breeders Association to promote good breeding in our area.

To look for good breeders, Mum and Dad, and Mr and Mrs Gorey, went to the Sydney Royal Easter Show to inspect the cattle. It was the biggest and most important cattle show in Australia, and Mum and Mrs Gorey packed their best clothes. We were left at home with Miss Thiele and Helen, and were quite put out at being abandoned. But Dad came back inspired. He had bought a beautiful bull called Progressor and several breeding cows from a Poll Hereford stud in South Australia, and had them trucked up.

'Always buy from the breeder,' Dad said, and he went on to buy other beautiful bulls from the same breeder for decades. 'Keeps your breeding consistent.'

Now Dad had the chance to show off his new cattle at the Alice Springs Show. To do that, he needed the right kind of help. He found a man from down south called Mr Browne, who arrived at Bond Springs about three months before the Alice Springs Show and took charge of training the bulls.

'Mr Browne with an E', as everyone called him, wore a jacket and tie every day with the kind of smart hat usually worn by southerners. He had a short moustache and spoke with a clipped accent. He was the most fascinating man we'd ever met. He was an expert at training cattle to walk around a ring and to be shown at their best. Mum's precious lawn was taken over as the training ground. Every day Mr Browne, and anyone else he could round up to assist, would lead the cattle around and around. The goal was to quieten them down to make them fit for 'showing'.

Given Mr Browne was a man of some sensibilities, he was, naturally, horrified by us. He considered us ruffians. Even in the freezing winter we would run around at night in our pyjamas with bare feet.

'These children!' he would scold. 'Where are their dressing gowns? Their slippers?'

'We don't have any!' we would retort gleefully as we raced through the kitchen in noisy pursuit of one another. Our feet were incredibly tough. We could run over gravel, dirt, prickles and hot and cold surfaces like gazelles. We were tiny but wiry from all our hard work. Mum would just shrug helplessly at his comments and continue cooking.

Charlie Gorey did not know how to deal with Mr Browne. He'd never met anyone quite like him. Mr Browne probably thought likewise about Charlie.

But we thought Mr Browne was a magician. He could take a group of wild cattle from the paddock and turn them into quiet, well-behaved show entrants, groomed to within an inch of their life, happily haltered and walking in a circle next to him.

Mr Browne took string off the hay bales to plait halters with which to lead the cattle around. They had the advantage of being soft, which suited Mr Browne because he wouldn't countenance anything that hurt the cattle.

One day Brett was with Mr Browne, putting a halter on one of the friskier steers. As they were struggling to get it over the steer's head, it took fright and bolted. Brett's leg got caught in the end of the halter and he was dragged along the dirt. The steer took off out of the house yard and up the hill, with Brett screaming behind him and Mr Browne yelling and tearing off after them. It was chaos. By the time Brett had worked his leg free of the halter, he was a mess. He had skin off everywhere and his little body was covered with bogan flea (the worst of prickles).

Mr Browne stopped plaiting halters after that. Leather halters— soft ones only—took their place.

Going to the show was a big deal. Two days before it began, the chosen cattle were loaded up into trucks to be taken on a slow, bumpy ride into the showgrounds at Traeger Park. Mr Browne stayed in a caravan nearby to guard them at night, and the next morning we were allowed to go in and help. We mucked out the yards. We helped wash and carefully brush the coats of the cattle and watched their tail tendrils flying in the breeze. We thought they looked beautiful, all brown and white and bellowing happily as they tucked into fresh water and hay.

The Alice Springs show was held at the most glorious time of year. The mornings and nights were freezing but the days were warm and sunny with huge blue skies. To make it all perfect, the Show brought a carnival atmosphere to inland Central Australia.

We met up with the Braitlings, the Goreys and lots of other friends. Even though we kids were still shy, we all had cattle in the show, and therefore a lot in common.

The cattle were judged over a two-day period, and Dad couldn't stop beaming like a proud father when Progressor received 'Poll Hereford Champion', and his heifers and steers second and third place in various classes. To finish off, there was a huge Grand Parade, where Dad led his beloved bull, and Brett proudly walked alongside him. Mr Browne led our other prize-winning cattle around the ring.

Brett was allowed to lead Progressor for some of the long, grand walk, and with his big stockman's hat over his little head and eyes, he was photographed by the newspaper, which ran a caption, '*Little man, that's a lot of bull!*'

We girls watched on, transfixed. What we really wanted wasn't to walk in the show—we wanted to *ride* in it.

We'd spent much of the two days gazing enviously at the show riders out on the oval. There were dressage exercises and competitions all day long, with horses and riders soaring over the gleaming red-and-white jumps. The riders looked so smart and confident trotting around in jodhpurs and coats and caps. It was as if they belonged to a different world—and they did: the mysterious and unknown world of pony club and show jumping and dressage.

M'Lis and I knew all about this through our reading. Our favourite series at that time was *Jill* by Ruby Ferguson. The heroine,

Jill, had it tough in her English village, but through sheer determination she had become one of the best show riders around (and beat the stuck-up, rich-kid riders). We loved her pluck.

Then there were sisters Josephine, Diana and Christine Pullein-Thompson, whose books were all about children having adventures without adults, usually hunting down the baddies and bringing them to justice. Set against a backdrop of English stables and dressage work and pony club and horse shows, their books enthralled us. We wanted to become like those kids.

There was just one stumbling block: we only had our naughty pony Lesley and the bony, old stock horses, none of which were really show material. I wasn't as confident a rider as my storybook heroines, but we were so inspired by those books, and the horses and riders we'd just seen at this show, we thought anything was possible. So, we started begging Mum and Dad to let us ride in the following year's show.

Mum said, 'We'll see. We'll ask Dad.'

Dad said, 'Depends on how good you are.'

That was Dad's default position. Even on his birthday, when we made him cards and gave him little gifts, he'd say, 'I don't need cards or presents. I just need you kids to be good. For Mum.'

We'd nod dutifully. Being good was definitely a day-to-day matter. A year of being good was just too hard to wrap our heads around.

In the meantime, now the cattle work was over we wanted to go to the sideshows, which were big and noisy and filled with people. There was a merry-go-round and the Ferris wheel and clowns with gaping mouths you could throw a ball into to win a soft toy and, best of all, fairy floss.

We couldn't *wait* to go.

Mum said we could go—under her supervision.

'I'm not letting you out of my sight, either,' she said firmly. 'If you get lost in there, I'll never find you again. But first, go and get money from your father.'

By now, Dad had retreated to the grandly titled Members' Bar. The bar was hidden away under the grandstand and children were not allowed in there. But we dived in, focused on finding Dad before the doorman found us. The bar was awash with noise and the smell of rum and beer. The concrete floor was sticky and men were standing five-deep at the bar. It was a maze of hats and boots. There were no women.

We found Dad in a corner. He looked resplendent in his smart town hat, smart blazer, smart Longhorn trousers and polished town boots. Mr Gorey and Mr Braitling and he were laughing over some joke. His eyes were sparkling, as they always did when he was happy.

"Scuse us, Dad, can we please have money for the sideshows? Mum sent us.'

Dad put down his glass and hunted in his pockets. 'What about this?' He fished out coins, then a fistful of notes. We grinned in delight, grabbed them and stuffed them in our own pockets.

'Thank you, Dad. Thank you!' We hugged him and raced out. Dad was tough, but at times like this, always generous.

Dad was a strange contradiction. He was born just before the outbreak of war, to parents who lived through the Great Depression, and so he was incredibly frugal. Like his mother, who had cupboards full of brown paper bags and pieces of string, he kept everything that could be reused, reworked or reimagined. He pulled nails out of boxes and straightened them so they could be used again. He kept the same big, square calculator on his desk for thirty-five years. If he ever saw food not eaten on a plate, he was furious. He could not abide waste in any fashion.

But at times like this, he didn't stint on letting us have fun too.

Tearing back to Mum, we chorused, 'We've got money! Let's go!'

Mum allowed us to buy the pink, feathery fairy floss and crunchy toffee apples, which were sickly and delicious, and hot dogs with sauce that ended up all over our special white show shirts. We rode on the carousel on wooden horses that went up and down to wonderful music, and bought tiny wands that swirled in the breeze. It was heaven.

———

For us, the fun of the show included staying with the Braitling family overnight in their sprawling house on Babbage Street. It was like being on holiday. In fact, we were now one big extended family. Whenever we left the station for an event, the Heaslips and the Braitlings went together.

With Mr Braitling, Dad was always able to unwind and laugh, which he rarely did at home. They were like brothers.

Mrs Braitling would say, with a wry grin, 'They're uncontrollable when they get together! But oh, such good men, nonetheless!'

We loved Mrs Braitling very much. She had brown, curly hair, a dimple in either side of her cheek and a ready laugh. She and Mum were like sisters.

Mum always sparked up when they were together. No wonder. Mum missed her girlfriends, and she and Mrs Braitling were able to talk about all the same kinds of issues and challenges that drove them both crazy. Mostly husbands, staff and kids.

———

We were great friends with the Crowson family, too—Faye and Brian, and their five children, Billy, Johnny, Catherine, Andrew and Annie. They lived hundreds of kilometres north on Montejinni Station.

They invited us, and the Braitlings, to join them at Katherine Show, which was held several weeks after the Alice Show, and to our delight, Dad said yes. The men would use the chance to look at the cattle and markets in the north. Dad was always exploring new sales opportunities, ever keen to expand his options.

There was something extra exciting about it all for M'Lis and me, too. We had found out that Mr Crowson had wooed Mum back in the 1950s, when she was a governess at Hamilton Downs. Mum had even considered staying up there with him, until the call of her childhood sweetheart (Dad) finally lured her back to South Australia.

'Brian was a gorgeous man,' Mum had told M'Lis and me, who'd hung off every word of the story. 'But he was a Catholic. Back then it simply wasn't done to marry between religions. Besides,' she'd sighed, 'I'd known Dad since I was thirteen and he was the one for me. And Brian then met Faye, who was also Catholic, and they were the perfect match.'

We thought this all terribly tragic and romantic. We were also fascinated that since returning to the Territory, Mum and Dad, and Brian and Faye, had all become great friends.

So, when I first met Billy, their eldest and my age, I thought it was practically written in the stars between us.

'Hello,' I'd said breathlessly and then spent the whole day staring at him. He was handsome like his father, with a gorgeous smile and gorgeous eyes, and I was smitten and decided we would get married. I told him about my plans, but he did not share them.

'Is she always this bossy?' he asked his mother,

I was undeterred; I knew we'd meet up again.

So, there we were, a month later, flying into Katherine. The Heaslips and Braitlings in their Cessnas, and the Crowsons in their low winger with *Montejinni Station* written in bright red right across it.

On arrival, it was bedlam. The motel had rooms in one long line that seemed to go on forever. Each family had a room or two. With thirteen children and six adults, the noise was at crescendo level.

The mothers decided it was time to let down their hair. Mum and Mrs Braitling especially believed they'd earned it after putting up with Dad and Mr Braitling at the Alice Show. The afternoon we'd left Dad and Mr Braitling in the Members' Bar was pretty much the last time we saw either of them again until the end of the show. They'd done what all bush blokes did when they came to town—got on the grog with their station mates, and left the women to do everything else.

'Right,' said Mrs Crowson, 'I'm getting out the brandy bottle!'

Mrs Crowson was feisty, smoked holding the tip of her cigarette up in the air, and swore deliciously. We were in awe and rather afraid of her.

On the first night, we had a barbecue outside the motel. The men drank beer and told stories. The women drank brandy in little glasses. We were allowed lemonade. I tried to sit as close to Billy as I could.

I also gazed a lot at Mrs Crowson throughout the night. She wore a tight, short white dress and long, white boots. She yelled at any of us if we stepped out of line. She seemed unafraid of anyone or anything. No wonder Mr Crowson fell for her.

The next morning we woke to find Mrs Crowson outside the rooms, stirring big pots over the barbecue burners, and still smoking vigorously. She was wearing a yellow blouse over yellow pencil slacks and seemed even feistier than the previous night. She'd been up for hours cooking porridge, and when she shouted, 'Line up!' we all jumped to attention.

Grabbing our bowls, we did as we were told. I was intrigued, holding out my bowl to be filled. I'd never tasted porridge before, even though it appeared regularly in Enid Blyton's books, not to mention *Goldilocks*, and this was my great chance. To my disappointment, it just seemed gloopy and had a funny taste.

'I don't like this, Mum,' I whispered. It wasn't 'just right', as I'd expected. But Mum had no time for such sensitivities. She was feeding Benny and he was throwing his food around.

'Well, there's nothing else. Eat it and be grateful. Think of the starving children in India,' she said crossly. Then she added, 'We're at someone else's place. Use your manners.'

Finally, we all got through the porridge, and headed to the show. Soon we were running around with our new friends, stuffing ourselves with toffee apples and fairy floss, and scoring a few rides at the sideshows. I even forgot about wanting to marry Billy for a while.

When it was over, Mr Crowson announced, 'Okay, kids, get your bathers. We're going to have some fun!'

Brian Crowson was the most jolly man we'd had ever met. We hurried after him as he directed us to a number of vehicles. 'Hop in,' he instructed with a broad smile, and soon we were tumbling out at the Low-Level Crossing on the Katherine River.

The Low-Level Crossing was made for fun. It was a part of the Katherine River that was safe for swimming, and had a beautiful, white sandy beach and shady trees. It looked like a cross between the sea and a billabong. We swam and splashed and played for hours. It was so different for us. We swam in the creeks at home if there was rain, or in the tanks if they filled up, but our water at home was brown and muddy—and often we had none at all. This river was clear and sparkling.

Dad took his sixteen-millimetre movie camera and captured the Low-Level adventures on film. Looking back, we saw images of numerous children jumping and laughing in the water, the three young mothers in their bikinis dipping their toes in and running after the little ones (Benny and Annie being the main two), and the two other fathers cheerily raising their stubbies to the camera and laughing.

We loved watching Dad's movie reel for years afterwards.

We felt like one big, happy family, everyone momentarily suspended from the stresses and strains of bush life.

24

Wild, Wonderful Bush Get-Togethers

The Katherine Show weekend reflected changing times in the bush.

Despite our families living so far apart—the Braitlings near the Western Australia border, the Crowsons near the Queensland border, and us in Central Australia—we were able to get together because each family had a plane.

There was a reason for this. From the late 1960s onward, bush people had been looking at ways to minimise the many down-sides of the isolation they faced, and at the same time Cessna was heavily marketing its planes to the bush. It was a match made in heaven. With an increase to the Elders GM or Dalgety overdraft, many bush families could acquire top-wing Cessna 172s and 182s, which were light and perfect for mustering, or occasionally, the heavier and faster lower-wing Beechcraft, which was better for long distances.

All they had to do then, apart from pay off the overdraft, was learn to fly them.

The pilots were mostly men, but women like Mrs Braitling flew too.

We would often hear Mrs Braitling's voice calling, 'Echo Foxtrot Whiskey, can you read me, Delta Quebec Golf?' when we were out flying with Dad, and we'd all shout out, 'That's Mrs Braitling!'

I longed to be brave like Mrs Braitling and another wonderful lady called Thelma Pye, who lived nearby and flew like a daredevil.

The other great thing about planes was that they expanded the ways bush people could get together and socialise. We would overnight at friends' stations when flying to Witchitie; we could fly to the Braitlings for New Year's Eve, and the Katherine Show each year was now possible. Then there was the 'fly-in' weekend.

Once a year, people with planes were invited to fly to Dalhousie, a tree-lined, hot natural spring that sat on Mount Dare Station in the middle of nowhere.

For an entire winter weekend, bush people would enjoy warm waters and cold beers. But the hosts, June and Rex Lowe, had one stipulation: children were not allowed.

'Sorry, darlings,' said Mum. 'It's too dangerous to have children around such a deep spring. The Lowes are just being careful. You could fall in and drown.'

'But Sandra and Donna are allowed to go.'

'Sandra and Donna are their daughters! Mrs Lowe couldn't leave them home all by themselves all weekend, now could she? Besides, they're quite grown up now.'

'Mmm.'

The long-suffering Miss Thiele and Helen were instead given the unenviable task of looking after us while our parents headed off. Our hearts plummeted as we heard the roar of DQG taking off and then disappearing into the sky until it was a speck. We were used to going everywhere with Mum and Dad and felt lost and lonely without them. The weekend dragged, and we took it in turns wondering what it would be like to sit up to our necks in hot water in the middle of the freezing desert.

On Mum and Dad's return, Dad said there had been thirty-two planes there.

'Gee! I wish I'd seen them,' said Brett, who really loved planes by now.

'I'll show you on Saturday night,' promised Dad.

When Saturday night came, Dad put up a little white screen in the sitting room and connected his camera. We sat cross-legged on the floor, impatient for action. In minutes, the whir of the camera delivered us thrilling images of a place up until now forbidden to our eyes.

'Oooh!'s and 'ahhh!'s filled the room.

There was sand as far as the eye could see ('the Simpson Desert,' Dad explained), then a huge billabong fringed by trees came into view. There were images of people jumping in and out of the waters and waving to the camera, before running back to the campfire and wrapping themselves in towels and thick jumpers and trousers. There was Mr Braitling shaving next to his tent, grinning and brandishing a bottle of beer. Next, Mr Crowson was charging him with a bleached set of cattle horns on his head. Dad was applying a branch fashioned into a branding iron to Mr Crowson's rump. They were all laughing uproariously.

There were also shots of a smiling Mum with little Benny wrapped in many layers (he was allowed to go because he was too young to report back on what happened there); and of Mrs Braitling and Mrs Crowson, each looking glamorous in pencil trousers and sipping brandy ('To warm up,' Mum explained).

There were also many shots of daredevil aeroplane activity during the day.

I thought of the old pilots' expression Dad had taught us: *Eight hours from bottle to throttle.*

At the fly-in, it seemed there were very tight margins.

———◦◦◦———

Wondrously, all bush kids were invited to the Central Mount Wedge Cricket Match.

Bill Waudby, or Wallaby Bill as he was affectionately known, was a gentle bear of a man, with a big moustache and stomach to match. He ran Central Mount Wedge, a cattle station several hundred kilometres to the north-west of Alice, and was a cricket enthusiast. Every year he hosted a cricket match 'to promote communications and camaraderie in the pastoral industry' (I read that in the local paper).

Wallaby Bill had the perfect spot for it, too—a big, flat plain, just down from the homestead, on which he graded a huge oval pitch. There was nothing around the oval; no fence, just a bit of scrub. But he built one large gate. It wasn't attached to a fence (because there wasn't one), but the cricketers had to walk through the large gate to get on and off the oval.

'Adds a bit of the big-smoke effect,' he once remarked. 'People will be more respectful.'

He also painted a sign marked 'BAR' and hammered it into a gum tree next to the pitch. Then he built two long drops covered in hessian over the other side of the hill. He declared the area in working order and sent out invitations. Cattlemen versus the stock and station agents along with any other associated 'townies', as we called them.

The two-day game was played over a weekend, with a day each way for travel, and the winners would receive a big silver potty, into which beer would be poured, and all the winners would have to take a big gulp. The winning team's name would be engraved on the potty and it would appear the following year for the next match.

There was a strict dress code. All the cricketers had to wear whites (where some of the bushies got them, nobody knew, but no allowances were made). Bill Waudby arranged for soft blue caps to be made for all the bush players, with 'CMW'—Central Mount Wedge—embroidered on the front. It was an honour to be invited to participate in the game. If you didn't abide by Bill's rules, or wear the cap correctly, you weren't invited back the next year.

Given Mount Wedge was so far from Alice, we always flew to it, as did a lot of other station people. Anywhere from between fifty to a hundred people arrived: cricketers, their wives, governesses and children, all milling about with swags, vehicles and cricket gear.

We loved Mount Wedge. From start to finish, it was an enormous thrill.

One of the best bits was flying into the match. Dad would duck down through the Mount Wedge ranges in DQG, head towards the oval, then drop into a steep dive to buzz those out there already practising. Through the windows we could see people fleeing, faces upturned, mouths open. We'd shriek, Dad would yell at us, and we'd cower in response: same routine, every time. But he would land DQG short on the nearby strip as lightly as a feather, with a wicked grin, and we'd tumble out, shouting and laughing once more.

No one could dive as well as Dad.

In the distance, we would see a cloud of dust and Bill's old ute trundling down to collect us, and the festivities would begin.

The first night was full of revelry as everyone caught up and made camp, food and lots of merry. We were off playing with the Braitling and Martin kids the minute we arrived. Some had driven in, some had flown, but we were all like extended family.

When Dad got dressed for the match the next morning, we hung around to watch, such was our excitement in seeing him don his 'special whites'. They were the same whites that he'd worn when he lived down in the Flinders Ranges and played cricket there, and so we believed they were imbued with something special. Mum had washed and pressed them in advance and it was quite a ritual as he put them on.

When Dad was called up to bat or bowl, we hung over the gate, cheering him on. He hadn't played since he'd lived down south, but he still had the touch, with a flick to the wrist in his spin, and the capacity to make big runs. We were incredibly proud of him. 'That's our Dad,' we'd say to each other with huge grins as he'd send a ball flying for six into the scrub.

While the men played cricket, the women ran around looking after the children, and then loyally stood on the sidelines when their husband went in (or came out).

In between times, we kids continued to make our own fun. We darted in and out of the nearby mulga trees, created games and visited our mothers only when we were hungry or thirsty. It was always hot but we didn't care.

Mrs Braitling was in charge of the bar under the tree. That was her domain for the weekend, year in, year out. There were eskies everywhere. Mrs Braitling stocked beer, rum and soft drink, usually lemonade and Coke. For at least the first day, she had enough ice to keep the drinks fairly cool. By the second day the ice had melted, and the beer was lukewarm, but by then nobody cared. She did a roaring trade.

At the edge of the pitch sat a dead mulga with many branches sticking up into the air. As blokes emptied their bottle or can, they would shove them onto one of the branch ends. In the end it looked like a beer tree, framed against a huge blue sky.

If we were good, we were allowed a soft drink or two. After a hot, busy time playing, when we finally stumbled in for food, we would clamour for the sweetness of the (otherwise) forbidden drink.

Everyone brought their own tucker, which was pretty much the same for every bush family: cold roast beef and corned beef, dry white bread, tomato sauce, fritz sausage slices and tomatoes. Mum always made sure we had fruit, so there were apples, and because it was usually winter she would have mandarins and oranges from the Peterkins' citrus trees in Alice. Lots of people grew lemons, oranges and mandarins in Alice Springs, and the fragrance in backyards was beautiful. As was the juicy sweetness of the orange segments we pulled out and sucked from the fruit.

The match was invariably fiery throughout, replete with sledging and dubious umpire decisions, much laughter and back-slapping, and the odd brilliant catch or run. Little boys like Brett and Matthew would hover, waiting for the opportunity to race after a ball, and then throw it back as though they were one of the team.

The nights were freezing. Everyone set up swags and made fires and there was a huge barbecue as the sun went down. The nearby ranges would glow with a deep red before turning orange, purple and then inky-black. By then, it was dark, and so we sat around on swags and played music. We loved it when Ted Egan came out, as he often did, because he was a great cricketer and played for the townies.

He would pull out his empty Fosters carton and start tapping away and sing our favourite songs, including 'The Drinkers of the

Territory'. We'd all join in, especially for the chorus, knowing that our parents couldn't stop us swearing in that moment. Joy! Ted always had a mischievous grin as we yelled out the word 'bloody' at the top of our voices.

Bill Waudby, our host extraordinaire, aka Wallaby Bill, was given his own verse. We loved it.

> I went to visit a mate of mine
> A run called Wallaby Bill's
> It was at Mount Wedge, right on the edge of the spinifex and sand hills
> When I produced a bottle of rum and asked if I could stay
> Bill said, 'Oh mate, let's shut the gate, and throw the bloody cork away'
> Hey!
> They've got some bloody good drinkers in the Northern Territory . . .

Most of the time, I had Benny with me. I looked after him wherever we went and whenever I could. But as the evening wore on, the mothers would descend, and hustle us into our swags. There were twelve swags in a row, all lined up so the mothers could account for everyone. Benny slept close to me. We would drift off to sleep under the stars, listening to Dad and Mr Braitling singing 'When Irish Eyes are Smiling' and 'Goodnight Irene'. We felt completely safe and cosseted and all was well in the world.

At the conclusion of the match the next day, there would be a presentation. Each team had their photo taken in front of the large gate. If the bushies won, we cheered and cheered, and hung around all the fathers, who would be in great form. If the townies won, we clapped politely, then turned away and went back to our games.

Best to avoid the fathers at that point.

Again, it was always a tight 'eight hours from bottle to throttle' timeframe from the end of celebrations to the time everyone flew out the next morning. But we knew Dad was the best pilot in the world and that he had a special twenty-four-hour pilot's watch on his wrist.

Squashed back in the plane, we'd watch his focused eyes, his sure command of the throttle, and hear him call out on the radio, 'Delta Queeeebec Golf', as he lifted us safely into the air. We'd watch until Mount Wedge was a speck in the distance and our eyes grew tired; then we'd sleep as Dad flew eastward towards the Bond, landing us safely at home, each and every time.

25

'We've Got Visitors, Mum!'

Even when there wasn't a bush event on, Mum always had an open-door policy for people near and far. This was especially important for those families who didn't or couldn't fly. When bush families (usually the mothers) took the long trek into town by car, Mum welcomed them into Bond Springs to stay with us overnight. It gave the mothers the chance to wash off the dust and tiredness of the long trip, and it gave Mum the chance to connect with girl-friends. Mum would feed them up and they would sleep in comfort and then head off on their last leg to Alice, restored.

We knew that driving in from out bush could be dangerous. Almost all the women had station wagons to carry their kids. They weren't very roadworthy vehicles, so the trips were long and difficult. There were often breakdowns, and always flat tyres. Most of the roads weren't sealed and they were all badly corrugated, and sometimes the cars had to drive up and down the banks of sand dunes that served as roads. When the car was full of children, it could be a hairy ride. If the car broke down, they were in trouble, because very few people came along that way, out in the middle of nowhere.

One evening, Mrs Braitling arrived with Mrs Martin from Mount Denison.

'Have we had a trip!' she exclaimed, staggering into Mum's kitchen. 'We broke down last night. Had to camp. We had no food, except a couple of eggs I collected from the chook yard just before I left home. So, we lit a fire, and I took the hub cap and filled it with a bit of water, put it over the fire, and put those eggs in it. Best boiled eggs we've ever eaten!'

Mum rushed to whip them up a hearty supper.

One of our favourite visitors was Marie Mahood.

She would drive for a whole day with her children from Mongrel Downs Station, way, way north-west of Alice Springs. Sometimes it would take her two days because she'd camp overnight. Either way, she would invariably arrive on dark, exhausted. She'd climb out of her car and, hands on hips, exclaim to Mum, 'I've just driven over six hundred kilometres on dirt roads today and this road into Bond Springs is the *roughest* road of all!'

Marie Mahood was a gutsy, smart and witty woman who endured the toughest of lives on Mongrel Downs and still kept her sense of humour. She wrote stories about all the hilarious incidents of their isolated life and her very resilient children Kim, Bob, Tracey and Jim. *Icing on the Damper* was perhaps her funniest and most famous.

Our poetry and readings in the bush always included Banjo Patterson and Henry Lawson. Marie's eldest daughter Kim reworked the much-loved and amusing *Mulga Bill's Bicycle* into a poem about her father. She called it *Joe Mahood's Motorbike*. It was side-splitting and brilliantly clever.

The poem was circulated around School of the Air, and I loved it so much that I memorised it. Then I went on to write my own version about *Mike Kimber's Motorbike*—a wild, bad and mad machine down at Witchitie that had thrown Mike off. I put my poem in the post to the Kimbers and wrote that I hoped 'they would enjoy my rendition'. Margaret wrote back and said that while Mike was still recovering from the dangerous bike, they certainly had, thank you.

———≫●≪———

Our lives changed yet again, most wonderfully, when I was nearly ten. The Gemmell family came to visit the Bond and ended up staying for two and a half years. Aunty Jill and Uncle Pete Gemmell were long-term friends of Mum and Dad from Adelaide. Mum called them the 'glamour couple'. Aunty Jill was tall and slim, with gorgeous silver–blonde hair she wore either twirled high into a French roll or straight and flicked out at the ends. Uncle Pete was dark haired and dashing and lots of fun. They had two children, Adam and Sharon, who were younger than me, and we loved them. More kids meant more chances to play. Uncle Pete was a builder and Dad needed help, so everyone was happy when they decided to stay.

The Gemmells moved into a tiny wooden cottage set back from the road entrance to the homestead. It had two floors—well, the second one was only half a foot up from the first, but I thought it marvellous. It was our first experience of a two-storey house! It was also on stilts to keep it safe from snakes.

While Sharon scampered around with Benny, Aunty Jill taught Adam his Correspondence School lessons from the cottage. She wore pencil slacks, fitted tops, lipstick and looked like a model, day and night. Adam came down to the 'big house'—the homestead—every day to speak to his teacher Mr Jamerson on the radio and shared School of the Air lessons with us.

Before long, Adam and Sharon were part of our gang, which meant they got roped in to do all sorts of jobs. One of those was taking care of the 'fairy stone'.

It was a beautiful old white stone, thick and square, that sat in the fork of the homestead road. Mum said it was the home of the tooth fairies. 'But the fairies will only come if you keep the stone perfectly clean,' she warned.

Every time someone lost a tooth, we would rush down to the fairy stone with buckets of soap and water and brushes, and scrub it from top to bottom. Once that was done, someone would be delegated to go and get Mum.

'Mum, come and look!' we'd say, pulling her by the hand until she came to inspect our handiwork. Her role was to declare whether or not it reached the Fairy Standard: glowing white. We would huddle around her anxiously as she inspected every part of the stone until she pronounced it fit for the fairies' visit.

The next morning we would race back to the stone, where it was always waiting for us, bright in the morning sunshine. The person who'd lost the tooth was allowed to put their finger underneath, while the rest of us crowded around, holding our breath. Lo and behold—there was always a sparkling silver coin underneath.

Magic!

Another wonderful thing about that year was that the Gemmells brought the first-ever television to Bond Springs. We could hardly believe our luck.

It was a small black-and-white box, with a very large aerial that Uncle Pete pushed high up into the sky. The reception was patchy, and it often lost coverage, but we were used to sounds of static, and just thrilled to see flickering, moving images when we could.

One day, Aunty Jill came down, smiling her beautiful smile. 'On Sunday nights, there's going to be an Australian serial starting called *A Taste for Blue Ribbons*. It's about horses and children. Would you like to come down and watch it with Adam and Sharon?'

Would we?!

'Thank you, Aunty Jill!' M'Lis, Brett and I fell over ourselves to say. We could hardly wait until the following Sunday night.

Mum made us eat dinner first, and then we rushed down to Aunty Jill's, where we curled up in front of the screen and waited for the show to begin. There was some lovely music and then a girl and a horse came on. Soon, we were completely lost in its spell. By the end, M'Lis and I were in love with the heroine of the show, who was heartbroken when she learned her father was going to sell her horse to help pay off the family debt. She was very pretty and brave, and a beautiful rider. Brett didn't care very much about the girl but was impressed by the horses and riding. We spent most of the next week discussing *Blue Ribbons* and hoped Aunty Jill would let us come back for the next episode.

Luckily, she did. It was our first television serial and we were hooked.

Around that time, we also started listening to a wireless serial. It was called *Cattleman*, and covered the sagas of a brave cattle-man from the bush called Dan McCready. It came on at 4.30 in the afternoon, beginning with the crack of stock whips and '*Har hup there!*' We felt like we knew Cattleman personally and huddled around the wireless in the kitchen to listen breathlessly as he faced his latest dramas and adventures on horseback.

We were drawn to these stories because they were all about our lives: horses, cattle, the bush, and they inspired us to make up and put on our own plays. Most of ours focused on cattle duffers, Cowboys and Indians, and life out in the stock camp. But after reading some of the Braitlings' comics, we decided to expand our repertoire. We decided to terrify the grown-ups with masks, ghosts and tragic deaths.

Our best-ever play was *The Deathly Murders*.

Rehearsals were serious business. We dressed up in Mum's sheets and painted our faces with black texta. We leaped about screaming and thrusting cardboard daggers into each other. With moans and groans we all fell about on the lawn until we were all dead. On the big night, we put chairs on the lawn and made the grown-ups sit and watch. We couldn't believe it—they collapsed off their chairs laughing.

We were outraged.

One Easter, Dad flew us out to Mount Doreen, and we kids decided to hold a church service. We set up chairs on the Braitlings' lawn and made everyone sit on them, while we all took turns solemnly reading out extracts from Mr Braitling's school bible.

'Now we will have collection,' I announced.

'What do you mean, hand over our money?' asked Mrs Braitling, perplexed, as we went to every adult with a tray we'd borrowed from her kitchen, requesting they put coins on it.

'It's collection time,' we declared. 'It's church.'

Surely it was obvious.

'Will we get our money back?'

'No.'

Of course not. Sometimes grown-ups asked very silly questions.

Our next idea was to set up a shop.

On the way out of Alice sat a small enclave of shops called Northside, and our favourite shop tucked away in there was Hoppy's. It was a tiny store that sold bread, milk, fritz sausages and other essentials—but best of all, lollies. Mum would invariably stop at it on the way out of town to pick up last-minute goods. We would tumble into the shop after our guitar lessons and gaze longingly at the milk bottles, red and yellow snakes, raspberry jubes, white-and-pink teeth and piles of chocolate freckles.

'Please, please, please, Mum, can we have some?'

'No.'

'Why not? Please please please!'

'Because they'll rot your teeth.'

'*Pleeeeeease*, Mum.'

'No, I said no. Enough, I'm getting cross.'

So, we had to come up with a better plan. And we did.

'Mum, we've got an idea. Can we please set up a shop, just like Hoppy's? We can buy the things from the shop and sell them to everyone at home.'

Eventually we wore Mum down. We borrowed the princely sum of five dollars from her and bought enough milk bottles, snakes, teeth and freckles to rot the teeth of everyone on the station. Then we set up a table with a tablecloth on the veranda and made everyone passing buy lollies from us. It was enormously successful.

We didn't see the money again. I suspect Mum took it all back from us.

26

All the Games That We Could Play

One of the big events on the station was the monthly outing to get a 'killer'. Dad would drive out in his Land Rover and shoot one of his cattle to provide meat for the station, and we always went to help.

Our first job was to pull leaves off the mulga trees and make a ground carpet to place the dead beast on. That way it wouldn't get dirt and ants on it when it was being carved up (or at least, it minimised the risk). Dad usually brought one of the stockmen to help and they used very sharp knives.

After doing our bit, we were allowed to blow up the lungs. This was the most fantastic game and we each waited impatiently for our turn. We'd grown up with branding, castrating and seeing dead animals throughout the bush, and were unfazed by a bit of 'blood and guts'. The lungs were always slippery, covered in gunk and hard to hold onto, and our mouths would be surrounded by a bright red 'O'. Huge amounts of huffing and puffing were required from our little chests but wow—the result was a miracle! It seemed amazing that we could blow into the lungs of a dead animal and see them rise and fall with our breath. It was like we were bringing it back to life. We laughed hysterically and fell over ourselves to do it again and again.

We could make a game out of anything, anywhere, with whatever we had. Then Dad would order us to gather more leaves, which meant the fun was over, and we'd be back to work. These leaves would be packed on the floor of the tray of the Land Rover. The men would then heave the lumps of quivering beef into the tray, and we would undertake our final, very important job: sitting on the meat all the way back to the homestead, using extra leaves to brush off flies, and stopping the meat from falling off.

One of the things we loved most about sitting on the back was the wind in our hair and our faces. We felt so free and alive being on the back of the vehicles and never sat in the front unless we had to. We were rarely offered a seat anyway, because the men always took them. 'Kids and dogs on the back,' was the old bush saying, and we never complained. Clutching the bars of the vehicle, with a 360-degree view around us and the ground hurtling underneath, was almost as good as flying.

Once we arrived home, the men took the lumps to the meat house, and further dissected it into its various cuts that could be stored. Some larger cuts would be hung up and left in the meat house if they needed to be tenderised over a long time. Cuts that would be eaten immediately—such as steak—were put into the cold room. The whole process was a long and difficult business and required great skill from Dad and whoever was helping him.

But once it was all over, it was time for a celebration. Rib bones on the barbecue!

It was the highlight of our month. We would all have a bath and clean up first. Mum would butter lots of bread and bring out tomato sauce. We would all gather around the barbecue, where Dad was in charge of cooking. It was a huge event and everyone on the station looked forward to the monthly feast.

When the rib bones were crispy and cooked perfectly, we would line up to get a plateful. Then we'd sit cross-legged on the lawn with our heaped plates, chewing and gnawing like happy dogs. Dad's rules were clear: we couldn't go back for seconds until we could show that our current bones were completely white. If there was even a tiny bit of meat left visible, Dad would shake his head.

'You can do better than that! Come back when you've done a proper job.'

Adam Gemmell became a pro at getting the rib bones white, and Dad always nodded approvingly at his efforts.

'Good work, Adam! You're showing 'em how it should be done.'

Dad also cooked what he called curly gut—the inside lining of the beast's stomach—but we hated it and wouldn't eat it. It was grey and rubbery and, we thought, tasted disgusting. Dad always told us it was good for us (and he ate it, as did the stockmen) but we knew we'd have fresh steak for the next week and said we'd wait for that. Fresh steak was the treat before we had to resume our usual diet of corned beef and curried beef, each dish created by Mum extending the life of the beef for the rest of the month.

After we'd stuffed ourselves with rib bones, it was usually time for a concert. We would make up plays with songs to entertain the adults on the lawn. Adam and even Sharon and Benny were dragged into it. Sometimes the Peterkins came out for the cele-bration, and the three Peterkin boys were forced into our plays whether they liked it or not.

———————⟶●⟵———————

'Does Uncle Grant always carry a stockwhip with him?' Adam asked me one day.

I thought about it, but not for long. 'Yep.'

Dad usually walked around the station with his stockwhip looped around his shoulder. He would unroll it and give it a crack if anyone or anything was out of line. The sound of that crack would make our knees tremble.

Stockwhips were also an important part of a cattleman's set of tools, along with his pocket knife used for cutting micky bulls and cutting out snake venom, a fence strainer to prop up leaning strands of wire, and of course, his saddle and bridle. All bush men had to be able to do whatever was required in the middle of nowhere: fix bores, drive trucks, muster cattle, break in horses, and a stockwhip always came in handy.

Stockwhips were so important that Slim Dusty sang about them. The incredibly sad ballad 'The Dying Stockman' summed it up for us. The young stockman's last request was to be buried with his stockwhip and blanket, deep below the coolibah tree, safely away from the dingoes and crows. He also wanted a picture of his stockwhip carved onto a sapling to be placed over his grave so other stockmen would know he lay there. That song always brought a terribly big lump to our throats.

Stockwhips were also dangerous.

As kids, we'd all tried to crack the stockwhip, and whipped ourselves by mistake. We all knew how much it stung. It bit into our bodies, removed skin in a second, and left us with long red welts that often bled.

If we did something wrong, Dad would make us all stand before him, and flick it up and down near his own leg. We'd flinch at the likelihood he might use it against us. Not that he ever did, but then again, there was always a first time, depending on how naughty we'd been. We never knew whether one day he might actually change his mind and use it. So, we'd all be white faced and beg forgiveness and say we'd never do it again, whatever 'it' was.

Didn't matter who'd misbehaved—we'd all be called to account— so Adam had a vested interest in knowing.

———◦———

One of the things we were never allowed to do was go anywhere near Dad's precious, private bar. And that was one thing we never, ever did.

Not one of us. Ever.

On winter weekend nights, though, we were all allowed to crowd around the sitting-room fire, which was next door to Dad's bar. Then we could play our records on our little red record player. We were even allowed to make noise and sing along. We loved those evenings. Adam and Sharon would join in and it was our own special time.

We always laughed at Slim Dusty's 'Pub with No Beer', because by now we knew how important beer was in the bush. And 'Cunnamulla Fella', because we all knew a cheeky stockman like that. We were also wide-eyed at the 'From the Gulf to Adelaide' where a bunch of hopeless drovers took on thirty thousand crocodiles. We certainly knew pessimistic bush blokes like 'Happy Jack' and felt deeply miserable but deeply connected to songs like 'How Will I Go With Him, Mate?' and 'By a Fire of Gidgee Coal'.

Charley Pride's songs 'Banks of the Ohio' and 'Cotton Fields' weren't much happier but they didn't relate to losses in our world. For us they were fun. We would listen to them on the record player and then we'd get out our guitars. We'd strum the first chord of

'Cotton Fields', then belt out the song like we were twelve-bar blues professionals.

Those songs helped M'Lis and me learn to harmonise.

We did a great take of Charley Pride's 'The Snakes Crawl at Night', because that's exactly what they did in our part of the world, and 'Kaw Liga', which ended with a fantastic opportunity to howl like a dingo. 'Kaw LigAHHHHHHHHH,' we'd all howl at the tops of our voices until Mum came rushing in to say, 'Keep it down, you kids. We can't hear ourselves think out here!'

And then there were all the really sad Slim Dusty and Charley Pride songs. Nor could we forget Ted Egan's unbearably poignant 'Drover's Boy'. There were just so many sad songs in the bush. Kids, dogs, horses, people, life . . . always loss, grief, hardship, because— as Slim Dusty reminded us, and we all agreed—it was a hard, hard country.

Nostalgia was built into us from an early age.

————⯈●⯇————

Benny and Sharon were both about four years old by now and joined at the hip. Because there were so many people around, they generally ran free and wild, and most of the time nobody really knew what they were up to. But mostly they were up to trouble.

One day Papa Parnell was visiting and he brought his old, long-haired cat, Sylvester.

Sharon and Ben thought Sylvester's grey coat was a boring colour and decided to do something about it. So they found some pink paint in the shed and painted a stripe down Sylvester's back. By the time Sylvester finally escaped their clutches he was most indignant and marched off with his tail in the air, meowing crossly. Benny and Sharon followed, giggling all the way and admiring their handiwork. At some point, they had the presence of mind to think they should wipe it off before Papa Parnell caught them. So they grabbed the poor old cat again and rubbed and rubbed his back. To their dismay, the very pink paint wouldn't come off. Sylvester meowed even more crossly. Undeterred, they thought they would clean it off instead. Heading to an outside toilet, they put Sylvester into the toilet, and flushed him. At some point Mum heard the cat's shrieks and raced out and saved Sylvester's life.

'I can't put up with another moment of you kids!' Mum declared furiously, after she pulled the equally furious cat out of the toilet. Turning to Benny and Sharon, now twitching before her, she said, 'Out of my hair. And Sharon, you have to go home to your mum now.'

Then she marched back to the kitchen to address the never-ending tasks of cooking and cleaning.

So, Benny and Sharon headed back up to Aunty Jill's house.

Benny put his head through the door and said, 'Aunty Jill, can I please have lunch here? Mum's a bit cranky today.'

Benny and Sharon's next exploit was branding the chooks.

Adam and Sharon's grandmother was up from Adelaide, and Mum brought her, and Aunty Jill, out to the west side of the station one day to see us doing the yard work. This involved drafting, branding and castrating (aka cutting) the micky bulls.

Dad always did the cutting if he was present, because it was a very important job to do well, and he was always careful and protective of his cattle. There were many micky bulls to be cut on that day and subsequently lots of bloodied bits of balls being thrown onto the ground. We started throwing them about and one hit Adam's grandmother in the face; she was not at all happy.

There was much apologising, but Benny and Sharon saw it all, as well as the branding, and they thought it was marvellous. When the pair got home, they decided they should brand the chooks. They didn't have a branding iron, so they came up with another solution. They snuck into the chook yard and grabbed every chook and shoved it into the water trough, head and all.

Mum rushed out of the house to the hideous shriek of drowning chooks. She managed to save them but they went off laying eggs for over a week after that and she was livid. Eggs were an essential daily ingredient in all her cooking. Steak and eggs for breakfast, and cakes, were staples of the station diet. Unfortunately for an entire week, things were a bit grim on the food front, as was Mum's 'health and humour', as she liked to call it.

None of this deterred Benny or Sharon in the least. They continued causing trouble and having a wonderful time.

At one point, Sharon loved *A Taste for Blue Ribbons* so much that she decided to become a horse. Every day, she would tie herself up in the stables with bags of chaff to eat, and spent hours there. Aunty Jill would be looking everywhere for her and then they would find her, happily hidden away from everyone. Except for Benny, who was usually there too, before they both went off to cause more mischief elsewhere.

Eventually Benny and Sharon were so naughty together that Aunty Jill decided Sharon should start school early. Most of Sharon's days were thereafter spent up in the cottage and Benny lost his playmate throughout the day. He still managed to get up to plenty of mischief on his own, but at least the cat and the chooks were reasonably safe.

>•<

We were all sad when the Gemmells left Bond Springs. Luckily they didn't go far: just out to the Braitlings at Mount Doreen. Uncle Pete did a lot of building work for them, and when he finished they moved back to Alice, so we continued to see them all. All the families remained very close.

⸺⸺＞•＜⸺⸺

One day I came into Mum's room after school to find her crying. She had clothes scattered over the bed and an open suitcase next to her.

'What's happening?' I asked, looking in shock at her red-rimmed eyes.

'Mr Crowson,' was all she managed to say.

M'Lis joined me, and we stood there, staring at Mum. Her shoulders heaved. 'There's been a terrible accident. Mr Crowson has been killed. In his plane.'

We were open mouthed, not knowing how to take this in. Mum and Dad's wonderful friend, who lived east of Katherine; husband of the feisty, glamorous Mrs Crowson; father of Billy, whom I intended to marry. Mr Crowson, who was always smiling, always fun, beloved by everyone.

It was impossible. Unthinkable.

Dad walked in, but didn't speak. Finally, we gathered that Mr Crowson had been flying over Montejinni in his beloved plane when it crashed.

That night Mum and Dad, along with the Braitlings, flew to be with Mrs Crowson, and we were once again left in the care of Miss Thiele and Helen.

The outcome was unbearable. Mrs Crowson had to take her five bush kids several thousand kilometres south and create a new life in suburban Adelaide, far away from Katherine and Montejinni, and the only life they knew.

Mr Crowson was gone. Forever.

Dad and Mr Braitling were bereft. As were Mum and Mrs Braitling. And I was never quite able to look Billy Crowson in the eye again.

The loss of charismatic, handsome Mr Crowson threw a huge pall over all of us and I felt the grief of Mum and Dad for a long time.

27

Eeyore John Wayne

Benny was growing quickly. Whenever Papa Parnell came to stay, Benny became Papa's little shadow. Papa would spend most of the day pottering in the garden, helping Mum with the endless sweeping of leaves and watering. Wherever Papa went, Benny was two steps behind, dragging a rake or bucket.

At lunchtime, Papa would come in and have his usual: meat and pickled-onion sandwiches. Papa was a man of habit. Benny would have the same. They would sit together: tall, silent Papa at the end of the table, with little Benny sitting by his side, eating meat and pickled onions in rough bread together.

Benny was pretty well behaved with Papa, because Papa was not someone you messed with. But when Benny wasn't with Papa, he was constantly into mischief and causing trouble. He would mess up our books or toys or little stations in the dirt. In turn we'd yell at him. We loved him but he drove us crazy.

Mum told us off when we complained.

'Benny's just lonely. It's his way of seeking attention,' she'd say. 'Go and play with him. Be kind to him. That's your job.'

I knew it was my job, for sure. I was the eldest. And it was a happy job. I loved looking after him. But M'Lis, Brett and I were growing up and either in school or doing serious stock work during the days. Our lives still overlapped at night, especially with cuddles and stories, but seven years between us made me his little mother, rather than a playmate.

So, during the day, Benny trailed around after the stockmen and bore men. No doubt he was desperate for attention from someone, anyone. For Benny, negative attention was better than no attention.

Mostly the men were patient and good with Benny, but he sorely tested their limits.

One day our Irish stockman Ray was up welding a rail around a trough. It was quite a way up the hill from the house. Dad wanted to ensure the trough was protected when the cattle came for a drink. Ray had his welding glasses and gloves on, and was focused, ensuring he got the sparks of the welding iron in just the right place. It was a hard job and Ray didn't want to have to go back to Dad until he'd got it right.

Next minute, Ray felt the shock of something ice-cold hitting him. He dropped the welding iron at his feet, yelling in shock. Spinning around, he saw Benny standing there, dangling an empty bucket. Ben had wandered up after him—quite a walk for a small boy—drawn some water out of the trough into the bucket, and thrown it all over Ray. Focused as Ray was, he hadn't even noticed Benny arrive.

'You wee leprechaun!' Ray was red-faced by now. He grabbed Benny by the straps of his jumpsuit and shoved him face first into the trough. Benny shouted and spluttered, and as Ray pulled him back out, Benny stumbled to his feet and hotfooted it back to the house, now soaking wet as well.

When Ray saw Mum at lunchtime, he told her what had happened. He was still shaking with rage.

Mum sighed. 'Oh well, it serves him right,' she said, serving cold meat onto plates. 'He was lucky that's all you did to him.'

I covered Benny with hugs and kisses whenever something went wrong, to remind him how much I loved him. But he drove even me to distraction with his next escapade, which involved a donkey and cart and a horse breaker called Barry.

Barry had a dark beard and dark eyes and wore a bush hat pulled low over his eyes. He came to work for us for a while and became Benny's next conquest.

Barry was a fascinating man. He always travelled with a couple of dogs and camels. We learned he'd led a whole train of camels along the railway line through the Heavitree Gap in Alice. We were aghast. What if a train had come along and run them all over? And what about the cars running alongside the railway line; wouldn't they spook the camels?

We called him a 'cameleer'. He reminded us of the brave and amazing 'Afghan' men who transported goods on camels across the outback in the 'olden days', back before even horses or Land Rovers were here. Those camel drivers wore turbans and had long beards, so Barry could have been one of them, except he didn't wear a turban.

Barry was also the first person we'd ever met who drank proper coffee. He brought ground coffee with him, which he brewed up in a pot. He wouldn't drink anything else and he certainly wouldn't drink instant coffee, which was the only type we knew. And there was no animal that Barry couldn't break in, and train or tame.

Benny was fascinated by Barry. He trailed around after the black-bearded man, watching him in action in the horse yards. Every day a few donkeys in the horse paddock came in for a drink at the house trough. One day Barry and Benny spied a little donkey with them. Benny coveted that donkey, and begged and begged Mum and Dad to let him break him in.

'Please, Mum, Dad,' he begged. 'Then I can have a friend.'

Dad said it was up to Mum.

Normally soft-hearted Mum refused. 'No, donkeys are a menace.'

The good and kind Barry eventually took pity on Benny. He put a halter on the donkey, brought him into the yards, and said, 'I'll break him in for yer.'

The donkey was christened Eeyore John Wayne, and Benny was ecstatic.

But Eeyore became a complete menace, just as Mum had predicted. He galloped everywhere around the house yard. He chased us kids and we'd have to run to escape him. If he caught us, he'd bite us, hard, and we'd howl. He pinched Mum's towels and clothes off the clothesline and ate them. And if we gave him the chance, he'd kick us too.

But Benny loved him.

There was an old cart down in the shed that Barry restored for Benny. It could fit just two people in a squeeze and had two high wheels. Barry harnessed Eeyore so Benny could take him for a ride. My baby brother was in heaven. He'd jump in the cart, stockman's hat squashed over his ears, shake the reins and drive Eeyore around the horse yard. After a while he became adventurous and started to ride Eeyore around the lawn. Mum was unhappy with this because it roughed up the lawn and made a mess of the dirt, and the donkey also tried to eat all Mum's precious plants.

So, Benny thought of something else: racing the donkey and cart out on the flat.

'Come with me, Tanya,' Benny pleaded one day.

'No,' I said firmly. I didn't like the donkey or the cart.

'Please, please, please,' begged Benny.

This went on for several days. Eventually Benny wore me down. So, I hopped up with him and said in my best big-sister voice, 'Okay, but we'll just go for a short ride round the yard.'

But Eeyore, sensing a change in the dynamics, took off at a gallop. Benny, delighted he had a conquest, urged Eeyore on. The donkey went flat-out through the yard, past the sheds, out through the gate and headed towards the creek. I screamed and clutched on, while Benny shrieked with laughter, and shook the reins to make Eeyore go faster. As we headed down the rocky flat towards the creek, the inevitable happened. The cart flipped and I fell out and sprained an ankle yet again. Benny was unscathed and thought it was a wonderful adventure.

It was my first and last ride in the cart with Eeyore John Wayne.

———◦◦◦———

I was sure that Mum was right. It wasn't Benny's fault he got up to mischief. He was just looking for somebody to notice him. But there was no end to the lengths Benny would go to in that quest.

A wonderful couple, Pat and John Govers, came into our lives and spent years with us, off and on. Pat was an amazing chef and had travelled the world as a photographer, painter, journalist and collector of art. John was a Dutch immigrant and a brilliant carpenter (well, he was brilliant doing almost everything with his hands). He was Pat's handsome toy boy. They lived in numerous places, stayed with us from time to time, and called each other Mr and Mrs G.

One day Mr Govers was carrying an incredibly heavy load. It was lengths of iron railway track he'd retrieved from the town scrap yard. Each weighed about thirty kilos. He was on his way to make a border for Mum's garden. As he walked, he balanced the sleepers on his palms above his shoulders, each step slow and deliberate on the way towards his Toyota. He was so focused that he didn't hear Benny climbing into the old Land Rover nearby. Benny was five by now and learning to ride and drive everything, just as Brett had done when he was the same age.

Benny opened the little chute below the Land Rover window so he could see through to the outside world, and then he kangaroo-hopped forward towards Mr Govers. On the last hop, he hit Mr Govers' rear end.

Mr Govers reared backwards, screaming as he toppled over. The huge lengths of iron crashed to the ground. When Mr Govers recovered, he chased Benny, shouting in Dutch, and belted him thoroughly.

'You're a mongrel kid!' Mr Govers finally said, in English, and let Benny go.

The object of Mr Govers' wrath was not seen for hours.

———⋙●⋘———

Meanwhile, I was continuing to explore life beyond our boundary fence, mostly through School of the Air, study and books.

Reading and writing consumed me. I constantly wanted to learn and understand more. I was fascinated by the adults' conversations. They seemed to talk about the important things in life. Dad didn't talk a lot, but when he did, he *only* talked about important things, so I thought that's what I should be aiming for and learning about.

But not everyone agreed. 'Off you go, flappy ears,' Mum would say to us if we came too close to the grown-ups when they were talking.

I soon learnt that when Dad started talking, he wouldn't stop for a long time, so if I sat quietly, Mum would usually forget I was there. What, with all Dad's table-banging and finger-pointing and thundering about the problems we constantly faced and what needed to be done to fix them, Mum would leave the table before he'd finished, and I could listen without interruption.

I'd go away and think about the many things he talked about, then store them deep inside. Mostly they made me feel anxious all over again, but after a while I realised that there were gifts in Dad's rants.

Yes, life was risky.

But if we were constantly alert we could be prepared, and preparation was a way to stay in front of the problems.

Dad spoke about it all the time. '*Always do your homework. Know your numbers.*'

Now I realised why.

When the bloody bureaucrats, communists and socialists turned up in their long white socks, holding their clipboards, we would be ready. It didn't necessarily mean we'd be safe, or saved, but we'd have a better chance if we were prepared, than if they arrived and caught us sleeping, or worse, slacking off.

Dad prepared by being proactive in every possible way he could dream up. He was so passionate about protecting and advancing the interests of cattle people on the land, he not only became the Chairman of the Central Australian Beef Breeders Association and the first Chairman of the Northern Territory Cattlemen's Association, but he also went on to become Vice President of the Cattle Council of Australia and Chairman of the Producers' Consultative Group, which reported directly to the Australian Meat and Livestock Corporation. He also became the leader of numerous cattle trade delegations throughout the world. He didn't stop pushing to make things better.

'You've got to be in there, taking charge, making things happen, rather than letting them happen to you,' he'd say.

Unlike me, he was fearless, and clear about what he wanted to achieve, and he didn't stop until he made it happen, or had at least given it his best shot.

The trouble was I didn't know how to apply Dad's approach to my own life. I didn't do homework (it wasn't required for our primary school lessons), and I wasn't very good at numbers (and probably would never be). I couldn't be in charge of anything, because I was just a kid under his dominant rule, so thinking about how to use his wisdom to improve myself just made me feel anxious again.

Nor could I talk to anyone about it. I didn't even have the words to express how I felt. Mum would probably just tell me to stay away from grown-up conversations in future, and there was no way I'd tell Dad anything of my fears. I was too ashamed of having them in the first place. But I knew that as long as Dad was there, I would be safe. If I listened carefully to the advice he gave us, and looked for the reasons behind his instructions, I knew I could work out how to be stronger, clearer, braver myself.

But what about when I went away to boarding school? Dad wouldn't be there to protect me, nor would Mum. But boarding school was several years away, so every time that scary thought popped up, I squashed it down.

28

Everard Park

I spent a lot of time thinking about my friend Janie Joseland, and how we could meet up again, face-to-face.

School of the Air wasn't enough for us. While we now knew what each other looked like and got to hear each other's voices in class each day, we wanted our *own* conversations. That wasn't possible in class because Mrs Hodder ran the class and asked questions of us all individually. There wasn't the chance for chat between students.

So, we tried to wangle moments on the afternoon sked. That wasn't easy either. There were many determined bush women wanting to talk in that precious allocated time, and they were not amused by two young 'giggling Gerties', as Mum called us. But through the giggles, we hatched a plan. The next time Dad flew south, we decided, he would drop me off at Everard Park for a visit.

Eventually we wore Mum down and she agreed to put our idea to Dad (I didn't have the courage to ask him myself; not for something so personal and frivolous—no way).

As it happened, Dad was flying south in a month, but the timing didn't work. But my darling Mum took on my plea and continued to look around for options. Several days later she came to me and said, 'Rex Lowe from Mount Dare is flying south from Alice in a couple of weeks, and is prepared to go via Everard Park and drop you off on his way home.'

I was thrilled—and then terrified.

'You know who Mr Lowe is, so you'll be fine,' said Mum comfortingly.

Yes, the Lowes held the famous fly-in event. But the thought of spending almost a full day with Mr Lowe—who was a much older man and very quiet—almost paralysed me with anxiety. I'd never travelled alone before, certainly not without Mum. It was a testament to how much I wanted to go that I was prepared to head off into the skies with a strange man, dry throat and no words.

Mum sent a telegram on the RFDS morning session to Mrs Joseland to arrange to talk to her on a sked, so they could make plans. I would take my correspondence work so I could do school with Janie and her governess. Mum was not going to let me miss lessons.

But not everyone was as thrilled. My beloved sister looked at me, her eyes bigger than usual. 'Are you coming back?'

'Of course, Lissy!' I tried to reassure her. A whole week apart was a very long time for us.

But I was drawn to visiting Janie in a way I couldn't explain. It was a chance to connect with an independent friend, my own age, in another place, and I was longing for the adventure. It was my own new land at the top of my very own Magic Faraway Tree that was calling me. It was such a grown-up and exciting thing to do.

Mum decided that the whole family should go south with Dad, which would give M'Lis a chance to spend time with her beloved

Nana Parnell. That made me feel better about abandoning my soulmate sister. It also meant they would come back via Everard Park and get to meet Janie. We would all have a fun time, and no one would miss out on anything, which Mum was always at pains to ensure happened.

'I love you all equally,' she would declare and make sure no one got any more or any less of anything. The scales always had to be equal.

On the day, Mum drove me to the light aircraft section of the Alice Springs airport. We arrived at a tin shed surrounded by small planes, heat shimmering off the tarmac. I was wearing my best dress and hair in tight plaits with two ribbons, and I thought I might be sick.

'Be good for Mrs Joseland, won't you?' They were Mum's last words as she hugged and kissed me goodbye.

Mr Lowe picked up my case, led us to his plane and spoke to the tower to get clearance for take-off. He took off fast to the east, and I quickly discovered that he flew like Dad—focused and silent. With the western sun beating on me through the window, I finally dozed off, hot and exhausted.

When I opened my eyes, we were descending towards a range of hills. They stretched as far as I could see and looked a lot like our MacDonnell Ranges—rugged, red and ancient. Either side was bare, flat landscape. Everything was different but utterly familiar.

We dived over the homestead so they would know we had arrived. I saw a cluster of corrugated-iron roofs, horse yards and a beautiful, expansive green lawn. We landed on a dirt strip that ran along the edge of the ranges, and as we came to a stop, an old ute rumbled towards us. Mr Joseland was behind the wheel and Janie leaped out barely before he'd stopped. We threw our arms around each other, this time without any awkwardness, just sheer happiness that our plan had come off and we were together again after so long.

Mr Joseland and Mr Lowe stood for quite a while next to the plane, sharing a cigarette and exchanging news, while Janie and I gabbled, each talking over the other. Eventually Mr Lowe said, kindly, 'Best be off. Enjoy your time, young lady.'

With a rush of gratitude, I held out my arms and hugged him around the waist.

'Thank you, Mr Lowe.'

He looked momentarily taken aback but then grinned. When I let him go he shook Mr Joseland's hand, ruffled Janie's hair, climbed back into the plane and took off. The drone of the aircraft mingled with the rumble of the ute as we headed back to the homestead. My great adventure had begun.

———————

My week at Everard Park was perhaps the most wondrous time of my life to that moment. I was utterly free—no jobs, no responsibilities, no one to look after—and my only duty appeared to be to have fun. Mrs Joseland made up a stretcher bed in Janie's room and we giggled well into the night, when we were meant to be asleep.

Mr and Mrs Joseland made me feel part of the family and didn't tell me off for anything, even the fact that Janie and I couldn't hold a sentence together without doubling up and bursting into hysterics, day and night. I kept expecting to get into trouble, but it didn't come. I also spent a lot of time gazing at Mrs Joseland, who was always busy, often with the horses. She wore jodhpurs and cream skivvies, with her blonde hair swept up into a bun, and silver jewellery that clinked. I thought she was a film star still, in every way. I was desperate to ask her if she might make another movie but I didn't quite have the courage. Mr Joseland was involved with cattle work most of the days and was always cheery when we saw him at night.

The very old, very English governess, Mrs Sparks, took a different view of our girlish behaviour. She didn't find it amusing; indeed, she was mostly displeased with us. She made us study our lessons every day in an enclosed veranda, and she told us off constantly. I couldn't imagine why she'd left England to come here to teach Janie, but I didn't have the courage to ask that either. Mrs Sparks's wrath and raised voice and threats of homework made no difference. We struggled to concentrate when there was so much giggling to be done.

And then Mrs Hodder had to endure us both talking at once during our School of the Air lessons.

'Really? How very interesting, Tanya and Jane. You are doing a lot of fun things together. Good luck when you go out riding again!'

Every spare moment we were down at the horse yards, with Janie's two mares, Lucy and Sugar. Lucy was the bay on whom Janie had won all the events at Oodnadatta. She graciously let me ride her, while she rode Sugar, a sweet blonde. My usual riding fears were dispelled as Lucy took me everywhere, perfectly: she was a beautiful horse and I felt safe on her. We galloped all around the place with the wind in our hair, me making up stories as we went.

Janie's Aboriginal friends joined us often and Janie spoke to them in their language, Pitjantjatjara. They tweaked Janie's white blonde hair a lot and giggled too. It was just fun, fun, fun.

One afternoon after school, Janie said, 'I've got somewhere special to take you. But no one else can come. It's secret.'

'Oooh. Okay.'

We saddled up quickly and I followed her, mystified and full of butterflies. We rode towards an imposing set of ranges that we could see in the distance from the homestead. It took an hour to get there and as we grew closer, the ranges grew grander and bigger.

'Through here,' said Janie, pointing to a track that led up through a gap in the rocks. 'It's a secret entrance.'

We clambered up and then pulled the horses to a halt. Before us lay a wide valley floor. It had been hidden from the entrance, but now that we were inside I saw that it was strewn with rocks and flanked by gum trees. The afternoon sun slanted on the high walls, offering glimpses of gold amid the shadowed gulleys. The trees swayed and sighed. It was slightly eerie.

'What is this?'

She grinned. 'This is where the cattle duffers bring their stolen horses and cattle! No one can ever find them in here.'

My jaw dropped.

She moved easily in her saddle. 'Let's go after them!'

Then we were off, whooping and hollering and galloping up and down the valley floor, chasing the cattle duffers, our horses' ears pricked back as we rounded up the imaginary strays and herded them into imaginary yards where we knew they'd be safe. We did this until the sun fell behind the hills and the wind picked up. Before long we could hear the wind whispering and moaning, echoing through the valley. As we finally pulled up, panting and laughing, I realised I was shivering. The valley was shrouded in darkening shadow.

Janie's eyes widened. 'Hear that noise? The wind?'

'Yes.' I shivered some more.

Janie paused. 'Maybe it's the Kadaitcha Man.'

'Really?' I searched the valley for signs. 'The Kadaitcha Man? Here?'

'Lots of spirits live out here in these ranges. The Aboriginal people won't come here because they are afraid of them,' she nodded. 'That's why we had to come alone.'

I stared at her as she added, 'They say the Kadaitcha Man *lives* here.'

'What?' My throat closed. 'Why—why did *we* come here, then?'

'Well . . . because this is where the cattle duffers are hiding, of course!' Janie leaned her head over Sugar's mane, listening hard. The wind hissed and smacked the stones near us, and I started to get a very uncomfortable feeling in my stomach. Janie, whom I thought was normally unafraid of anything, looked this way and that, swivelling her head back and forth.

Then we heard a crack and a bang from the nearby hill, as though something—or someone—had thrown a rock. Janie turned, her eyes wide and flickering.

'I think it's the spirits! I think they're coming.' She stared wildly up at the hill. 'I think the Kadaitcha Man is on his way!'

We both started shrieking at the same time, terrifying ourselves as our cries echoed back to us from the valley. 'Ahhh! Ahhh! Ahhh!'

'We've got to get out of here!' Janie screamed as though the spirits were about to descend any moment. Wheeling our horses around, we raced towards the valley edge. The stones were loose underfoot and I prayed we wouldn't slip. Janie found the path down the rocky side of the hill, and we headed forward, urging our horses on as we slid our way to the bottom. It was only as we reached the foothills that we slowed slightly. Our mouths were dry, our horses' nostrils flaring, and we reached out and grabbed each other's hands.

'You look behind,' I urged Janie. 'See if we're safe.'

She turned her head and gulped. 'I can still feel them, hear them, they're coming. Keep going. Across the plain!'

We gave our horses their heads. It was a broad stretch of land—miles and seemingly miles of it—that lay between the ranges and the homestead, and the safety of home base.

'Once we get to the edge of the plain, we'll be right, they won't follow us that far,' Janie shouted through the wind.

I desperately hoped she was right. The fear in my throat made me want to gag.

We clutched our reins, bent low, knees tucked in like jockeys, driving our horses harder. The edge of the plain came into view but it hovered in the distance as though a far-away mirage. Would we ever reach it?

Finally, we crossed a creek and to our relief, spied the homestead roof shimmering in the late afternoon light. It was only then we thought it safe to slow to a canter and then a trot.

Then we both swivelled our heads behind us, hearts still pounding. My tongue was so dry it was stuck to the top of my mouth. I could barely swallow.

Behind us, the plain lay flat and innocent in the evening light.

'Okay, now we've got to walk!' gasped Janie. 'We've got to walk to cool the horses down before we get home.'

So, we slowed our pace even further, and as we walked our horses, we gabbled, expelling and rationalising our fear. The horses were traumatised too, we could feel it. They snorted and pranced sideways and I could smell their sweat from under the saddles.

By the time we got back to the yards, unsaddled and fed them, darkness had descended. I was worried we'd be in trouble, but Janie seemed unconcerned. 'First one to the house tells Mum!' she shouted.

I followed her at a slow jog, my legs and lungs already aching. I would rather not have talked about it anymore, in the hope that silence might banish the fears from my mind. But when I arrived,

Janie was inside, telling her Mum at top speed and in top voice what we had experienced, and how lucky we were to have survived and made it home in one piece.

Mrs Joseland was cooking a roast and didn't seem to be in the least bit concerned we were late. She just tinkled her charming laugh as Janie finished her breathless monologue.

'Complete nonsense,' she smiled, pulling the sizzling beef out of a roasting pan. 'You two have just wound each other up! Now, go and clean up before dinner.'

———◆———

My Everard Park visit ended all too soon.

The next day Mrs Joseland confirmed that Dad had been on the radio from Witchitie. They would arrive mid-afternoon.

I was torn between the relief of being with my family again and the end of this new adventure I was enjoying so much. Even though at home I often felt scared and anxious about many things, here I felt slightly older and bolder, just from being with Janie.

Mum and Dad were very strict, and as the responsible eldest, I was always desperate to do the right thing for them. I was scared of risking their anger, so I rarely did anything that I knew they wouldn't approve of. That meant that every step I took to learn more about life was a small one.

At Everard, on the other hand, I felt I'd taken very large steps. Being around Janie's free spirit was intoxicating. I'd never experienced anything like it. It seemed to me Janie was capable of being light and courageous all the time—because that was her nature. She wasn't afraid of anything or anyone, except perhaps the Kadaitcha Man.

I soaked up her energy, in awe.

Of course, it helped that Janie had three older brothers. They'd toughened her up and taught her to be bold. Plus, she had a worldly mother and a very easygoing father. Mr Joseland and Dad were polar opposites when it came to strictness and scariness.

So somehow, I felt stronger and able to do more, be more, in this place.

Despite this growth spurt of independence, from about midday onwards I kept looking at the sky. When I finally heard the familiar drone of DQG at about 2 p.m., I thought my heart might explode right through me. Hopping up and down, I yelled to Janie, 'It's them! They're here! Time for the *plan!*'

Janie's plan, which I thought marvellous, was to gallop to meet the plane as it landed. Very heroic and like something out of a movie. Especially something out of Mrs Joseland's movies. And because Mr Joseland was on a bore run, Mrs Joseland was going to take the Toyota down to collect the family, and we hoped she'd understand.

Janie and I raced to the horse yards, grabbed our horses, which we'd conveniently left saddled up, mounted them and galloped like wild Cowboys and Indians towards the airstrip. As DQG circled the homestead and then landed on the strip in a cloud of dust, I felt overwhelming joy. My family, my connection, my source were here, and I was with them again.

The little plane taxied to a halt, the doors sprang open and M'Lis and Brett tumbled out, racing towards Janie and me as we slowed from a gallop to a respectable canter along the strip. I jumped off Lucy and threw my arms around them both. Then I ran to Mum, who was getting out of the plane holding Benny, and hugged them both. Then I took Benny myself and kissed his cheeks until he squirmed and complained loudly. Finally, Dad emerged, with that grin and twinkle. I threw myself into his arms too and he pulled me into a hug.

It could not have been a more perfect reunion.

I'd gone on this brave adventure and survived and now had many tales to tell. I was bursting to share them with my family, who I hoped would be proud of how I'd grown up this week.

Mrs Joseland arrived in a cloud of dust and there were more hugs. M'Lis and Brett wanted to ride back with us, but Mum drew the line at them climbing on the back of Lucy and Sugar, so we agreed to meet them back at the horse yards. I felt such a thrill as we waved goodbye to them and headed back; the wind in my hair, the reins loosely between my fingers, beautiful Lucy galloping under me with such ease. It was an afternoon I would always remember.

It was the first time M'Lis and Brett had met Janie. Like me, they were incredibly shy to start with, but nobody could be shy around Janie for too long. We all went down to the horse yards to feed the horses. It was dusk by the time we'd finished, as Janie and I regaled M'Lis and Brett with stories of our flight from the spirits.

'They were there,' I said earnestly. 'You could hear them. Feel them. We were so scared. It was so lucky we escaped.'

'The Kadaitcha Man was angry we'd come,' said Janie, solemnly. 'And you don't want to get him angry . . .'

As she said this, out of nowhere came a wind. The shed door, which had remained stationary for the past hour, suddenly moved and creaked. Ominously. We swivelled around to look at it. The door creaked again and we realised darkness had fallen. The yards were silent and shrouded in blackness. And there was just the *creee-ak*.

We started shrieking as one. Then we turned on our heels and ran for our lives.

29

More Show Adventures

When autumn came, M'Lis, Brett and I started begging Mum and Dad to let us enter our horses in the Alice Springs Show at the Traeger Park showgrounds.

Janie Joseland was coming up for the show and bringing her beautiful horse Lucy. Jacquie and Matthew Braitling were going to ride too, along with Simone Dann, our School of the Air friend from Amburla Station to the west of Alice. There would be great events including 'Best Boy Rider', 'Best Girl Rider', 'Novice Pony Hack' and 'Pair of Hacks'. Then on the Saturday, there would be gymkhana events, such as the Bending race, the Pole and Bending, and if we were lucky, the Barrel race.

We pleaded our case. If Bond Springs was going to enter cattle, why not horses too?

Dad was now the Chairman of the Central Australian Beef Breeders' Association and had no time to think about horses. He was busy promoting a Meat Hall to showcase Centralian beef to the locals and out-of-town visitors at the show. Dad's mantra was 'buy local, support local', back before it became fashionable. However, after some cajoling, he said we could—that was, if Mum agreed, as she would have to manage it all.

We held our breath.

Mum said yes.

Dear Mum. All the responsibility of managing four kids, three horses and the logistics of getting us in and out of Alice fell to her. That was a huge amount to do, on top of her existing workload. But Mum's ever-present desire to help us engage with the outside world, and with kids our own age, won out. She supported our new project as though it were her own.

'Thank you, Mum!' we shouted in delight.

We had already begun training in anticipation and now doubled our efforts as if we were preparing for the Grand National. Every day after school, we rushed out into the Horse Paddock, got the horses in, saddled them up and practised. We had read everything we could about cantering in circles on the right leg, changing legs and keeping our hands low, our backs straight and toes pointed.

Charlie took a dim view of all this unnecessary poncing around. Our focus was meant to be on learning how to manage and work cattle, not trying to ride as though we'd stepped out of *Horse & Hound* magazine.

'Waste of time,' he'd mutter, as we'd shout happily, 'Look at us, Charlie!'

At this time we had a wonderful jillaroo called Pips. She was tall and angular with long, dark plaits, and was brilliant with horses and cattle. Although she spent most of the time working with Mr Browne with an E, who had returned for this year's show preparation, she gave us tips on our riding when she wasn't walking the cattle around Mum's lawn. We took every chance to learn from her.

There was another reason I wanted to ride in the show: I had the chance to show off my new horse, Sandy.

Sandy was a gentle-natured skewbald mare. She was also one of Janie's many horses I'd encountered at Everard. When the Joselands had seen how I'd fallen in love with Sandy, they generously offered to give her to me. After some conversation, Dad agreed to buy her. Sandy was put on the next truck going north and I had been her proud owner for some months.

On Sandy, I felt safe. With her calm nature, I knew she wouldn't chuck me off, so that made riding a lot easier for me. We were a great team from the outset. She changed my whole riding experience. Perhaps Dad realised I needed that too.

Finally, the Show weekend arrived.

The day before the Show, Dad entrusted Pips and Mr Browne to take his precious cattle into the showgrounds in the truck. He would follow in his vehicle and together they would unload and settle the cattle in.

Everything with the cattle went well.

Everything with the horses went wrong.

At the last minute, we realised we didn't have transport for the horses. Dad's truck was stuck in town and no one had time to bring it home. Mum had to rush around and find another truck. When she finally did, 'those fools' (Mum's words) dropped the horses at the wrong place. By the time we finally found them, we had to walk them along the railway line to get them back to the right place. That took about three hours in the fading light and winter chill.

As neither we, nor the horses, had ever walked through town before, much less on the railway line, we were sick to our stomachs with fear. The horses shied constantly at passing cars and trucks, we were worried they would go lame walking on such a hard surface, and we were cold and frightened. Most of all, we were petrified a train would come.

We certainly didn't feel like courageous Jill or any of the heroines in the Pullein-Thompson books. We wished Dad would turn up to save us. He always knew what to do in crises. He would have gone and sorted out 'the fools'. He would have made everything better, especially for Mum. He might even have arranged for a truck to collect us halfway.

But he didn't, because he didn't know where we were, and we had no way of contacting him, so Mum walked the whole three hours with us to keep us safe. She had dressed up for the day in a gold-and-brown top with long sleeves, sunshine-yellow flared pants and long boots. By the time we got to the right place, it was dark and her beautiful outfit was ruined: covered in horse slobber and bridle grease and red dust. Darkness had also descended. By now the horses were drooping by our sides. Our teeth were chattering. None of us could speak. We were dead beat.

Fortunately, Pips and Mr Browne were still at the showgrounds, because they were staying in a caravan next to the cattle, to guard them. Grabbing their torches, they helped us find our stables and settle the horses.

'Think the Boss headed to the Members' Bar,' they added, helpfully, 'some hours ago.'

That was the last straw. Mum stomped all the way to the Bar. We trailed behind her, adrenalin kicking back in.

We found Dad thumping the bar and telling stories, surrounded by lots of blokes doing the same. There was smoke and noise. Everything smelled like beer. Dad looked as though he had no intention of leaving.

I'll never forget Mum's fury. She held three bedraggled, starving, desperate children in front of her and asked Dad why the hell he hadn't returned his truck so that we could use it, and further, not given a thought to how we might be managing without it. Did he realise it was a miracle we were all still intact? And how the hell did he think we were going to get back to the Braitlings' house, where we were staying? Had he forgotten about us *altogether*?

Dad didn't seem to have any answers, probably because he'd had such a lovely time with all the local station men and judges and breeders up from the south, and had indeed forgotten all about us.

'I'll take you back to our house,' Mr Braitling stepped in. 'My LandCruiser's just outside.'

It was a good fifteen minutes to get back to the Braitlings' house, so Mum used every second of that time to tell Mr Braitling—who was like a brother to her—what she thought of bush men and their behaviour at the show: irresponsible, selfish, self-indulgent—she'd *had enough of them all*! Including the fool of a driver who hadn't understood his instructions. *When she got her hands on him ...*

Mr Braitling murmured agreement (sensibly, I thought) as M'Lis, Brett and I huddled in the back, silent and awed.

As he dropped us off, he added (again, sensibly, I thought), 'Tell Barb I'll be back soon. And I'll bring Grant, don't worry.'

Inside, Mrs Braitling was waiting.

Mum burst into tears.

Mrs Braitling handed her a strong brandy and then, because there was nothing to be done, they set about dealing with eight shattered children (Benny was there and crying by now as well). Mrs Braitling fed us her famous hot corned beef with white sauce and cabbage while Mum changed out of her ruined clothes and had another brandy.

I thought about what Mum said. It was true. Bush men like Dad became different creatures when they came to town, especially for the Show. At home they carried enormous responsibility for staff and stock, had to keep both the stock agents and the Land Board pacified, and could never forget they were the boss. But when they got to the Show, or anywhere that involved other bush men, they lived it up. And they could do it because the bush rules said it was all right for the blokes—it's just what they do.

It was almost expected; that's what bush blokes were *meant* to do.

There was no chance for the mothers to behave in the same way. They still had to look after their many children. They had to behave 'appropriately', whatever that meant. The double standards of being a woman, and a bush wife as well, infuriated Mum so much. She felt so helpless, and she was, because there was nothing that could be done about it.

Worse, the men didn't seem to notice or care.

Except, perhaps, for dear Mr Braitling, who more than redeemed himself that night.

Luckily, Dad and Mr Braitling turned up not long after that. Dad put his arm around Mum. We all went to bed and things calmed down.

But as I went to sleep, I thought to myself, *Who would want to be a wife in the bush?*

Not me.

The next morning, we were up before it was light, focused only on the day ahead, yesterday's problems gone. Winter mornings in Alice were always the same: below zero, with huge blue skies promising a beautiful day. We dressed in jodhpurs, polished our boots until we could see our faces in them, and grabbed coats and hard hats. We'd bought these flash clothes from Don Thomas in Alice Springs—the place every bush man and woman bought every piece of clothing (from hats down to riding breeches); we loved the smell of saddle leather and riding boots, and Aunty Lil—the big cheerful lady who ran it—and were very proud of how we looked.

Then Mum and Mrs Braitling took two carloads of us to the showgrounds. We raced to find our horses, pulling out oaten hay for them to eat. The sun came up and melted the frost on the ground.

It was great fun all being together. We groomed our horses until their coats shone, plaited their manes with frozen fingers, then saddled them up with our beautifully polished saddles and bridles. Today we *were* acting out a Pullein-Thompson story; about to join that mysterious, exciting world of pony club and horse events. In that icy morning, we were ready to compete in events, make new friends and win ribbons.

Janie finally arrived. We flew into each other's arms, giggling immediately. I led Sandy over, shyly, and Janie patted Sandy's nose.

'Sandy looks very happy with you,' Janie said, and I felt a warm rush inside.

The first event was 'Best Novice Pony'. Janie had been competing for years and so she and Lucy looked the part, relaxed and self-confident.

The pony club members were assembling now too, just as I remembered from last year. Smart, beautifully groomed—both the horses and riders. Janie rode over, said hello and chatted to them easily as they moved off towards the oval.

I looked on from a distance, trying not to tremble. No matter how much Brett, M'Lis and I had wanted this moment to arrive, now it was here, my stomach was filled with butterflies and my throat was dry.

'Come on, Sandy,' I whispered, as we bush kids headed to the oval too. Sandy pricked her ears as though she understood. I gave her a reassuring pat, although it was more for myself than for her.

Mum and Mrs Braitling waved us off, as did Mrs Joseland, who had arrived looking like she should be competing herself: wearing smart jodhpurs, riding boots and a pink skivvy that matched her lipstick. The three of them beamed at us. With a final adjustment to the itchy strap under my neck, we were gone.

It was a stomach-churning day. We competed in everything. Most of the time, I didn't really know what I was doing, and my nerves were so intense I thought my heart might burst out of my chest. At the start of each event, the judge would tell us where to line up and remind us what we had to do: canter here, turn there, change legs, ride in pairs. But I had a sense of accomplishment as I cantered off after each event, simply knowing that I'd done it. Furthermore, I'd become like the characters in the books that I loved.

I've finally ridden in a horse show.

At the end of each event, we had to line up to receive the prizes. Janie and the pony-club goers won blue ribbons for almost everything. Simone was close behind. M'Lis, Brett, Jacquie, Matthew and I received a handful of red and orange ribbons (second and third). I received an orange ribbon for coming third in 'Quietest Horse or Pony'.

A huge achievement!

Even though I was too shy to talk to the regular pony-club members, Janie was soon on first-name terms with everyone. I could only watch and wish I had her sunny, easy disposition, rather than the shyness that threatened to paralyse my every step when I came in contact with someone new.

But my shyness disappeared in the thrill of the Grand Parade. This year M'Lis, Brett and I were finally able to ride in it. We felt a mix of excitement and pride as we joined the long line of competitors to enter the oval.

Dad was there, with Mr Browne and Pips, and all his prize-winning cattle. He took the lead of the Grand Parade with his new Champion Poll Hereford Bull, Electra. He had a huge grin on his face, which told us the Show had been a great success for him.

Dad hadn't watched us ride. We hadn't expected him to. We knew that cattle came first.

But Mum was very supportive. She watched us in everything, and hugged us even if we'd won nothing (which in my case was almost every event).

Even Charlie Gorey came and watched. Despite him telling us that it was a waste of time, he supported us, as he always did. He even gave us a wolf-whistle and thumbs up as we entered the Grand Parade.

In my short life to date, the Grand Parade was the most marvellous thing I'd ever done. I thought I might burst with pride as we made the long walk around the side of the oval, with the noise of the crowd and the band filling the air. In that moment, I was so overjoyed I had a ribbon around Sandy's neck. Being in the parade was like being on the stage; it was like performing. I loved every minute of it.

'Thank you, Sandy,' I whispered to her as I waved to the cheering crowd.

It was hard to say goodbye to Janie, but we promised each other we'd be back on air next week. And to top the weekend off, both Dad and Mr Braitling remembered to come home in time to get ready for the Alice Springs Show Ball, the social highlight of the weekend.

Mum and Mrs Braitling looked like true princesses as they swept off in their long gowns and gloves, with their hair up in beehives.

The next day we heard stories of Dad and Aunty Dawn from Hamilton Downs performing together around the piano. Aunty Dawn yodelled (that was her specialty) and Dad sang 'Danny Boy'. Everyone danced wildly until the wee hours.

Later we saw photos of Mum in Dad's arms at the Ball, and the special smiles they shared melted our hearts. Despite the tough times, we knew that Mum and Dad loved each other deeply, and their passion for each other, for us, and for Bond Springs, was like a shining, golden thread that held us all together.

30

Writing and Music

Mum always made our birthdays special. We would rush into breakfast and there would be a present on our chair, carefully wrapped by her. On the top would be a card she'd filled out on behalf of herself and Dad.

The year I turned ten, Dad told me I was really growing up. When I came into the kitchen on the big occasion, I looked at my chair and it was empty. I quickly looked up and around, surprised. Everyone was smiling at me. Then I realised there was a big parcel on the table. Perhaps double figures meant I'd graduated from a chair to the table.

When I ripped the paper off, I was unable to speak. 'Ohhhh!' I breathed in, staring at a beautiful, orange typewriter. 'Ohhhh!'

'Well, you write so many stories—this will help.'

I wanted to cry with joy over this, the best present ever, in the whole wide world. I could hardly bear to go to school that day. As soon as lessons were over I raced back and set up my typewriter on the kitchen table. Mum gave me some paper and I was away—typing with one finger.

Reading and writing my own stories had helped my imagination flourish over the years. But now I had my own typewriter, my imagination was off the clock and the number of stories I could create endless. The only thing that stopped me were the tiresome matters of cattle work, jobs for Mum, and school work. Oh yes, and eating and sleeping.

Breakfast was non-negotiable, and after we ate, we had to finish our jobs and get to the schoolroom by seven-thirty. Dinner was equally non-negotiable, and we also had to do jobs beforehand (watering plants, cleaning our boots), then have a bath, and then it was bedtime shortly afterwards, by seven. Afternoons after school were the obvious times for reading and writing, but we were regularly dragged off by Dad to work; there was always cattle-yard work, or the need to fix up a fence or pipe, or to ride out and bring in recalcitrant cattle. Or we lost afternoons altogether because we were mustering for the whole day.

I figured the only time I could potentially escape and have free to myself was lunchtime. So, I set about persuading Mum to let me skip lunch.

In the homestead, lunch was always a big affair, with hungry men arriving after the morning's work. There would be about twenty people around the table, an enormous amount of noise and chatter, and Dad firing questions. There was meat, either hot or cold and sometimes both, usually mashed or baked potatoes, with coleslaw, tomato-and-onion salad, iceberg salad, sometimes boiled eggs and lots of damper and butter. Preparation, serving, eating and cleaning-up could easily take an hour and a half. I couldn't bear losing that much of my own precious time. So, whenever Mum let me, I'd sneak an apple and head out to the lawn where

I could read or tell myself stories, or prop up my typewriter and start typing.

Mum didn't like me skipping lunch, so she didn't always let me do it. I used every trick in the book I could think of to escape. The downside, which Mum warned me about, was that after a flurry of creativity I would be ravenous, and by about three in the afternoon I would be heading to the kitchen looking for food. But by then, the kitchen would be full of women preparing dinner, and they wouldn't want me in there, hanging about and getting in the way. Sometimes I'd sneak some Weet-Bix and have that with powdered milk, or spread it with butter and Vegemite, but that only made Mum cross.

'Mealtimes are mealtimes,' she would say. 'I haven't got time to put up with children making more mess. There's enough to deal with as it is. If you don't come for lunch, you have to miss out.'

So, it was always an anguished juggle: the overriding hunger to get to my typewriter and escape into my imaginary world versus the mundane but essential task of feeding my body.

There was another problem to contend with, too: I needed somewhere permanent to keep my typewriter. Somewhere I could type undisturbed (where Benny and others couldn't interrupt and grab my papers and throw them about for fun), and where I could store my stories safely when I'd finished typing for the day. After all, Dad had an office where he sat down at a desk and wrote things, undisturbed, and left them on his desk overnight, so I decided that's what I wanted too.

Why not? Dad's life was the one I wanted to emulate. I wanted my own space, the chance to make my own rules in it, and to be entitled to work there, alone.

Luckily for me, Mum understood my longing for a room of my own. And she was already tired of me and my typewriter and my endless streams of paper messing up her tidy house. My natural state of disorder did not suit her natural state of order.

So, Mum emptied out a corner of her and Dad's bedroom and set up a little table facing the wall. She found a portable screen that divided my space from theirs and gave me some privacy. I could sit there and type undisturbed after school. I still had to pack my typewriter up when I'd finished, and put my papers in the drawer of the table, but at least it was my space, and nobody else's.

I was ecstatic. I loved their bedroom. It had wide windows looking over the lawns and the horse yards. The afternoon sun dappled its way through the trees. My greatest happiness was being able to finish school for the day to spend the rest of the afternoon in there, typing frantically to create yet another story of children having adventures between England and Australia.

But my time in Mum's precious space was only temporary until she could think of somewhere more permanent. Finally, she did, and emptied out a corner in the veranda of one of the outside rooms. Then she brought in a medium-size cupboard, which had compartments underneath in which I could store all my papers and books. My typewriter could sit on top and I could sit on a stool. I was away! Pure bliss. I'd rush there after school every day, relieved to find it undisturbed, and smash out my next story.

Often M'Lis would sit with me and wait for each finished page to come out of the typewriter. She would read it while I started busily typing the next page.

All with one finger.

'Doesn't it get sore?' she asked me one afternoon, looking at my right index finger in full flight.

I looked at her with amazement. I didn't feel a thing once I started typing.

Typing out stories was a passion over which I had no control. It was the only thing I wanted to do all the time and the only thing that made me really, really happy. M'Lis and Brett's real passions were horses and the station, but I was a daydreamer and happiest in my own world of words and magic.

My stories started to grow more complex. They were racy, page-turning tales of children on cattle stations having adventures, infused with Enid Blyton expressions like "'I say!" ejaculated Peter, in excitement. "Super muster today, ol' chap!"'

Peter, and his many friends, including girls, were often ejaculating about this and that, in their very own 'super' and 'smashing' way.

When I read sections of my stories out loud to Mum or Miss Thiele or Helen, they would bend over double and stifle back laughter. Mystified, I'd put my nose in the air and march off.

Mrs Hodder would write careful notes back, like, 'My goodness, Tanya, your children do have a lot of fun! Perhaps we could have fewer ejaculations from Peter and his friends, though. How about a simple, Peter *said*?'

Much as I adored Mrs Hodder, I thought 'said' was a very boring word. Why use that when I could write in a way so that M'Lis could *see* the words actually spouting from Peter and his friends' mouths?

Finally, a full book emerged. I titled it *Adventures at Cutters Creek Station* and it boasted six chapters: 'The Ride', 'The Muster', 'Branding', 'The Picnic', 'Christmas Holidays' and 'The Breaking of the Drought', etc. Janie and her brothers appeared throughout, just with slightly different names.

Mrs Layton from the Correspondence School told Mum about a children's book competition—the most successful story would be published—and suggested that I submit *Adventures at Cutters Creek Station*. For weeks I was driven to make it the most beautiful book ever. Tongue sticking out of my mouth, I laboriously drew and redrew a picture of me for the front. When it was finally done, it depicted me galloping along on a beautiful horse, hat squashed over long blonde plaits, cracking a stockwhip and chasing a beast, with dark-brown ranges in the background. Then I coloured in the drawing and put my name at the bottom.

On the back page in careful cursive script I wrote, 'About the Author', just like I'd seen in other books, which went as follows:

> I am ten years old and in Grade 6.
> Because I live on a cattle station, I receive my lessons from the
> Correspondence School in South Australia. My brother and sister
> and I attend school in our own schoolroom on the station, and
> our lessons from the Correspondence School are supervised by
> a governess.
> I learnt to type with one finger, and I'm now quite quick at it.
> This story is all my own work.
> Tanya J. Heaslip,
> Bond Springs Station,
> Alice Springs

Under the words, I put a tiny coloured photograph taken of me by Mrs Joseland when I was at Everard Park. Mrs Layton had told me a photograph would be looked upon favourably, and I thought this one was perfect. There I was, astride Janie's horse Lucy, with Janie's other horse Sugar in the background. And not only was I revealing long blonde plaits, jeans, boots and a little checked shirt, but also some bare chest. Being so small, we were all flat-chested, and often rode with our shirts flapping open for coolness. It didn't strike me that there was anything odd about this when I put it onto the book.

'Do you think, darling,' began Mum tentatively, 'that perhaps we should find a photo of you with your shirt done up? I'm sure we could take one. That might be better.'

I looked at her indignantly. 'But I've got two horses in this photo, Mum, and it's special, because it was taken by Mrs Joseland.'

I thought the film-star effect might permeate through to me from the great Mrs J.

Mum gave up.

We carefully bound the book and sewed it together with wool. Then Mum packed it up for me and sent it off. I waited anxiously for days, and weeks. Every time she came back from the post office I would rush to her, heart in mouth, wondering if I'd had a response. Eventually, several months later, she returned home with a package that had my name on it. Hardly able to breathe, I ripped it open, and there was a handwritten note on the inside cover: '*No publisher etc. You have put a lot of work into your book and we like it very much. A good effort.*'

I put my head in my hands and sobbed.

I was inconsolable for days. Didn't they know about Mrs Joseland's magic touch? Had all my work been for nothing? What did this mean for the rest of my work?

These were big, existential questions for a ten year old.

But there was something deeper in this for me. I knew I was never going to be a useful, long-term talent on the station. Unlike M'Lis and Brett, who were naturals with stock and horses, I knew I had no destiny there. Besides, I was a girl, and the rules were as old as time: the land would eventually go to the boys. And even though nobody ever said so, my lack of interest in the yards and stock work held me back from ever being as good as M'Lis and Brett. My handicap was like a painful sore that festered away, with flies all over it.

The one thing I was good at, and in which I overflowed with interest, was school. There I could earn Dad's praise, and Mum's, too. But unfortunately, excelling at school was of no use to the station. On the other hand, it meant I wasn't completely useless, which was about the greatest sin of all in Dad's eyes. And publication of my book would have been proof that I wasn't useless in life.

But even that strategy had failed.

I had no words to explain the depths of my grief at this rejection. I wept in Mum's arms and she tried to comfort me, then reason with me; then she got desperate.

Dad was called in. Well, to be more accurate, I was sent to his office.

I put my hand on the doorknob, swallowed hard and opened the door. Dad was sitting behind his desk with pages of bookwork in front of him. He pushed his glasses up on his head as I entered. His eyes looked tired.

'Hello, Dad.' I stood in front of him, shifting from one leg to the other.

Dad pushed away the bookwork. 'I want to tell you something I've learned over the years, Tanya. About losing the bullocks at night-time.'

I looked down at my feet, unsure of what was coming.

'This is how it goes. You muster all day to get those bullocks, it's hard work. Finally you get 'em back to the yards. Last bit of the day's the hardest. Trying to get those bullocks through the one gate isn't easy. You risk losing them.'

I nodded, still shifting my feet.

'So, by the time you actually get them in the yards, you're just thankful and dead beat and ready to hit your swag.'

Yep, I could smell the dust and grime and feel the ache in my bones.

'And then, sometime later, you hear it . . . that sound of bellowing, hooves, the sound of bullocks on the move . . .'

Yep.

It meant somebody had left the gate open. Or hadn't latched it properly. Either way, the bullocks had pushed it open and escaped into the night. All the hard work—sometimes days of it—was lost in a few minutes. All the effort put in, useless, gone. It was like the end of the world when it happened, particularly if you were the fool who hadn't shut the gate properly. It was virtually a sackable offence on our place.

Dad looked directly at me. 'When that happens, you're wild, furious, upset, but there's nothing you can do.'

I chewed my lip.

'And then what to do next, Tanya?'

I didn't say anything, so Dad answered for me.

'Nothing. You get in your swag and you have a good night's sleep. That's all you can do. Have a good camp so you're right next morning. Then you get up, and you go out and find those bullocks, and you bring them back again.' Dad took his glasses off his head. 'And that's it. Nothing else to be done.'

Dad pulled his bookwork towards him again.

'Righto? Got to get on that horse again, Tanya, and bring those bullocks back.'

He smiled and put his glasses back on his nose.

I whispered, 'Thanks, Dad,' and stumbled out of the office.

My eyes stung, hotly. I felt a mixture of shame at my weakness, yet hope at Dad's story. He had imparted something special, just to me. He'd given me his hard-won wisdom, honed over the years. He'd given me something of *him*.

No time for self-pity or weakness. It was time to grow even stronger, like my book heroines; like Florence Nightingale; like a true bushman.

M'Lis and Brett were waiting anxiously when I returned from my talk with Dad. They wondered if I was going to be belted, and whether in fact I had been. They hadn't heard me shout or scream, so they thought not, but you could never be too sure if you were summoned to Dad's office, especially if you were Brett.

We went back outside and fed the horses. I told them Dad's story. I called it 'Losing the Bullocks at Night'. M'Lis and Brett were silent. In that moment, they too realised the precious gift Dad had passed on.

I returned to my typing and produced a lengthy tome entitled, 'The Red Red Rose of Triumph'. It was seventy-seven pages about horses, children, love and loss.

I defiantly wrote inside the book, *'First published in 1974 by Heaslip Press.'*

I wasn't taking any chances with anyone else.

It was also *'illustrated by the author'* and *'dedicated to my favourite sister, M'Lis, who gave me helpful hints all through this book'.*

The fact that I didn't have another sister escaped me. The one favourite sister that I did have sat faithfully at my feet as I typed all seventy-seven pages and read each one as it rolled off my orange typewriter. And her helpful hints were our secret.

31

It'll Take the Time It Takes

About this time, the Schmidt family came into our lives. The Kimbers had moved on from Witchitie and Dad needed a new manager. Mick and Lorna Schmidt turned up from Western Australia and moved into the role. Mick was a brilliant stockman, his wife Lorna was a sensational cook, and they had two small children, Robbie and Rhonda, who were used to bush life. We never looked back.

Mum and Dad went down to meet and settle the Schmidts in, as they'd done with the Kimbers. I wondered whether there would be a snake crawling into the kitchen at the first meeting, forcing Mum to tear through the house in pursuit of it.

'No snakes, thankfully,' Mum confirmed when she and Dad returned home. 'And the Schmidts are going to come up for mustering in a few months. Mick will be your new Head Stockman.'

M'Lis, Brett and I looked at each other. A new Head Stockman?

Our beloved Charlie Gorey had moved on, so Dad decided to split Mick's skills and time between Witchitie and Bond Springs.

Several months later, just before the mustering season began, the Schmidt family arrived in a cloud of dust, with swags, cases and billycans atop their station wagon. Robbie and Rhonda peered through the windows, then stumbled out, blinking in the bright Centralian sunshine. They stared at us, as we stared at them.

Mum greeted them all. 'This way,' she said, leading them towards the house, Benny chasing after her. 'Time for a cup of tea. Grant's on a bore run but he'll be back soon.'

'Robbie, Rhonda, come with me,' said Lorna.

M'Lis, Brett and I stayed put, staring up at our new Head Stockman.

Mick was as tall as a tree. We only came up to about his knees.

'G'dayyy,' he said in the longest drawl we'd ever heard. He seemed to be talking through his nose as he looked down at us and grinned. It was a long, wide grin that lit up his eyes. 'So, you're my new young stockmen, eh?'

We shuffled our feet in the dirt, grinning back shyly.

He pushed his hat back. 'Yer goin' to show me yer horses?'

Brett was the first to speak. 'Yep, this way, in the horse yards.'

He darted off and M'Lis and I followed. Our new Head Stockman was wasting no time getting down to business. We hoped he'd approve of our morning's work. We'd headed out into the horse paddock before breakfast to muster in the main stock horses for Mick to meet, and then spent several hours grooming them. Our work had paid off. In the morning sun, the horses' coats shone, and as we walked through the yards, they were munching contentedly on a bale of chaff in the corner.

It was always a big moment when the Head Stockman first met his stable of horses, and we wanted him to be impressed.

'Yer, yer, yer . . .' Mick nodded to himself, clicked his tongue, ran his hands across the manes of a couple of the quieter horses, and leaned against the rails and took it all in.

We hovered anxiously.

At Mick's request, we then took him to the saddle shed so he could inspect the riding gear, the blacksmith forge with the requisite horseshoes for shoeing, and the second saddle shed with the packhorse equipment. He walked fast between sheds; we could hardly keep up.

'Righto,' he nodded after a lengthy perusal of everything we thought he might want to see. 'What about that cup of tea, eh?'

Then he turned and headed to the house, fast.

We were panting by the time we caught up with him outside the kitchen door. We looked at each other, stunned, as Mick took off his hat and bent his head to enter the door.

We soon discovered that Mick walked very fast, everywhere, and that he hated slackers. We always had to run to keep up with him. 'Keep up or go home,' was his motto. If you couldn't keep up with him, you were of no use, so we did a lot of running, as his legs were several times the length of ours. One day M'Lis was determined to walk as fast as she could, and ideally as fast as Mick. By putting in a huge effort over a short distance, she almost managed to match his pace.

Mick looked down in surprise and uttered a rare compliment. 'Good walking, M'Lis.'

Life under Head Stockman Mick was a steep learning curve. Most of the time he was tough and gruff, with people at least. With horses and stock, it was a different matter. He was brilliant and skilled. And he taught us many of his bush techniques.

One day we were out mustering and the flies were everywhere: all over the eyes and the tails of the cattle and the horses.

They were in our eyes and mouths and all over our clothes. Every time we blinked, we blinked out or in a fly. They were driving us insane.

When M'Lis finally swallowed a mouthful of them, she erupted in rage. 'Ahhh! These *mongrel, stinking* flies—I'm *sick* of them!'

Mick looked over. He pushed his hat back and drawled, 'Don't worry about 'em, M'Lis. Waste of time.'

She looked up, surprised that Mick had even noticed her.

'Yep, they'll always be here,' he drawled. 'Just get a switch from a tree and flick from side to side slowly. Keep doing that, and after a while you won't notice them.'

M'Lis gulped. 'Yeah?'

M'Lis headed to the nearest mulga tree and pulled off a switch of leaves. She started flicking it from side to side. When a stirry cow and calf broke from the mob, she had to focus on chasing after them, and dropped the switch, but once she'd got the recalcitrant cattle back, she found another tree and another switch. Then she flicked the leaves from side to side for the rest of the day.

By the end of the afternoon she was grinning.

Mick had changed her life with flies, she said.

Not mine. I continued to complain about them just as much. But M'Lis never complained again.

Apart from flies, Mick helped us all with another part of droving cattle that we (well, I, particularly) found unbearable— the boredom. Mustering was an adrenalin rush, yes, but once the muster was over, we were usually stuck on the tail of the slow mob. Time seemed to go on forever when on a long, boring drive, or when it was scorching hot, or we were just so tired. I likened it to being stuck in Purgatory. Couldn't go backwards, couldn't go forwards; stuck in the violent white heat and blinding red dust; our throats swollen, parched; thick bulldust haze over everything; with no say over our time, or our own lives. Some days the awfulness of it all threatened to eat me from the inside out.

M'Lis and Brett usually coped better than me but it often got the better of us all.

'Mi—ii—ck?' we'd chorus. 'How much longer till we get there?'

Destination 'there' could be anywhere: the end of the road ahead winding its way into the distance, or beyond the shimmering mirage at the foothills, or over the ranges where we knew the cattle yards lay. 'There' differed depending on wherever we were mustering at the time. But inevitably, on long, hot afternoons, 'there' was always a long way away.

Mick would have the same response, every time. He'd push his hat back and drawl, 'It doesn't matter how long till we get there. It'll just take the time it takes.'

Our new Head Stockman had the capacity to live in the moment in a way I'd never seen before. He never wore a watch. He told the time by the sun. He worked with the sky and the seasons, not against them. For him, time was never the issue. His sole focus was getting the mob back safely in one piece. He was a man truly born for the saddle.

I had none of Mick's self-control or restraint. I coped by escaping into my imagination and daydreaming about what it would be like to live in those cooler, northern climes with Heidi or Enid Blyton's characters. Most the time I would then drift off into that other world, and by default, let the tail drift off as well.

Mick's yells would bring me back to reality with a jolt.

'Oi! What d'yer think yer doin', girl? Wake up—and get them bloody cattle back!'

When I'd finally get them back, he'd say, 'Yer *here*, Tanya. Yer gotta be here, *now*; not *there*, in your head.'

But, oh, how much I wanted to be *there*.

Mick also had an extraordinary capacity to beat time when it did matter.

On the morning of a muster, Mick was always ready first. By the time we got up, dressed, and got down to the horse yards, Mick would be sitting on his horse, all saddled up, ready to go, waiting. It didn't matter how hard we tried, we never beat him. We were always late, and it seemed to take us forever to saddle up with our childish fingers and thumbs.

One day, when we got into the yards, Mick was on a young colt. As we rushed in, falling over ourselves to saddle our horses, the colt started pig-rooting. Mick was taken completely by surprise. The next minute he was on the ground, looking up at the colt. We couldn't stop laughing as Mick dusted himself off, but he was furious.

'If you kids hadn't been late, I wouldn't have had to stand around like this with this colt getting narky. If you kids had been here on time, we'd have been gone by now, and I wouldn't have got chucked off.'

We quickly stopped laughing.

Going anywhere with Mick and the horses was a learning experience for us. Apart from that colt, he was rarely thrown off horses and we admired his riding style. He always sat loosely in the saddle, his long legs pushed out in the stirrups, stockwhip looped over one shoulder, completely at ease.

I would often get tense and nervous before getting on a horse, particularly if I wasn't feeling confident. The horse would inevitably sense it and react badly.

'They can *read* yer, Tanya, *feel* yer,' Mick would click his tongue. 'Yer gotta be calm and yer gotta be the boss with 'em. Otherwise they'll play up on yer and yer'll never get 'em to do what you want. Remember, your horse will work well with you if *you* control 'em.'

Once I felt cheeky enough to say, 'Like you did with the colt?' but just before that smart-alec response reached my lips, I swallowed it right back down. Getting the Head Stockman offside was not worth it. And besides, he knew what he was talking about. The colt had been a one-off. Mick was always the boss and horses obeyed him and he therefore got the best out of them.

I never remember a time when Mick was not working. Even when we weren't on horseback or dealing with stock, he'd be tinkering with the Land Rover. He could repair anything. If any of the workshop tools came apart, Mick was so resourceful he could work out how to mend them with very little. One day he lost the handle off an axe, so whittled a piece of wood to replace it. Good as new!

At night, he plaited belts, made ropes out of hide; he made stockwhips, and counterlined saddles and bridles. He had an old Singer machine that was built for sewing leather and used it to fix bridles and saddles. We'd crowd around him and watch open-mouthed as he put the leather under the needle and pushed it through. Magically, the broken bit of bridle would soon be joined again.

He was self-taught, so if anybody wanted to learn anything from him, he was gruff. 'Learn the right way—or don't waste my time,' he'd say.

Mick would get cranky when things went wrong. And things went wrong, regularly. We were always losing cattle during musters, despite our best efforts, which meant we wouldn't have the numbers for Dad when we got back to the yards. That would delay trucking because we'd have to go back out and get them in again. Sometimes we'd box cattle in the yards by mistake, which meant they were mixed up and had to be re-drafted, delaying trucking yet again. Worst of all was when the horses got hurt or went lame.

Mick was incredibly protective of his horses. It also delayed proceedings if we were a horse down. All of these problems affected Dad's end objective, which was having the right numbers of the right cattle at the right time to truck to market, so there would be money for the station.

The worst was when Dad applied too much pressure on Mick, which Dad was wont to do on a regular basis. On those bad days, Mick would stride around, short-tempered, yelling at anyone who got in his way.

But we kids were conditioned to being yelled at by tough men, and we were pretty tough ourselves, so we were never offended by Mick. That was just how blokes on the land were: of few words, tough and uncompromising. And because we didn't really know many other kinds of blokes, we assumed that was normal behaviour. His words slid off our backs, because we knew deep down he was deeply kind and caring. If we were ever in trouble, he was always there for us. He reminded us of Charlie in many ways. Both men were different, but they each looked out for us.

Mick had a great sense of humour underneath, and he had a special kind of chuckle, which was contagious. If he chuckled, we always laughed out loud. It made working with him fun. It helped pass the endless hours.

We were very sad when Mick told us that he and his family would be leaving at the end of the mustering season to return to Witchitie. However, Dad brought in a number of other stockmen to ease the transition. We were then happy about that, because more workers meant more support for M'Lis, Brett and me, and potentially more fun having new people around.

The overlap with the new stockmen took place a month before the Schmidts' departure. Mum and Lorna barely left the kitchen during that time.

Lorna was a wonderful cook, and in the afternoon the kitchen would be filled with the fragrance of the puddings and tarts and casseroles she was baking. Mum was so relieved to have Lorna's skill and presence that it eased the burden that fell on her shoulders. Helen still worked side-by-side with them, and Miss Thiele helped when we weren't at school. But Lorna really did transform the kitchen and our lives during her time at Bond Springs.

32

Bush Life—Lost and Found

Janie Joseland loved Everard Park with all her heart. Her Aboriginal friends were there. She belonged to that land. It had shaped her very being. But when she was ten, her life changed. Her parents moved on from Everard Park. As they drove away from the homestead for the last time, Janie couldn't speak. She sat in the back seat of the station wagon staring up at the ranges, a last glimpse of gold in the morning light. Her soul split with grief, her inner being howled like a wounded animal. Mr Joseland was moving to a station called Mittiebah in the Barkly Tablelands far to the north. Mrs Joseland would stay in Alice Springs so that Janie could go to school.

Mrs Joseland and Janie moved to a block of land to the east of Alice in what was called the 'farm area'. There was room for Janie to have her horses. They were coming up on a truck soon. She could then join the pony club and start competing seriously in the many different horse events in and around Alice. In the holidays, she would go straight to Mittiebah to the stock camp. Her new life would revolve around horses to keep her sane and happy.

I couldn't believe it. I'd lost my best friend on School of the Air. But now I could see her in Alice Springs, in person. She could even visit me at Bond Springs and become part of our family too. It was a time of mixed emotions.

I thought about what it would be like to be in Janie's shoes. To be told I had to leave Bond Springs. That the only life I'd known was over. It was impossible to comprehend, but I did try. Would it be like going to boarding school? Would this be how I would feel in a few years? Transported to a new world, far away from my existing one, the place that was part of me, that *owned* me?

No, Janie's situation was much worse than boarding school. She could never go home, whereas I could return for holidays. The hazy horizons of blue and curving lines of the ranges would still be there, the ridges and circles of waterways, the sunrises and sunsets, the night skies full of stars, the endless horizons. My favourite creeks and valleys and horses, the house and my bed would always be there to welcome me back. My world wouldn't be ripped away, as it was for Janie.

Janie's pain haunted me. Yes, I hated long musters and fantasised about overseas lands, but *this* landscape was home. It was the place where I was me. My body and soul *were* this country.

I wanted to wrap Janie in my arms and whisper, 'It'll be all right, it's just a bad dream, soon you'll be safely back at Everard Park.' I longed for there to be a happy ending for her, but I saw in Mrs Joseland's eyes there would not be. Janie couldn't even talk about what had happened.

In her dreams, the spirits of her land called her back, night after night. But when she woke, she had to get up and put on a school uniform and shoes that pinched her toes and get on a bus and go to a school with people she didn't know. Until that moment, she'd lived in jeans and boots, wild and free. She'd had a governess and Aboriginal friends. Her schoolroom had looked out onto the horse yards and Everard ranges.

Janie's move made me think long and hard about my own departure to boarding school. In just a year and a half I would be sent south. Dad and his whole family had gone to boarding school in Adelaide, and we'd all been booked in the year we were born. Years ago, Dad had even bought blocks of orange trees in Waikerie, South Australia, to fund future school fees.

Mum didn't want us to go south to boarding school and leave her, or our home, but there were no strong high-school options in the Territory. The NT government even *paid* bush people a subsidy to send their kids south for a proper secondary education.

But Janie wasn't going south. She was stuck here, in some dreadful no-man's land.

Instead of the sked, Mum could meet Mrs Joseland face-to-face to arrange catch-ups. In the early days, Janie visited almost every weekend, and we enfolded her into our family. Mum felt the depth of Janie's grief as only someone as sensitive and intuitive as Mum could, and she cared for her with all the love she had. Dad adored her too. At Bond Springs Janie was safe, and we loved her with all our hearts and protected her as best we could.

In town, Janie had to develop survival strategies. Her loss was so beyond words, she pushed it deep down where she couldn't see or feel it. In true Janie form, she gathered all that she had learned in her life to date to build a new one. She was not going to go down with her grief; she was going to outshine it.

In Alice she quickly made friends and became popular. Her infectious giggle and charm endeared her to everyone. Her horse skills and general sense of adventure meant she was soon involved in all sorts of activities. She was a natural leader of groups, and a winner in competitions, and people wanted to be around her.

And while her new life only dulled the deep ache, it did help her survive.

Before long, Janie was riding out to Bond Springs every weekend with the friends we'd met at the show, Donald Costello and Joanne Castle (whom we called Jo).

The ride would take a full day, along the long, winding creek beds that had seen Dad bring his first lot of cattle to Bond Springs the night of the wild storm and flood. M'Lis, Brett and I invariably rode to meet the three of them halfway. It was an unmarked trek through the rocky hills and sandy beds, and we always imagined we were cattle duffers as we cantered along. Before leaving, we would saddle up our horses, fill our water bags and tucker bags, ready to meet Janie, Donald and Jo in a hidden tea-tree gully, and have a picnic.

Mostly no one fell off and hurt themselves, or got lost on those long, isolated treks. We had no communication with each other, much less our respective parents, and should anything have gone wrong no one would have known where we were, or at least not without a protracted and difficult search, and it would have taken a long time to find us in those rocky, remote hills.

But Mum encouraged us in our adventures. She knew we knew this landscape better than anyone. By now, we could tell the time from the sun, draw a map of each paddock with a stick in the dirt, tell our location from the shape of the hills or curve of the creeks or line of the fences. We never got lost. We were home.

———>●<———

One winter's day, we decided to hold our own gymkhana. The stock camp (including Dad) were away on the far boundary, so we planned it for that coming weekend. We had already competed in the MacDonnell Range Gymkhana several times and knew what the events were and what to do. We were just like sponges with ideas.

We invited Janie, Donald and Jo out, and it just so happened that Jacquie and Matthew Braitling were in town, so they came too.

We held the gymkhana on the Saturday morning up on the long flat of the Horse Paddock.

M'Lis, Brett and I had prepared the gymkhana site earlier that week. We lugged up empty drums for our horses to jump over and race around. We collected long sticks to erect for the Bending race. We pulled all the empty hessian chaff sacks out of the feed room, along with buckets, apples, hard-boiled eggs (collected from the chooks by us and cooked by Mum) and spoons (which Mum threatened us with our life if we didn't return to her), and piled them all in the back of the Toyota. We drove them up there, and arranged them all, ready for the big day.

This was going to be a proper gymkhana; the real deal just like in our *Jill* and Pullein-Thompson books, just like at MacDonnell Range.

We also persuaded Mum and everyone else at the station to join in. What that really meant was that we needed some grown-ups to help pull it all off. Luckily, we had five of them available: Mum, Miss Thiele, Helen and another couple that Dad had recently employed: a bore man, Harry, and his wife, Carol. They lived in the Gemmells' old cottage and Carol was very good with her hands (she was building a beautiful stone wall around it). They generously offered to help make ribbons and Harry carried some of the heavy drums for us. He even found a whistle and agreed to be the judge.

Saturday morning, we were up before the sky was light. We all put on jodhpurs, shirts and ties, and hard hats. We groomed our horses, saddled up and cantered towards the long flat of the Horse Paddock for a 10 a.m. kick-off.

Our gymkhana field stood shining in the early-morning sun.

We'd painted the drums for the jumping event in white and red and set them up at a proper distance apart. In the centre we'd stuck up the poles in four lines for the Bending race. At the end of each line was a barrel on which we'd stuck home-made flags on sticks, which would be used for the flag and barrel race. In the far distance we'd laid out the last three drums into a triangle for the barrel race.

M'Lis, Brett and I looked at our handiwork with great pride. It was as good as the MacDonnell Range Gymkhana. Benny, who'd helped where he could, joined us, gleefully.

Mum drove her station wagon up and brought chairs for the ladies to sit on (very thoughtful of her, because otherwise they'd have to squat or sit cross-legged in the red dirt). She also brought lots of oranges, to keep us hydrated and give us something sweet. Harry brought up a big drum of water on the Land Rover, pulled out his whistle and shouted, 'I hereby declare this Bond Springs Gymkhana officially open.'

'Hurrah!' We waved our hats in the air.

The competition was fierce. Harry had to do a lot of refereeing. Janie won most events, as usual, but we all put in a huge effort. And once we'd got through the serious events, there were three fun ones to finish—the egg-and-spoon race, the sack race and the apple-dunking race.

In each of those events, we lined up, waited for Harry to blow the whistle, then galloped several hundred yards towards a long line where Mum stood. That was where we'd set out the buckets and sacks.

For the egg-and-spoon race, we had to gallop up, dismount, pull a spoon and egg out of the bucket, and then run back to Harry at the start line, leading our horse, without dropping the egg out of the spoon. Nobody made it intact but there was a lot of cheering and laughter. Lucky the eggs were hard-boiled.

The sack race was similar. Gallop to the long line, dismount, jump in a sack and, leading your horse, shuffle back to Harry at the start line. This was difficult and everyone kept falling over. The main thing was to make sure your horse didn't walk over you in the chaos if you and your sack were sprawled on the ground.

Mum divided the water equally into the buckets for the apple-dunking race. Then she dropped apples into them, and Harry blew the whistle. Again, we had to gallop up and dismount, then shove our head in the bucket, and try to get the apple out with our teeth. Everyone was drenched in seconds. Those who got the apple out had to hold it between their teeth, get back on their horse and gallop back to Harry at the finish line.

That was perhaps the hardest event, but it was also hilarious. We did it last because by the end we were all soaking wet, laughing and falling about.

'You cheated!' We all yelled at each other, in hysterics.

Only M'Lis and Mr Pip did it properly and won outright.

After the gymkhana, we returned to the house for lunch and the presentation.

We had persuaded Mum to hold this big event on her precious lawn (and let us walk our horses across the lawn to accept our prizes), which she agreed to because of its importance. There, she royally pinned ribbons on the winners amid claps and cheers.

'What a great day,' we all agreed, and I was so happy to see Janie shine.

When it was all over, we unsaddled our horses and rode bareback down to the creek. There was some precious water left from recent rains and we spent the next few hours riding around and through it, splashing each other, and then hopping off and letting the horses roll freely. The horses loved it and so did we. Finally, we turned them out into the paddock, and spent the rest of the afternoon planning our next event.

It didn't occur to us that our lives and games might have been different to those of kids elsewhere, and particularly in the cities. All our friends on nearby stations did the same things and lived the same kinds of lives as we did.

We just thought our life and games were completely normal, because they were to us.

—————◦——————

M'Lis, Brett and I took our guitars everywhere with us now. We would sit against our swags and sing in the stock camp at night, or around the lawn at home, or in the sitting room after dinner. During the School of the Air Get-Togethers, our guitars always went, too. We usually had a night camping in the Simpsons Gap creek bed, or the Old Telegraph Station creek bed, and we would sing for the other bush kids. They would always join in because we were singing songs they knew, songs of their own lives. Slim Dusty and Charley Pride were always the favourites, although Olivia Newton-John was on our song list now, too. And John Denver's 'Take me Home, Country Roads' made us all misty-eyed.

Brett had become particularly skilled on the guitar, and M'Lis and I put melodies and harmonies to every tune. Benny was still too young to join in, but he would beat an old stool along in time if he was with us, and then there'd be the four of us, singing along.

M'Lis and I didn't notice that there were few songs about women in the Australian outback. We never thought about the fact that the fabled bush heroes were men; the wild, romantic 'Man from Snowy River' types. They were the ones who took danger in their stride, cracked a stockwhip over their head as they wheeled the mob fearlessly down flinty mountainsides, and never seemed afraid (just like Dad). They were the characters we desperately wanted to be like.

We never thought about the fact that we weren't those men and nor could we ever be. On the contrary, we just thought of ourselves as little men working with big men, and eventually we would grow up to be big men too. We wanted to be the kind of worker that Dad was proud of.

Nobody wanted to be a weak, girly sissy.

No, we all wanted to be strong and courageous and loyal and legendary.

33

The Nightmare of Shearing

We loved Christmas down south at Witchitie, but it came with a downside.

The happy time spent with Nana and Papa Heaslip, Nana Parnell and Aunty June and Uncle John was short lived, followed immediately by the dreaded three-week sheep-shearing period in early January. During that time there was no chance for me to read, write or do anything creative. We all knew that Christmas holidays, like all our holidays, meant work.

Dad would say, 'A change is as good as a holiday,' and that's just how it was.

But Dad seemed to drive us harder than usual at shearing time. Perhaps he hated it as much as we did, and had to steel himself to do it, especially as the Flinders Ranges rivalled Alice for heat in the new year. Most days the temperature reached forty to forty-five degrees.

There were a number of practical reasons Dad chose January for shearing, though. It never rained, which was important, because you couldn't shear wet sheep. He had M'Lis, Brett and me with him, so he had a strong workforce ready to go. Now he had Mick, too. The shearers were locked in at that time every year, and they delivered up lovely, thick wool for Dad to sell.

The shearing shed was at Nana and Papa Heaslip's property, Glenroy, so Dad spent most of the three weeks there, managing the shearing process, sorting the wool and overseeing the numbers of sheep in and out.

We kids were stationed at Witchitie, with Mick.

Our job was to muster the sheep, draft them into Dad's required lots and load them onto the semi-trailer that Mick would then drive to Glenroy. Then we had to unload the shorn sheep when they returned. It was non-stop. Mick drove in and out several times a day.

The blazing January temperatures made mustering the sheep out of the paddocks slow and difficult. They sheltered under trees in their hot, woolly coats, and didn't want to move. They panted and sometimes lay down and wouldn't move at all. I was convinced they were more stupid than cattle, but, in fact, perhaps they were just more cunning.

'C'mon,' Mick would say, giving them a push, 'Yer'll be glad when it's all over. Yer'll be much cooler.'

We used Witchitie horses for the mustering, and also some others that Mick brought in, but that was always fraught with risk because the horses didn't know us, and we didn't know them. I got chucked off that summer, and ended up with not only sore muscles and bruised bits, but prickles stuck in my hands, legs and face.

By the end of each day, we were exhausted.

Mum would greet us three times a day with piles of food but we were usually too tired to eat. She would always be dead beat too, from cooking continuously over a wood oven in a little kitchen where temperatures exceeded forty-five degrees. She also had to keep Benny out of mischief, which was always difficult, especially because the woodheap was as big a draw to him as it was to the snakes.

At night, we collapsed into bed at the usual time—7 p.m. But South Australia had daylight saving, so the sun didn't go down until at least 9.30 or 10 p.m. It seemed ridiculous to be in bed when the light poured brightly in through the windows. We put our pillows over our heads and Mum pulled the curtains across tight, but our rooms were hot and stuffy, and we tossed and turned in damp sheets and woke up weary after broken sleep.

Mick made jokes as often as he could to cheer us up. He reminded us on a daily basis to ignore the flies, to ignore the monotony and the heat, and just get on with the job, because it would be over soon enough.

One day, when we were so hot and tired that all we could do was snap and argue with each other, he let us travel with him to Glenroy with a sheep load.

'Yayyyy!' we yelled, recovering our energy in an instant, and squashed ourselves into the dirty, hot semi-trailer cabin. Mick slowly reversed out and we headed off, sheep in the back. We were making so much noise that he grabbed his water bottle, ripped open the lid and chucked water on our heads.

'Ahhh!' We all shrieked with shock, then delight. The water was cool and refreshing and we were so hot. Brett grabbed the water bottle, and threw some back at Mick, who shook his head like a dog, while trying to focus on the road. M'Lis and I wrestled it off Brett, and soon the cabin was a free-for-all.

Before long, the water bottle was empty.

A total sin.

Mick shouted, 'You useless kids! Now we'll all perish.'

Mick saved us with his humour and sense of fun. He also saved me during one of the last days of mustering in the third week.

It was blindingly hot as usual—over forty-five degrees—and neither we, nor our horses, nor the sheep could move beyond a plod. We'd stashed water bottles in trees along the route—even Dad conceded we needed something to drink during the day in January—but by the time we got to them, the sun's heat had made the bottles sweat inside and turned the water putrid.

It stunk, like it had been in a smelly, dried-up dam full of dead cattle. Its stench made me want to vomit, but not M'Lis and Brett. They were so parched, they drank it. But I couldn't. Mick refused as well—but he was tough, like Dad, and could keep going.

We set off again, by which point I was starting to feel delirious. Ahead of us we finally saw the next paddock gate. The blinding sun glinted off the barbed-wire fence.

'Go ahead and open the gate!' Mick ordered me.

I was glad to do so, because I was desperate for a distraction. I had gone beyond the capacity to make up stories and escape into my imagination; I was just lost in a world of dehydrated, overheated misery. It took a long time for me to get there because my poor horse was struggling to put one hoof in front of another. And once I got to the gate, I stared out at the shimmering mirage in the distance, and couldn't get off my horse. The coordination between my hands and feet didn't seem to be working. I slumped over his neck.

'Oi, what the hell do you think yer doin?' Mick shouted.

I tried to pull myself together. Voices were driving me, bouncing around in my head.

Push on, keep going, push on.

Then came another one.

I can't, I'm finished.

I stayed slumped.

When Mick got no response from me, he rode as fast as his horse would move to the gate, then dismounted and opened it himself. Then he walked towards me, his reins looped over his arm, his horse coming in behind.

'Yer right?' He sounded sceptical.

But I couldn't answer him. Stars spun before my eyes. I felt sick.

'Righto, you go home,' he said, finally.

I stared at him, letting those magical words waft through my non-compos brain.

'C'mon, Lis and Brett,' he added, swinging his leg back up over his horse. 'Push those sheep up.'

Poor M'Lis and Brett—I left them there in the heat. M'Lis's face was a study in anxiety. Brett thought I was faking it so I could get out of the afternoon's work. Fair enough. But through my deluded brain, I couldn't think of anything but getting home.

It felt like several hours before my horse and I stumbled into the yards. I wanted to vomit, but I had nothing in my stomach. I felt feverish, my throat parched. I hoped that Mum would be there. I imagined her cool hands, her cool touch on my brow, her kind words, her putting me gently into bed, and me fading off into the distance, to wake again only once shearing was over and we could go home to the safety of Bond Springs and my typewriter.

But as I sat unmoving on my horse, unable to get down, I saw a figure moving out of the corner of my eye. It was Dad. Suddenly, I panicked. Why wasn't he at Glenroy?

I could just make out the red-and-white tip of DQG through the trees. He must have come home to refuel.

I waited, steeling myself to be told off.

Dad marched straight towards me, but by the time he got to the yards he must have realised there was no point saying anything.

He simply pulled me off and hoisted me from the yards into the house. Through the blur, I finally found myself in the bathroom. I heard the noise of water. It was the shower. Dad had turned it on, and it was running, first boiling hot from the pipes, and finally, tepid warm.

'Here, boots off.' Dad then picked me up and pushed me under the tepid water. I collapsed, curled on the shower floor, with all my clothes on, except for my boots.

It must have been an anathema for Dad to see so much precious water from the tank being wasted. Even as it poured over me, I realised the gift he was giving me.

Finally, Dad turned off the tap, and pulled me out.

I leaned over the bath, shivering, shaking, dripping everywhere. He handed me a cup of water.

'Sip this slowly. Very slowly.'

I slurped, gagged.

'Where's Mum?' I finally managed.

'She and Benny have gone to Glenroy. She'll be back later.'

Tears welled up, the first sign of moisture to actually come out of my body. I wanted Mum with every part of my being. But she wasn't there.

'You need to sleep this off. I'll head out to the mob on the bike.'

I crawled into bed in my wet clothes.

'You'll be right,' were Dad's firm, departing words. 'Just a bit of heatstroke.'

As I lay there curled up, I heard the motorbike rev and Dad roar off.

Then I realised.

I was at the Witchitie house, all alone.

You'll have to be alright, Tanya, no choice.

You can't get any worse. There's no one around to save you if you do get worse.

Fatigue finally won out over my overwrought imaginings. Even guilt at abandoning Mick, M'Lis and Brett, and forcing Dad to leave Glenroy for the mob dissipated.

I slipped into sleep.

Much later, there were voices, and eventually Mum's cool, gentle touch. By then, there was no sun through the window, and the curtains were closed tight.

In Mum's arms, I cried, really cried.

The next morning, I was a bit slow, but by midday I was back in the sheep yards, pushing up the recalcitrant, bleating, woolly animals with Mick, M'Lis and Brett, like I'd never been away at all.

'No more slacking,' said Mick, and I couldn't tell whether the glint in his eye was amusement or not.

'Yeah,' said Brett, who still thought I'd put on a turn to get out of the last leg.

But M'Lis stayed close and protective. 'I was so worried,' she said, her beautiful eyes clouded.

I felt lucky.

Mick had sent me home.

Dad had poured his precious water over me.

I'd had an afternoon off.

Mum and M'Lis had cared for me.

Admittedly, I was a letdown; I'd failed the standards of the legendary stockman.

But at least I wasn't dead.

34

My Last Year

When I returned home, I started grade seven. It was a year of happy firsts and melancholy lasts.

Aunty June and Uncle John had a baby, whom they named Fleur. We couldn't wait to see her. A first cousin, at last! Babies Nicholas and Susan would follow and finally we would have a real family of cousins. We felt like other families, finally.

It was also my last year before boarding school. Now that it was really on the horizon, Mum swung into action. She ordered name tags and uniforms. The list of clothes included strange things like 'gym slips' and 'bloomers' and 'brown regulation pants'. The school sent schedules, timetables and advice that we would go to bed at 8 p.m. after 'supper' and 'prep'.

'But Mum, we go to bed at seven o'clock here,' I said, panicked. 'Eight is a whole extra hour later. D'you think I should try to stay up a bit longer each night, so I know what to do?'

Mum's face went a strange blotchy colour. She bowed her

head back over the name tags she was sewing onto brown socks. Eventually I saw a tear drip down her cheek. Dad talked about 'preparation' all the time, but this was harder than anything I could have imagined.

⟶•◦•⟵

Lea Turner from Jinka Station and I were the only two students left in our School of the Air year, and we'd graduated to a new teacher, Mr Walker. He was very funny and I loved my classes because Lea and I could talk with him to our heart's content.

Mrs Hodder was teaching the younger children, and I still got to see her every time we went into the School of the Air office. Mrs Layton, who had taken me from grade one to grade seven, was still at the Correspondence School. She looked unchanged in each annual Correspondence School Magazine—earnest and clever—and I loved her with all my heart. She'd given me gold stars and written comments of support as I'd grown as a student, and I couldn't have asked for a more wonderful teacher.

The previous year Miss Thiele had celebrated her twenty-first birthday on Bond Springs and it was a wild night where everybody partied until dawn in Dad's bar (of all places) and danced out on the patio (no problems about heels and spilt beer). Aunty Jill and Uncle Pete jived, and Mr and Mrs Gorey waltzed; Mum caught it *all* on camera. Miss Thiele had presented us with our own invitation. The dress code was 'jodhpurs, please!' This year she would get married, to Ken Watts, a handsome helicopter pilot from Alice Springs. Another wedding! It was especially thrilling because the reception would be held on Bond Springs. Mum would make identical long dresses for us girls (she drew the line at us wearing jodhpurs to a wedding).

Miss Thiele would stay with us until I went away to boarding school. Then Mum would have to find another governess. The whole challenge of bringing someone new in would begin again. Benny would be starting school and the governess would have to deal with grades one, five and seven, in one classroom. Not an enviable task.

———————

My writing continued apace. Mum and M'Lis continued to support everything I created. And I had wonderful encouragement from two women outside my family.

'How are your compositions going, Tanya?' Mrs Gorey from Yambah Station would ask me whenever she came to visit. Mrs Gorey still looked like Sophia Loren and wore glamorous jewellery and I was inevitably tongue-tied in her presence. But for an adult to express interest in my writing was like being given a gold star, face-to-face. I adored Mrs Gorey.

Rosie Johnson, a dynamic actress, singer, dancer, poet and radio host in Alice, even took one of my poems and read it aloud on her 8HA radio show 'The Rosie Johnson Show'. She and her husband knew Mum and Dad well and she made me feel like a real star.

None of this entirely removed the feelings of failure I still felt about *Adventures at Cutters Creek Station* not winning the competition, but I'd got my confidence back. And Mrs Gorey and Rosie Johnson really helped.

I had started to think about my future, and about whether I perhaps could grow up to be a writer and singer and performer. But as we drew closer to the end of the year, my departure to boarding school consumed every other thought. I didn't even know how I was going to survive the next five years in Adelaide, so it seemed pointless worrying about what I would do beyond it, when I grew up. A blanket of blackness hung heavily over my waking hours and sleepless nights.

My fears weren't helped by the fact that it was also a year of terrible bushfires.

After the long drought of the 1960s, the seventies brought a great deal of welcome rain, which had led to good feed; every pastoralist's dream. Feed meant fat and happy cattle, and good sales. However, good feed also meant bushfires. And while we'd been shearing at Glenroy, the brutal summer heat had dried off the feed, and we knew it was only a matter of time.

Most days peaked beyond forty-five degrees, and long-awaited thunderstorms brought lightning, but no rain. We learned from the two-way radio sked that the lightning was starting fires all over Central Australia. We could only guess when it would reach us, too.

The level of dread in my stomach grew in line with the amount of time Dad spent watching the skies and listening to reports on the two-way radio. Before heading south he had spent most of December grading bushfire breaks, day after day, coming home exhausted at night, unable even to eat. Bushfires in the outback spread far and wide, and about the only way to control them was by grading breaks. Dad had never had to deal with bushfires before he came to Central Australia and, as with everything else on the Bond, he'd had to learn on the job.

By the time we returned home in late January, the skies were black with clouds and the humidity was suffocating. Everyone was praying for rain. Surely God would not impose such an evil thing as fire upon us, especially if we prayed hard enough. But as dusk drew in one evening, a lightning storm hit with a vengeance.

Dad's jaw was tight. 'There'll be fires by the morning,' he said.

Before we went to bed, bright bolts of electricity were already scarring the blackness. And sure enough, we woke to waves of red and black engulfing the sky to the north and west. Dad said the fires would rip through the tinder-dry grass and he just hoped his fire breaks would hold. The air over the homestead became heavy with smoke hanging like a thick, grey blanket as though Revelations from the Bible was on its way.

'Will we be alright?' I asked Mum, as she hurriedly packed the tucker box with sandwiches and water.

'Yes, it's just going to be a very busy time for us all,' said Mum, doing her best to sound practical and no-nonsense.

We kids would be involved in every part of protecting Bond Springs.

'Get dressed everyone,' said Mum. 'Long-sleeved shirts, jeans, boots, hat.'

'It's too hot,' we whinged. 'Can't we wear shorts with our boots, instead?'

'No.' Mum was firm. We were to be kitted out in full protective gear for this big job.

Dad flew out in DQG that morning under a cover of smoke. He rose through it until he was high enough to see the fires. He returned, grimmer than ever.

'It's in the spinifex and travelling fast.'

It was too hot to come face-to-face with an out-of-control fire until nightfall. We didn't have the equipment or special clothes like the Alice Springs firefighters did, and Dad said we had to be 'strategic about conserving our energy and resources' to fight the fire—especially as half the resources were us kids. By 7 p.m. we had all piled into the Land Rover with Mum and Dad. We had emptied out hessian bags from the feed shed, which we would use to beat the fire back, and filled little petrol cans to light firebreaks when Dad instructed us to.

Our direction was Orange Tree Bore. We drove for what seemed like miles under the stars, the horizon flaming ahead of us like some weird, detached dream of hell, with scarlet licking the sky. Behind us came the rest of the men from the station, in two Toyotas.

On the back of one of those vehicles, the men had roped in a solid water tank for emergencies. It came with a big hose and a pump that everyone would have to take a turn of to get water if needed. Its contents were precious, and not to be used on the fire—that would have been like throwing a bucket of water into the sea—but it was there should we need it for our own protection.

We crossed the foothills and arrived at the base of a wide sweep of spinifex. It was a roaring wall of red, and burning fast towards the ranges silhouetted behind it. The flames were leaping into the air; they looked like they could reach the stars.

'Righto,' Dad shouted, as we pulled up about a hundred metres from the flames. The howl of the angry flames was deafening, so we leaned forward to catch his last words. 'Stay together.'

Clutching our hessian bags and our petrol cans, we jumped out into the heat of the night. The scorching air sucked at our lungs. The men assembled, ready to start our back-burning tasks. Anxiety rushed up to my head like a firecracker.

We knew from Dad that spinifex areas were the worst. Spinifex was filled with oil, which created pockets of heat, and explosions that could leap from one mound to another, with such ferocity they could even jump firebreaks. Our job was to find patches that would burn back on themselves, right into the existing fire, and burn out.

But there was spinifex burning ahead of us in a conga line of white-edged flames. We had no chance against this ferocity.

'Follow me!' I heard Dad's voice through the noise of falling branches and sizzling bushes. Adrenaline finally kicked in, as did the sense that we were doing something important. Something that mattered. Helping Dad, saving our beloved home. I pulled myself together, as I'd taught myself to do every time we went on a big muster.

We worked all night, side-by-side with the men. They moved here and there, shouting, tackling the burning mounds with bare hands and branches, pumping water from the tank where needed. M'Lis, Brett and I trailed after them, beating back flames with the bags, and using our petrol cans to light up spinifex areas wherever we were told. Before long we were filthy, covered in petrol and dirt and grease. Mum drove the Land Rover slowly behind us all, with Benny tucked in beside her, water and sandwiches at her feet. The dim lights of the Land Rover rose and fell eerily through the darkness and the smoke and the flames.

The adrenaline soon wore off.

The heat was suffocating, debilitating. The fire sucked out life; it was all about death. It made me think of an angry dragon that had come to destroy the world. I kept looking up at a God who was looking down, indifferently it appeared, as the land was blackened. The precious mulga trees destroyed behind us; burned, dead kangaroos and scorched wallabies all around. We worked until the rays of the morning sun blended with the orange glow covering the horizon. We kept working as it transformed into a savage, sweltering bloodshot vision of hell. Days flowed into nights, which flowed into days, and soon we were all walking zombies.

With fires spreading across such large areas, there was no way of putting them out. We just had to try to contain them.

So, Dad changed strategy. At nights we burned back; during the day Dad graded more firebreaks.

But Dad couldn't be everywhere at once. So, various stockmen were delegated the task, often with Brett on the back of the Toyota as a spotter, clinging on for dear life and helping direct the blades of the grader cutting into the earth as they sought to head off the different fire fronts.

It also became a race to protect the cattle. The firebreaks were designed not only to halt the fire but isolate the cattle into secure areas and keep them safe. But it was difficult to know where the cattle were. The paddocks were large and the cattle had dispersed in every direction in panic. So, before long, Dad was in the air in DQG more than he was on the ground.

Flying the fire, as he called it, was perhaps his most effective fire-fighting strategy, and one that hadn't been used by anyone here before. It was his very own idea, and we were both terrified for him and immensely proud.

Dad flew over every corner of every fence-line. He identified where the cattle were and pushed them along in his plane if he could. He sent the men out on motorbikes during the day, ensuring the cattle made it to the dams and bores. It was too hot for the horses, so we were spared mustering in the heat, but we ended up in the back of the Land Rovers, jumping in and out to open and shut gates, move cattle and turn bores on and off.

No cattle would die on Dad's watch, if he could help it.

Dad's use of DQG became an incredibly useful way of managing the fires generally. They moved so quickly that it was difficult to know how widespread the fronts were. Dad would be gone before daylight in the plane, the drone of his little Cessna dying away into the air as he headed back to the next fire front, reporting back over the two-way radio. He also flew over any neighbouring stations that were affected, and reported back to not just them, but also to the Bushfire Council in Alice Springs.

But it didn't come without risk.

'Be careful, Grant!' Mum would plead.

Flying the fires was incredibly dangerous. Dad had to stay high enough in the air so that the turbulence created by the heat and flames didn't send him and DQG spiralling downwards into their fiery centre. But he had to dive low enough so that he could locate the areas engulfed, identify the areas at risk, and importantly, find any cattle that should be moved. Before long he was taking the stockmen up to spot for him so that he could keep focused on the job of staying in the air.

Mum wouldn't let us go.

And the stockmen hated it.

'Give me a horse anytime,' said Jim, emerging pale-faced from the plane, and rushing behind a mulga tree to throw his guts up. The heat and turbulence rocked the little plane around and only the sturdiest stomachs could handle it.

We were also lucky to have the support of the Bushfire Council in Alice Springs. With other cattlemen in the region, Dad had pushed some years earlier for the establishment of a Council. The men from the bush had argued that they too should have firefighting support, not just those living in the town.

We called these firemen the Bushfire Mob. They were wonderful. Their role was to help coordinate firefighting efforts on stations via the two-way radio, and to join in the efforts where possible. They had huge vehicles with correspondingly huge water tanks on the back. They could travel long distances with a lot of equipment. They would turn up like the cavalry.

On one particularly bad fire front, when we'd been out for several long, exhausting nights and were making no headway, they arrived through the darkness, like angels in answer to prayer. I'll never forget the relief on Dad's face as a group of strong, fresh men joined our efforts, especially because they were actually able to use the water in their tanks to spray spot fires. They had travelled three hours to get to us, and their efforts changed the direction of that particular fire front.

By the time February came, despite our best efforts, the wild-fires had scorched and decimated most of our beautiful landscape. They had spread to the east and the west, too. Dad spent those months flying north and south, east and west, across the different cattle stations, passing on fire information and sharing details over the two-way radio. He was the first 'eye in the sky' for Central Australia.

On the last occasion, he was gone for two weeks. The day he called Mum on the two-way radio to say they had turned back the last fire, and he would fly back home that afternoon, Mum's face crumpled, and her shoulders heaved.

It was as though Dad had gone to war, and we hadn't known when or if he would return.

When he dived over the homestead in DQG to let us know he was home, we all jumped in the Land Rover and raced down to the airstrip to meet him. He emerged out of the cockpit, black all over like a chimney sweep, his grin reaching up through his stubble. We threw ourselves on him, and for a short, sweet moment he held us all in his arms. Then he wrapped Mum into his hold as well, and for that time, we were the tightest unit there ever was.

Dad was a true hero; we were sure of it. He even received an award from the Bushfires Council for his innovative and dedicated efforts in the air. Dad and his beloved DQG were a force to be reckoned with.

Momentarily, I forgot my anxiety about leaving all of this.

35

Remember the Bullocks

The dawn sky was milky, touched with stars. From my swag I could make out the dying glimmers of the Southern Cross. I knew they would dim then disappear until another day passed across this desert land. In defiance, the hovering mountain ridge flirted with the sun's kiss, before surrendering and lighting up in gold splendour.

I soaked in the beauty, just for a moment longer. But the hobbles of the horses were clinking, the fire was crackling into life, and the billy already hissing. Morning in the stock camp had begun. No more time for dreaming. I had to find my boots at the bottom of my swag and head out to get my horse.

'Tanya! Wake up!'

I blinked and slowly opened my eyes. Mum was leaning over me. I was in my bedroom at home, not out bush. My new suitcase was in the corner where I'd left it last night, neatly packed, with clothes for the trip laid out on the chair. M'Lis was still asleep, her dark curls spread across her pillow. The birds were squawking in the gum trees outside, and the scent of eucalyptus spilled through the open window. The morning was already hot.

'I dreamed I was in the stock camp, Mum,' I said, with tears in my eyes.

Mum tried to put a smile on her face, but there were tears in her eyes too. 'Oh darling, it's all right. Up you get. We don't want to miss the plane!'

I squeezed my eyes tight again. Maybe if I kept them shut, the day wouldn't start, and I wouldn't have to go to boarding school. But from a distance I heard Dad's boots clomp along the gravel, and I jumped up. That sound was like the crack of a stockwhip, a call to action. It would never do for Dad to think I was weak, or slacking off. Especially after he'd said last night, 'I survived boarding school, Tanya, and if I could—when I wasn't very good at study—you can!'

Mum took the maroon tunic off the hanger and put it on the bed. She was still trying to smile. But I couldn't. That tunic would turn me into someone new.

I knew that, because yesterday I'd dressed up in my whole uniform (white shirt, tie, tunic, belt, shoes and socks) and walked down to the horse yards to show everyone how I looked. Head Stockman Mick, who was visiting and had been down at the other end of the horse yards, looked up at me in surprise, and said to M'Lis, 'Who's that girl?'

'Tanya.'

'Nahhh.'

'True. It is. Look closely.'

Mick peered in my direction and shook his head. 'Strike me pink. Would never have known it was her. Never seen her in a dress before.'

Well, here I was, about to become the 'new me'—someone I'd thought about being for so long—yet already I was unrecognisable to people who knew me. What would that make me, then? Who would I become?

I tried instead to think of the fun things that lay ahead. For the next five years, I could study and read as much as I wanted, without being interrupted by stock work and the need to go to stock camp. I could embrace a new life of adventures, as though I were actually at Malory Towers or St Clare's.

'If you get up now, you'll have time to say goodbye to the horses,' said Mum, so I got out of bed and went down to the horse yards. M'Lis, Brett and Benny were up by now, too, and came with me. I buried my face in Sandy's mane. The tears started as I smelled her sweetness. She nuzzled me and my tears flowed.

'Come on,' said Mum, coming in behind us. We'd been there a long time. She sounded desperate. 'Breakfast.'

I couldn't drag myself away from Sandy, but Mum put her hand on my shoulders, and we all walked back up to the house together. I ate a piece of toast that tasted like cardboard. Then Mum said it was time to finish packing.

M'Lis, Brett and Benny handed me a little parcel, roughly wrapped and held together with a pink ribbon. 'This is from us kids, so you won't forget us,' said M'Lis. 'We hope you like it. We hope it will help at boarding school.'

I squeezed it in at the bottom of my case so I could open it when I got there. I squeezed my eyes as well, hoping to keep the tears inside, but it was useless. They started coming, rolling faster and faster down my cheeks. I was twelve years old and going away. I would no longer be able to look after Benny, or the others. I would no longer be the big sister. I would no longer have a home, a family. I didn't know how to live without them. How would I do it? I wrapped my arms around them and we all cried.

'Time to go!' Mum's voice was tight.

I tried to remind myself of all the things to look forward to. Next year, M'Lis would follow me to boarding school, and we would be together again. Brett would go to his boys' school the year after, and Benny, many years on again. We would all end up crippled by homesickness, but on that morning I didn't know what was to come. All I knew was that my life was unravelling into shapes I couldn't see, loose threads spilling everywhere.

Dad pulled me back from the nightmare in my head.

'Come on, Tanya,' He strode towards me. 'Enough of this, in the car, all of you. I've got to head off and check Bulldust Bore in DQG.'

I thought my heart would stop.

'You'll be right, Tanya. No tears for Mum, okay? You'll be home before you know it.' Then Dad paused and looked hard into my eyes. 'If you're ever having a tough day down there, just remember the bullocks' story.'

I threw my arms around him and smelled the dust, the diesel and the dirt on his shirt. His face was rough against mine and I soaked in his strength. I wanted to stay like that, against him, held by him, forever, where I was safe. I loved him with my whole heart. But then, with a kiss to my cheek, he was gone, striding off to his Land Rover, and I was on my own.

'We've got to go,' said Mum. Her voice sounded strangled. I swallowed back the sobs, remembering Dad's words. I had to be strong for Mum.

We all climbed in the car. The others let me have the front seat.

As we drove out, I looked behind at the ochre hills that framed the homestead with their high peaks. I pushed the image hard into my mind's eye, so that I could see it in my memories, and hold it in my heart.

There was so much ahead of me that I couldn't know.

As the rear-vision image grew smaller and smaller, until it disappeared in our dust, something happened. I remembered some words that had come to me some months ago, as we were heading home after an afternoon playing cattle duffers.

'I will go away and live in the other places I've read about in my beloved books. I will do exciting things. Then, one day, I will write about this life and this land, so it's always with me, forever.'

Author's Note

One of the things I couldn't know back then, as a despairing twelve year old, was that Mum would go from strength to strength, and become like one of the inspiring, creative women she used to talk about in such reverent tones.

She would turn her grief at sending us off to boarding school into action, becoming a national leader pushing for equal education opportunities for kids in the bush. She would become a founding member of the renowned Isolated Children's Parents' Association (ICPA), Alice Springs Branch, and the Inaugural State President. She would help start the most extraordinary secondary school in Alice—St Philip's College—so that bush kids could stay there, rather than being forced to go south. She would lead the College as its Chairman for many years. She would design bedrooms for the boarders that faced the ranges so they could see their land from the school and not be homesick. She would receive an OAM from the Governor General of Australia for her decades of devotion to bush children.

Not bad for a girl who had to leave school at fifteen.

Adelaide Miethke and Molly Ferguson would have been proud.

Acknowledgements

Writing this book has been a roller-coaster of emotions and memories and I have many people to thank for helping me reach the end.

First, my precious family—Mum, M'Lis, Brett and Ben—for sharing their memories and their stories and allowing me to write about them.

With only fourteen months between each of us, M'Lis, Brett and I spent our entire childhood as though in a three-legged race. We moved as one, in work, play, riding, school, and the stock camp. M'Lis and Brett gave me so many stories to include and allowed me to shape them into my own, supporting me as I wrote. Thank you—they are yours as best as I've been able to honour them.

Ben was so very young during the years in which this book is set; he only reaches age five in the last chapter, but he gave me some great (and naughty!) stories as well—thank you, Benny 'Slipsta'!

Mum gave me some fabulous stories that don't appear here because I ran out of room—but her life is a book in itself. There aren't enough words to thank you, darling Mum.

To our dear family friend, Mrs Braitling, thank you for sharing some wonderful stories too, as well as a lifetime of support and friendship to our family. And to Anne Schearer for the photos!

A huge thanks to Ray Murtagh and Adam Gemmell for bringing back great memories of their time on the Bond; likewise, dear Lorna Schmidt, and a huge hug of thanks to my beloved lifetime friend, Janie Jo. Big hugs also to the beautiful Mrs Gorey and Rosie Johnson for inspiring me over the years.

And, of course, Dad, for giving me as much as you did, and could (including your precious diaries), before you died.

———⟶⦾⟵———

The 60s and 70s were a very different time in the bush and much has changed, including attitudes to work, how hard children should work, physical punishment and the rights of girls and women.

That change is welcome.

But I have no doubt the toughness we endured taught us some good things: hard work, never giving up, independence, and a love of the land. And despite how tough Dad was on us—which was a reflection of both how he was brought up, and how he learnt to survive himself—he and Mum gave us an incredible childhood on Bond Springs, which I'll always treasure.

———⟶⦾⟵———

A huge thanks to my wonderful writing friends, neighbour Renée McBryde and cousin Fleur McDonald, who read the first drafts, and gave equally wonderful advice. Renée literally did it in 'sickness and in health' and I'm so grateful. Thank you also to Annette Every for kindly proofreading for me once more, and my beautiful friends

Andrea Davies, Jodeen Carney, Kellie Hill, Jane Aberdeen, Jane Carpenter, Anne Fulwood, Katie McGregor, Melissa Perry, Stephanie Mallen, Penny McCann, Rebecca Scott and Chris Noonan, all of whom have gone above and beyond to help me get my books out into the world. There are many more dear friends I don't have room to mention but please know I'm grateful to each and every one of you. A particular thanks to the fabulous team at Coleman's Printing. And of course Kim Mahood, Ted Egan and Toni Tapp Coutts— three fine Territorians who generously made the time to read my story and provide me with endorsements. Thank you all.

There are also people who profoundly shaped my life who sadly are no longer here. Mrs Judy Hodder died far too young. She was a wonderful teacher who inspired so many bush children, including me.

And the wonderful men of my childhood who are no longer with us either—Mr Crowson, Mr Gorey, Mr Braitling, Uncle Pete, Mick Schmidt.

And now to my wonderful Allen & Unwin publishing team. Without you, there would be no book out in the world, so thank you with all my heart for making it possible to tell this story. A huge thanks to my wonderful publisher, Annette Barlow, her brilliant assistant, Jenn Thurgate, and my talented and inspiring editor Samantha Kent. You are all the best!

Finally, I want to thank my amazing and wonderful husband, Steve, for his constant love and support. He tells me I can do it even when I think I can't and he never stops believing in me. Thank you, my darling, for everything, as ever.

It seems appropriate to finish with a story M'Lis told me about Dad and his beloved horse, Limerick. Many years after this book was set, Dad found Limerick, dead, in the Horse Paddock. Dad didn't say a word. He got his old camera and went out to take a last photo. When Dad came back, M'Lis saw his shoulders heaving. He was wiping his eyes with his dirty shirt sleeves. He couldn't speak. He had the photo printed and put it on his office desk. The picture was heartbreaking: Limerick was already half eaten by crows and dingoes. But on the back, Dad scribbled in his almost illegible writing: '*Limerick—the horse that made Bond Springs.*'

Dad kept that photo on his desk for the rest of his life.

Vale—Grant Frank Heaslip.

You, like Limerick, fought the good fight, and died on the land you loved so much.

The stories told in this book are either from my memory, or they are my interpretation of the collective memories of others of times in our life in the 1960s and 70s. Any mistakes herein are mine and mine alone—apologies.